CHANDRAGUPTA MAURYA AND HIS TIMES

CHANDRAGUPTA MAURYA AND HIS TIMES

Madras University
Sir William Meyer Lectures, 1940-41

RADHA KUMUD MOOKERJI

MOTILAL BANARSIDASS PUBLISHERS
PRIVATE LIMITED • DELHI

3rd Reprint: Delhi, 2016
Fourth Edition: Delhi, 1966

ISBN: 978-81-208-0405-0 (CLOTH)
ISBN: 978-81-208-0433-3 (PAPER)

MOTILAL BANARSIDASS
41 U.A. Bungalow Road, Jawahar Nagar, Delhi 110 007
8 Mahalaxmi Chamber, 22 Bhulabhai Desai Road, Mumbai 400 026
203 Royapettah High Road, Mylapore, Chennai 600 004
236, 9th Main III Block, Jayanagar, Bengaluru 560 011
8 Camac Street, Kolkata 700 017
Ashok Rajpath, Patna 800 004
Chowk, Varanasi 221 001

Printed in India

by RP Jain at NAB Printing Unit,
A-44, Naraina Industrial Area, Phase I, New Delhi–110028
and published by JP Jain for Motilal Banarsidass Publishers (P) Ltd,
41 U.A. Bungalow Road, Jawahar Nagar, Delhi-110007

PREFACE

To the First Edition.

This work embodies the Sir William Meyer Lectures I was invited to deliver by the Madras University in October, 1941. The publication of the Lectures has been delayed by the conditions created by the War.

As a teacher of Indian History, I have felt that a comprehensive work dealing with the life and times of India's first historical emperor, and a picture of the civilization of India in that early period of the 4th Century B.C., will satisfy a long-felt need. This work is meant to fill up a gap in our knowledge of Ancient India.

The question of the extent to which the unique Sanskrit work, the *Arthaśāstra* of Kauṭilya, may be treated as a source of Maurya history, has been amply answered in the pages of the book. I have utilised much material found in the *Arthaśāstra*, which is not yet sufficiently known or noticed. I am indebted for its interpretation to the erudite commentary known as *Śrīmūlam*, written by the late T. Ganapati Sastri on the basis of the earlier Sanskrit commentaries by Bhaṭṭasvāmī and Mādhavayajvan, and also a Malayalam commentary discovered by him, which are of great value as preserving older traditions. The work also embodies collation and comparison of evidence from different sources, Classical Works, Sanskrit, Buddhist and Jain Texts, and the Inscriptions of Asoka.

I have added to the work a Table of Contents to serve as an Index of Subjects, besides an Index of Technical Terms, three Appendices, and a Plate of typical Maurya Coins.

The system of transliteration adopted in the work will be understood from the following examples: *Kṛishṇa*, *Lichchhavi*, *Mahāvaṁśa*.

Lucknow University,
January, 1943.

RADHA KUMUD MOOKERJI.

PREFACE

To the Second Edition

The first edition of the book which was published by the Madras University was exhausted within a year of its publication. The second edition has been somewhat delayed by my pre occupations, including my Parliamentary work. I am indebted to Dr. Dashrath Sharma, M.A., D.Litt., Professor, Hindu College, Delhi, for his kind assistance in correcting the proofs of the work and suggesting some necessary revisions of the text. I am grateful to the Madras University for permission to have this work republished.

December 5, 1952 RADHA KUMUD MOOKERJI

TABLE OF CONTENTS

CHAPTER I

ORIGIN AND EARLY LIFE

CHAPTER II

CONQUESTS AND CHRONOLOGY

CHAPTER III

ADMINISTRATION: IDEALS: DIVISIONS

CHAPTER IV

THE KING

CHAPTER V

MINISTERS : RULES OF SERVICE

CHAPTER VI

ADMINISTRATIVE DEPARTMENTS AND OFFICERS

CHAPTER VII

LAND SYSTEM AND RURAL ADMINISTRATION

CHAPTER VIII

MUNICIPAL ADMINISTRATION

CHAPTER IX

LAW

CHAPTER X

THE ARMY

Chapter XI

SOCIAL CONDITIONS

Chapter XII

ECONOMIC CONDITIONS

CHAPTER I

ORIGIN AND EARLY LIFE

Chandragupta's Achievements : His Historicity. Chandragupta Maurya ranks as one of India's greatest rulers. There are many titles to his greatness which, in several respects, is found to be even unique. He figures as the first 'historical' emperor of India in the sense that he is the earliest emperor in Indian History whose historicity can be established on the solid ground of ascertained chronology.

Earlier Emperors. India had seen many great kings and emperors before him like Mahāpadma, Nanda, Ajātaśatru, or Bimbiśara whose reign was enlivened by the moving personality of the great Buddha. And even before these we read in the texts of earlier emperors with high-sounding titles acquired by conquests and formally conferred upon them with appropriate religious ceremonies announcing such achievements. Indeed, the tradition of such great kings and emperors goes back to the Vedas. The *Ṛigveda* tells of Sudās who had achieved his overlordship of Ṛigvedic India by his victory at the Battle of Ten Kings (*Dāśa-rājña*) [*Ṛv.* VIII. 33, 2, 5 ; 83, 8], representing about forty different Ṛigvedic peoples.

Terms and Ceremonies of Imperialism. The conception of paramount power and imperial sovereignty was so well established even in these early days that it expressed itself in appropriate technical terms, such as *Adhirāja*, *Rājādhirāja*, or *Samrāṭ*, liberally used in the Vedic texts. The *Aitareya Brāhmaṇa* [VIII. 15] even uses the more significant term, *Ekarāṭ*, and, together with the *Śatapatha Brāhmaṇa* [XIII. 5, 4], enthuses over the 'world-wide' conquests of the two Bharata kings, Dauḥshanti and Sātrājita Śatānīka, stating that "the great deeds of Bharata neither men before or after him attained, as the sky a man with his hands." These two texts also mention as many as twelve other such great kings. Even different ceremonies are described for different grades of kingship : the *Gopatha Brāhmaṇa* prescribes *Rājasūya* for the Rājā, *Vājapeya* for the Samrāṭ, *Aśvamedha* for the Svarāṭ, *Purushamedha* for Virāṭ, and *Sarvamedha* for *Sarvarāṭ*, while the *Āpastamba Śrauta Sūtra* [XX. 1, 1,] reserves the *Aśvamedha* only for a *Sārva-bhauma* sovereign.

Importance of Chronology. Chandragupta follows in the wake of this imperial tradition. But in his case the tradition becomes a reality, and acquires historicity. The older kings are mere names and cannot be related definitely to space and time which alone can make them historical characters. In the case of Chandragupta, we are able for the first time in the long annals of ancient Indian kingship to locate him accurately in both time and space, and establish his history on the basis of chronology. In one sense, History is limited by Chronology, and what is history proper is chronological history, comprising an arrangement of facts in order of time. Chronology is not so essential to the history of thought or cultural history, made up, as it is, not of isolated and individual dated events, but of large movements of the spirit embracing a long interval of time, though even such cultural history must rest on and present a sequence in thought, what Max Muller has called 'the inner chronology of ideas.' But Chronology is essential to Biography. An individual cannot rank as a historical person unless his life and work are placed in time. The dates of Chandragupta's life and reign may be worked out with considerable precision.

Other Titles to Greatness. We may now examine his other titles to greatness. He is the first Indian king who established his rule over an extended India, an India greater than even British India. The boundaries of this Greater India lay far beyond the frontiers of modern India along the borders of Persia. Chandragupta is again the first of the Rulers of India to be able by his conquests to join up the valleys of the Indus and the land of the five rivers with the eastern valleys of the Ganges and the Jumna in one Empire that stretched from Aria (Herat) to Pāṭaliputra. And he is also the first Indian King who followed up this political unification of Northern India by extending his conquests beyond the barriers of the Vindhyas so as to bring both North and South under the umbrella of one paramount sovereign. Earlier in his career, he was again the first Indian leader who had to confront the distressing consequences of a European and foreign invasion of his country, the conditions of national depression and disorganisation to which it was exposed, and then to achieve the unique distinction of recovering his country's freedom from the yoke of Greek rule. It may be recalled that Alexander's invasion of India covered a period of about three years from May 327 B.C. to May 324 B.C., while it will be seen that Chandragupta was able to rid the country of all traces of Greek occupation by 323 B.C. Very few Rulers of India have to their credit the accomplishment of so much within the short time of his reign which, according to the *Purāṇas*, embraced a period of only 24 years. To crown all, Chandragupta, as the founder of the imperial

Maurya dynasty, gives to India for the first time a continuous history as well as a unified history, a history affecting India as a whole, and as a unit, in the place of merely histories involving only particular peoples and regions of India. This imperial history thus inaugurated by Chandragupta could not long survive him. It soon lost itself in local annals. The political unity of India attained under the Maurya emperors was not maintained by their successors. One political authority no longer shaped her history. India was again split up into a multitude of smaller States and Kingdoms, each having its own history.

Sources : Greek and Latin Works. An advantage of Mauryan History lies in the abundance, authenticity, and variety of its sources. One of the greatest discoveries of Indian History (which we owe to Sir William Jones) is the correspondence of the Greek name Sandrocottos or Androkottos to the Indian name Chandragupta [*Asiatic Researches*, IV. p. 11]. This led to the consequential conclusion that Chandragupta was a contemporary of Alexander whom he had also personally interviewed. We get this fact from Plutarch who states: "Androkottos himself, who was then but a youth, saw Alexander himself." The result of this discovery has been a bountiful crop of evidence bearing on Chandragupta Maurya and his times, furnished by the historians of Alexander's campaigns in India. Foreign sources thus throw a flood of light on what might have remained a most obscure chapter of Indian History, though it was so glorious by its achievements. To these sources, Indian History is also indebted for what has been called 'the sheet-anchor of its chronology,' for the starting-point of Indian chronology is the date of Chandragupta's accession to sovereignty.

Of the companions of Alexander on his campaigns, three are noted for their writings on India, viz., (1) Nearchus, whom Alexander deputed to explore the coast between the Indus and the Persian Gulf; (2) Onesicritus, who took part in the voyage of Nearchus and afterwards wrote a book about it and India ; and (3) Aristobulus, whom Alexander entrusted with certain commissions in India.

The writings of these companions of Alexander were supplemented in the third century B.C. by those of some European ambassadors who were sent by the Hellenistic kings to India. Of these, Megasthenes was unfortunately the only one who utilised his opportunities properly and has left the fullest account of India in classical literature. His account, however, is lost in the original and can be traced only in the citations of later writers among whom the following may be noted :

1. Strabo, who lived *c.* 64 B.C.—19 A.D. and wrote an important geographical work, of which Book XV, Chapter I, deals with India : its geography, manners, and customs, on the basis of material drawn from the companions of Alexander and from Megasthenes.

2. Diodorus who lived up to 36 B.C. and wrote an account of India taken from Megasthenes.

3. Pliny the Elder, the author of *Natural History*, an encyclopaedic work published about 75 A.D. and giving notices of India drawn from the Greek books and also recent reports of merchants.

4. Arrian who lived between *c* 130 A.D. and at least 172 A.D. and wrote the best account of Alexander's expedition (*Anabasis*) and a tract on India, its geography, manners, and customs, drawn from Nearchus, Megasthenes, and Eratosthenes, the geographer (276—195 B C.).

5. Plutarch, *c.* 45—125 A.D., whose *Lives* includes a Life of Alexander in its chapters 57-67 and deals with India.

6. Justin who lived in the second century A.D. and composed an *Epitome*, of which Book XII gives an account of Alexander's campaigns in India.

Indian Works. Besides these Latin and Greek sources, there are also Brahminical, Buddhist, and Jain sources throwing light on Chandragupta's life and times. The Brahminical sources include the *Purāṇas*, the *Arthaśāstra* of Kauṭilya, the *Mudrārākshasa* of Viśākhadatta, and partly works like the *Kathāsaritsāgara* of Somadeva or *Bṛihatkathāmañjarī* of Kshemendra. The Buddhist authorities are mainly *Dīpavaṁsa*, *Mahāvaṁsa*, the *Mahāvaṁsa Ṭīkā*, and *Mahābodhivaṁsa*. The Jain authorities are mainly *Kalpasūtra* of Bhadrabāhu and *Pariśishṭaparvan* of Hemachandra. Other minor sources, texts, inscriptions, or coins, will be indicated in the course of the narrative.

Age of *Arthaśāstra.* Of the above authorities, there is a controversy regarding the *Arthaśāstra* as a document of Maurya history. Professor F. W. Thomas holds the view [*Cambridge History of India*, I. p. 467] that the date of the work "clearly falls within or near the Maurya period." This was the view taken earlier by scholars like the late Dr. Vincent A. Smith in his *Early History of India*, Dr. H. Jacobi, and Dr. K. P. Jayaswal. This view is followed in this work. It will be seen from the contents and details of the work that, whatever might be the time of its composition in its present form, it is a picture of early conditions applicable to Mauryan India. As F. W. Thomas further points out [*Ib.* p. 474] : "Concerning the condition and organisation of the vast Maurya empire, the Greeks have provided us with a considerable body of valuable information: and, as the *Arthaśāstra* furnishes the means of describing the complete polity existing at the time, its land system, its fiscal system, its law, its social system, with some view of literature and religion, we shall not forego the opportunity, so rare in Indian history—we must wait for the time of Akbar and the *Āīn-i-Akbari*—of dwelling a little on the picture."

Origin. The lineage of Chandragupta is a subject of controversy. One view holds him to be of high birth, a true-born Kshatriya eminently worthy of royalty, while the other view slanders him as a man of base birth, a Śūdra, not eligible for kingship. We shall have to decide this controversy by a consideration of all the evidence adduced on both sides.

Extracts from Classical Works. We shall first consider the evidence of foreign authorities on account of its double advantage. Firstly, it is earliest in time, and nearest to the time of Chandragupta, and, secondly, it is based on contemporary Indian reports, the current stories and traditions on the subject gathered by some of the Greek historians at first hand.

The following extracts are made from the classical sources as being relevant to the issue:

(1) From Curtius (of first century A.D.): Porus (the Indian king who was defeated by Alexander in the battle of Hydaspes and the greatest personality of the times in that region) reported to Alexander "that the present king (the Nanda king who was later to be supplanted by Chandragupta Maurya) was not merely a man originally *of no distinction*, but even of the very meanest condition. His father was in fact a barber" who stealthily became the queen's paramour and encompassed the assassination of the king by treachery. "Then, under the pretence of acting as guardian to the royal children, he usurped the supreme authority, and having put the young princes to death begot the *present* king who was detested and held cheap by his subjects."

(2) From Diodorus: Porus informed Alexander "that the king of the Gangaridai (the Nanda king) was a man of quite worthless character and held in no respect, as he was thought to be the son of a barber."

(3) From Plutarch. "Androkottos (Chandragupta) himself, who was then but a youth, saw Alexander himself and afterwards used to declare that Alexander could easily have taken possession of the whole country (of 'the Gangaridai and the Prasii' under the Nanda

king), since the king was hated and despised by his subjects for the wickedness of his disposition and the meanness of his origin."

(4) From Justin (writing, as we have seen, in the second century A.D. on the basis of a Greek work of first century B.C.): "India, after Alexander's death, as if the yoke of servitude had been shaken off its neck, had put his prefects to death. Sandrocottus (Chandragupta) was the leader who achieved its freedom. He was born in humble life but was prompted to aspire to royalty by an omen. By his insolent behaviour he had offended Nandrus[1] and was ordered to be put to death when he sought safety by a speedy flight."

Base Origin of Nandas. It will be seen from these passages that none of them contains any reference to Chandragupta's lineage except the passage from Justin. Justin's statement only points out that Chandragupta was of *lowly* and not *low* or base birth, that he was a mere commoner who had no royal blood in him but who was 'aspiring for royalty.' The other passages cited indicate why Chandragupta was aspiring after royalty. They are full of aspersions on the character of the then reigning Indian king who was a man of disreputable origin, the illegitimate offspring of a barber, "detested and held cheap by his subjects." We are further told by Plutarch that it was Chandragupta himself who had reported to Alexander the "meanness" of Nanda king's origin. Does not this statement itself definitely demonstrate that Chandragupta himself was of no mean origin? Ancestral "meanness" will then be also his by descent. Thus Chandragupta by his own statement frees himself from any taint of relationship to a disreputable royalty as well as any mean origin for himself. The passages cited above only show how the political conditions of the times were paving Chandragupta's way to royalty after which he was thus naturally "aspiring."

Thus the evidence of foreign sources based upon the reports of the Indians of the day and the stories then current in the country does not at all contain any insinuations as to the sopposed base birth or disreputable origin of Chandragupta. On the contrary, that evidence imputes it to the then reigning Indian king of 'Eastern' India and describes the consequent weakness of his position, inviting his overthrow. At first, Chandragupta thought that Alexander might easily displace him, considering how he lacked the best defence and protection that a king could have, the love of his people. For the people's

1. "*Nandrum* has been here substituted for the common reading *Alexandrum* which Gutschmid has shown to be an error" [McCrindle's *Invasion of India by Alexander*, p. 327].

feelings were outraged by the usurpation of sovereignty by a man of low origin, the son of a barber, and Śūdra, and a murderer to boot of the last lawful soveieign, and a man of an equally low character possessed of an inherently "wicked disposition." When Chandragupta found that Alexander was out of the way and unable to carry further his conquests and exploit in any way the political situation prevailing in Nanda's empire, he himself thought of undertaking that task and was inspired by 'aspiration after royalty,' as stated by Justin. But how could he undertake that mission if he was himself not free of the taint which made Nanda so unpopular ? If he had to seek the support of the people in ridding the country of its despicable usurper, and count on their moral opinion outraged by Nanda's disreputable origin and doings, he could not hope to do so without having a clean record of lineage for himself. One who was making political capital out of the base birth of his rival could not himself be base-born. Justin also makes Chandragupta free of any trace of royal or even aristocratic blood, far less of any connexion, remote or illegitimate, with the Nanda kings, which some later Sanskrit traditions seek to ascribe to him. He was not out to oust the Nanda king as any jealous kinsman of his. He was out only to free his country from the dearly despised domination of the Nanda king, as an instrument of his people's will, as he had already freed the country from the yoke of foreign rule.

If, then, the trustworthy foreign histories based on Indian evidence collected at first hand are innocent of all uncomplimentary references to Chandragupta's lineage, who first started the story of his disreputable origin ? A careful analysis of all available evidence will show that the source of this story is rather out of the way and not quite authentic.

We shall now examine all the Indian texts on the subject, Brahminical, Buddhist, and Jain.

Evidence of '*Purāṇas*.' The principal Brahminical text is that of the *Purāṇas*. It will be seen that the *Purāṇas* are more concerned with the origin of the Nanda kings than that of Chandragupta. They are very much concerned at the ending of Kshatriya rule in the country and its displacement by a Śūdra rule under the Nandas whom they openly brand as *adhārmikās*, 'immoral people.' The founder of the Nanda dynasty is described as the 'offspring of a Śūdra woman' (*Śūdrāgarbhodbhavaḥ*) and a 'Mahāpadmapati,' 'exceedingly avaricious,' as translated by H.H. Wilson. According to the commentator, the term *Mahāpadma* may mean limitless army or limitless wealth amounting to 100,000 millions [Wilson's *Vishṇu Purāṇa*, p. 184].

The *Purāṇas* tell us that the previous Śiśunāga kings were Kshatriyas (*Kshatra-bandhavaḥ*). They were followed by the nine Nandas, Mahāpadma Nanda and his eight sons. Mahāpadma became 'a second Paraśurāma,' as 'the exterminator of the entire Kshatriya race' (*sarvakshatrāntakaḥ*), 'one who uprooted all Kshatriyas (*sarvakshatrānuddhṛitya*), 'the destroyer of Kshatriya's (*Kshatra-vināśakṛit*), and established himself as 'the sole sovereign of the realm' (*eka-rāṭ*) placed 'under the umbrella of one authority (*eka-chchhatrām*) which no one could challenge' (*anullaṅghita-śāsanaḥ*). Then the *Purāṇas* state that this race of "irreligious" kings "will be uprooted by a certain Dvija," "the Brāhmaṇa Kauṭilya," and that "Kauṭilya," will anoint Chandragupta as the sovereign of the realm" (*rājye-abhishekshyati*).

They know only of Nanda's base origin. These passages from the *Purāṇas* tell their own tale in no equivocal terms. They clearly point to the following propositions: (1) that the Nanda kings were base-born, and had inaugurated unrighteous and unlawful Śūdra rule which the *Śāstras* do not approve; (2) that it remained for a militant Brāhman, the redoubtable Kauṭilya, as the custodian and upholder of *Dharma*, to rid the country of its usurpation by Śūdra rulers and restore it to the lawful rule of the Kshatriyas; and (3) that, after accomplishing this mission of his life by 'uprooting' the race of Nandas, Kauṭilya chose Chandragupta for the throne to which he was consecrated by the performance of the ceremony of *abhisheka* or anointment prescribed for royalty. The formal anointment of Chandragupta to sovereignty by an orthodox Brāhman of unbending strictness, a master of the *Śāstras*, and an uncompromising champion of *Dharma*, like Kauṭilya, is a proof positive that the man of his choice must have been one of noble lineage, a Kshatriya who was eligible for kingship.

The *Arthaśāstra* bears the same evidence. It is interesting to note that the *Arthaśāstra* of Kauṭilya itself renders explicit the meaning and implications of these passages from the *Purāṇas*. At the end of the work occurs a passage which states that "the *Arthaśāstra* has been compiled by one who forcibly (*amarsheṇa*) and quickly (*āśu*) achieved the liberation of the mother-country, of its culture and learning (*śāstra*), its military power (*śastra*) from the grip of the Nanda kings." This passage shows that Kauṭilya considered it to be an urgent and imperative religious duty to extirpate, as soon as possible, and by violent means, the unlawful rule of Śūdra kings who could not be trusted with the spiritual and cultural, nor even the military, interests of the country. The social order and system for which Kauṭilya stands is known as *Varṇāśramadharma* which rules out royalty for the Śūdra and reserves it to the Kshatriya whose occupations are prescribed to be the 'pursuit of arms' (*Śastrājīva*), and 'protection of living beings', *i.e.*, military and administrative functions. The Kshatriya king is to function as the *Daṇḍa* or the Executive to uphold and enforce *Dharma* as the ultimate Sovereign, the rule of Law. It is thus quite absurd to suppose that Kauṭilya who was out to rescue this Dharma or system from the outrage inflicted upon it by a Śūdra sovereignty could have chosen as his agent in the fulfilment of his sacred mission a person of the same disqualification. He could not consecrate to sovereignty one Śūdra in place of another. To add to this, we have Kauṭilya's own opinion as to the merits of a king who is high-born (*abhijāta*) and one who is lowborn (*anabhijāta*). Kauṭilya prefers a high-born king, even though he is weak and powerless (*durbalam*), to a king of low birth but of great power (*balavān*). His argument is that the people (*prakṛitayaḥ*) of their own accord welcome a prince of noble lineage (*svayam upanamanti*) and are prepared to follow him (*anuvartate*) out of their natural regard for the greatness that springs from birth (*jātyaṁ kulotpannam*) and character (*aiśvaryaprakṛitiḥ aisvaryārhatā*). On the contrary, the people are naturally averse to a base-born prince whose intrigues (*upajāpam*) they are not prepared to support (*visamvādayanti, na anuvartante*). For, as the saying is: 'Love is kindled by Virtue' (*anurāge sārvaguṇyam*) [*Arthaśāstra* VIII. 2]. This reads like the self-defence of Kauṭilya in preferring a humble prince like Chandragupta, a true-born Kshatriya, to the Śūdra king Nanda, with all his power and pelf.

The term 'Maurya' The theory of the base birth of Chandragupta Maurya was first suggested by the derivation which a commentator was at pains to find for the epithet *Maurya* as applied to Chandragupta by the *Purāṇas*. The commentator on the *Purāṇa* text takes *Maurya* to be the son of *Murā* who was one of the wives of king Nanda [*Chandraguptaṁ Nandasyaiva patnyantarasya Murā-saṁjñasya putraṁ Mauryānāṁ prathamam*]. Heavens save us from commentators who supplement texts by facts of their own creation! The commentator here makes the astounding statement that Chandragupta was a son of the Nanda king against the silence of all the *Purāṇas* on the subject. Such a fact completely militates against the context of the references which the *Purāṇas* make to Chandragupta, as already indicated. It may be noted that if there is any sort of connexion between a preceding and succeeding dynasty, the *Purāṇas* as a rule do not omit to mention it. For instance, in the case of the Śaiśunāga dynasty which was succeeded by that of the Nandas, it has been clearly stated that of the ten Śaiśunāga kings, the ninth was Nandivardhana, and the tenth was his son named Mahānandin, and that, "as son of Mahānandin by a Śūdra woman will be born a king, Mahāpadma (Nanda), who will exterminate all Kshatriyas. Thereafter, kings will be of Śūdra origin." If this history had repeated itself in the case of the Mauryas, and if the first Maurya king were also related to the preceding Nanda king in the same way as the Nanda king was related to the preceding Śaiśunāga king that history could not have been omitted by the *Purāṇas*. It is nothing but a pure and simple invention of the commentator to explain grammatically the formation *Maurya* from *Murā*. But he is as innocent of grammar as of any concern for truth. It is impossible to derive by any grammar *Maurya* as a direct formation from *Murā*. The derivative from *Murā* is *Maureya*. The term *Maurya* can be derived only from the masculine *Mura* which is mentioned as the name of a *gotra* in a *Gaṇapāṭha* to Pāṇini's *Sūtra* [IV. 1, 151]. It is strange that the derivation of the term has not been traced by this track. The commentator was more interested in finding a mother than in grammar ! The only redeeming feature of the commentator is that not merely is he innocent of grammar and history : he is also innocent of any libel against Chandragupta. For he has *not* stated that Murā, the supposed mother of Chandragupta, was a Śūdra woman or a courtesan of the Nanda king. He is severely silent about her caste, while he describes Murā as a lawfully wedded wife of the king. Thus even this commentator of the *Purāṇa* cannot be held responsible for the theory of Chandragupta's low origin.

The question is : On whom are we to father this slanderous story ?

Evidence of '*Mudrārākshasa*': the terms '*Vṛishala*' and '*Kula-hīna*.' It is generally supposed that the true source of the story is the *Mudrārākshasa*, of which the relevant passages may be now critically examined. It would appear that the whole story rests upon the meaning of the two words, *Vṛishala* and *Kula-hīna*, applied in the drama to Chandragupta. The words should not be torn from their contexts and interpreted independently. The term *Vṛishala* has been applied to Chandragupta at several places in the drama and is taken in its ordinary sense to mean 'the son of a Śūdra.' It is, however, to be noted that the term may bear another meaning as one of compliment instead of opprobrium. A passage in the drama itself [III. 18] uses the term *Vrishala* as a term of honour to mean 'one who is a *vrisha* among kings, the best of kings.' In several other places, the term is used as one of endearment by Chāṇakya for his favourite pupil and almost as his personal nickname. It is left only to the enemies of Chandragupta to use it as a term of abuse against him [VI. 6], and that also by way of a pun on what is taken to be his nickname. Thus the derogatory meaning of the term *Vrishala* is not at all established in the drama. A similar meaning is sought to be found in the other term *Kula-hīna* as applied to Chandragupta [II. 17] and pointing undoubtedly to his 'inferior lineage.' But the context in which the term is used only shows that it should mean *lowly*, and not *low* or degraded lineage, and does not cast any slur on it. It practically indicates what Justin has stated, viz., 'that he was born in humble life.' It really means that Chandragupta was born of a *hīna* or 'humble', *kula* or 'family,' as contrasted with the Nandas described as '*prathita-kulajāḥ*,' 'of illustrious lineage,' or of 'high birth' [*uchchairavijanam* (VI. 6)]. The point emphasised against Chandragupta by his enemies in the drama is that he is a mere upstart, of a family unknown to name and fame (*aprathita-kula*), having no trace of any aristocratic or royal blood in him, and, as such, utterly unworthy of the throne which was adorned by the Nandas of noble lineage. This is undoing the *Purāṇas* with vengeance. While the *Purāṇas* represent the Nanda as Sūdra kings of odious origin, the tables are completely turned by the *Mudrārākshasa* which gives to the Nandas a proud pedigree and reserves to Chandragupta all the opprobrium attaching to a mere commoner, and an upstart of unknown family of indifferent status. But dramatic partisanship and prejudice cannot be taken as sober history, nor should a drama separated by an interval of about eight centuries from the time of Chandragupta prevail against the *Purāṇas* as a historical source.

Evidence of the Commentator. But though the *Mudrārākshasa* cannot thus be invoked in support of any calumny against Chandragupta, there is no escape for him from the clutches of its commentator who definitely fastens it on him. Dhuṇḍhirāja, a commentator on *Mudrārākshasa*, of the eighteenth century, is responsible for some new history. In the *Upodghāta* of his commentary, he introduces Sarvārthasiddhi as the father of two sets of sons by two wives, viz., (1) the nine Nandas by his wife Sunandā and (2) Maurya by his junior wife named Murā. It was left to Dhuṇḍhirāja to make the discovery for the first time in the long history of these Chandragupta traditions that the woman Murā was a *Vṛishalātmajā*, the daughter of a *Vṛishala* or Śūdra. Dhuṇḍhiraja stands alone in this statement which may be taken for what it is worth. It is also implied that Sarvārtha-siddhi was of high caste along with his nine sons, the Nandas, born of his Kshatriya wife, Sunandā. According to Dhuṇḍhirāja, Chandragupta was a son of Maurya who was entrusted with the command of his army by his father Sarvārthasiddhi in preference to his *Nanda* sons, whereupon the Nandas contrived the murder of Maurya and all his sons except Chandragupta who escaped. This united Chandragupta with Chāṇakya in a common hostility to the Nandas.

Other points in *Mudrārākshasa.* A few other points are revealed in the *Mudrārākshasa* on the subject. It may be noted that the attitude of the drama towards Chandragupta is not always consistent or constant. It shows an anxiety at times not to point the finger of scorn at him as *Vṛishala* but to hail him as a prince, a scion of the Nanda house, a *Nandānvaya*, a *Maurya-putra* [II. 6], and the same note is struck by Rākshasa, the faithful follower and minister of Nanda, in describing himself as Chandragupta's *pitṛiparyāyagata*, i. e., as the holder of the hereditary office of minister of his family. He also mentions Chandragupta as his *svāmiputra*, his master's son. It may be noted that the drama describes Chandragupta as a *Maurya-putra* and not as a *Nanda-putra.* Yet he is called 'a scion of the Nanda house,' because he is son of Maurya who was a son of Sarvārthasiddhi, the father of nine Nandas, and of Nanda ancestry himself. This old king was called a Nanda. He is seen in the drama to have fled from Pāṭaliputra to the forest at the suggestion of Rākshasa, as all his sons, the nine Nandas, were killed one after another by Chāṇakya and Chandragupta. And yet Chandragupta could not be called a parricide, because he is not called *Nanda-putra* : the son of any of the nine Nandas. The other description of him as a *Maurya-putra* saves him from that heinous crime [See C. D. Chatterji, '*Observations on the Bṛihat-kathā* in *Indian Culture*, I. p. 221].

Thus the drama departs from the tradition of the *Purāṇa* which does not assert any connexion by blood between Chandragupta and Nanda. The drama here draws upon the commentator of the *Purāṇa* who first attests that connexion, as we have seen.

The *Mudrārākshasa* shows other points of divergence from the *Purāṇas.* While the *Purāṇas* know of nine Nandas, the drama knows of a tenth Nanda named Sarvārthasiddhi whom it describes as a *Nandavaṁśīya*, a scion of the Nanda dynasty, and whom it places on the throne after the death of the last Nanda. Thus the enemy whom Chāṇakya and Chandragupta are to fight is not the Nanda king proper, as stated in the *Purāṇas*, but a kinsman of his. The drama opens with the statement of Chāṇakya to the effect that he has already "exterminated the nine Nandas from the earth and rooted out the stem of Nanda. But he fears that he cannot consider his work to be finished so long as there still survives a single offshoot of the Nanda family." And so, in that view, he did not refrain from accomplishing the assassination of Sarvārthasiddhi then living as a hermit in the forest, because he happened to be the last surviving "shoot of Nandas' stem."

Kashmir tradition. We owe a different version of Chandragupta's lineage to two Sanskrit works of Kashmir, the *Kathāsaritsāgara*, and the *Bṛihaṭ-kathāmañjarī*, both as late as the eleventh century A. D.

These texts do not know of the nine Nandas, nor of their father, Sarvārthasiddhi, known to *Mudrārākshasa.* They mention only two Nandas: (1) *Pūrva*-Nanda, stated to be the father of Chandragupta (whereas his father is named Maurya in the *Mudrārākshasa*); (2) *Yoga*-Nanda, father of Hiraṇyagupta or Harigupta.

The relation between these two Nandas is not specified, nor is any connexion asserted between them, and between them and the nine or ten Nandas known to *Mudrārākshasa.*

It is not also stated whether *Pūrva*-Nanda was even a prince. We are only told that the second Nanda or *Yoga*-Nanda was a king who succumbed to the *kṛityā* or magical spell practised against his life by Chāṇakya who installed Chandragupta as king in his place. This Nanda is also stated to be a *Śūdra,* and to have his camp at Ayodhyā.

On the whole, it is thus clear that beyond the mere names of Nanda, Chāṇakya, and Chandragupta, there is hardly any link of connexion between the tradition of the Kashmir texts and that of the *Mudrārākshasa* which is very widely and wrongly supposed to have been based upon either the *Bṛihatkathā* of Guṇādhya, or its later Kashmir redaction, or even the *Bṛihatkathāmañjarī.* The Kashmir tradition moves on different lines altogether, and has hardly any points of contact with the *Mudrārākshasa* story [C. D. Chatterji in *Indian Culture,* Vol. I. pp. 210 ff.].

Buddhist Tradition. We shall now turn to the Buddhist traditions which describe the 'Nandins' as of unknown lineage (*aññatakula*) and testify to the noble lineage of Chandragupta without any doubts about it. Chandragupta is described as a scion of the Kshatriya clan of Moriyas, an offshoot of the noble and sacred sept of the Śākyas who gave the Buddha to the world. According to the story, these Moriyas separated from the parent community to escape from its invasion by the cruel Kosala king, Viḍūḍabha and found refuge in a secluded Himalayan region. This region was known for its peacocks, whence the immigrants also became known as Moriyas, i.e., those belonging to the place of peacocks. Moriya is from '*Mora*' which is the Pali word for peacock, corresponding to the Sanskrit word '*Mayūra*.' Another version of the story mentions a city called Moriya-nagara after the fact that it was built with "bricks coloured like peacocks' necks." The people who built the city became known as Moriyas. The *Mahābodhivaṁsa* [ed. Strong p. 98] states that "Prince (*kumāra*) Chandragupta, born of a dynasty of kings (*narinda-kula-sambhava*), hailing from the city known as Moriyanagara, which was built by the *Sākyaputtas*, being supported by the Brāhmaṇa (*dvija*), Chāṇakya, became king at Pāṭliputra."

The *Mahāvaṁsa* also states that Chandragupta was "born of a family of Kshatriyas called Moriyas." [*Moriyanaṁ khattiyanaṁ vaṁse jātaṁ*]

The Buddhist canonical work *Dīgha Nikāya* [II. 167] mentions the Kshatriya clan known as the Moriyas of Pipphalivana.

In the *Divyāvadāna* [ed., Cowell, p. 370], Bindusāra (Chandragupta's son) is mentioned as a lawfully anointed Kshatriya king (*Kshatriya-mūrdhābhishikta*), while Asoka (his grandson) is described as Kshatriya.

Jain Tradition. Jain tradition also relates that Chandragupta was born of a daughter of the chief of a village community who were known as 'rearers of royal peacocks' (*mayūra-poshaka-grāme*) [Hemachandra's *Pariśishṭaparvan*, VIII, 230], while it describes Nanda as the son of a barber by a courtesan (whom the Greeks specify to be the queen of the last king) [*Ib.* VI. 232]. This imputes to him a double infamy due to both parents being tainted. The *Āvaśyaka Sūtra* (p. 693) which also knows of nine Nandas (*navame Nande*), describes the first Nanda as begotten of a barber (*nāpitadāsa . . . rāja jātaḥ*).

It may, however, be noted that the *Pariśishta-parvan* [VIII. 320] relates the story that while the deposed Nanda king was allowed by Chāṇakya to leave Pāṭaliputra with all the luggage that could be accommodated in a single chariot, he had with him two wives and one daughter who fell in love with Chandragupta at first sight and was permitted by her father Nanda to marry him, "because it is customary for *Kshatriya* girls to marry according to their choice" (*Prāyaḥ Kshatriya-kanyānāṁ śasyate hi svayamvaraḥ*). This seems to imply that Nanda was still claiming that he was a Kshatriya.

Monumental Evidence. The Buddhist tradition as well as the Jain tradition connecting the peacock, *Mayūra*, with the Moriya or Maurya dynasty receives a curious confirmation in striking monumental evidence. The Asoka pillar at Nandangarh has been found to bear at its bottom below the surface of the ground the figure of a peacock, while the same figure is repeated in several sculptures on the Great Stūpa at Sānchi, which are associated with Asoka on the basis of the stories of his life which these sculptures translate into stone. Both Foucher and Sir John Marshall agree with Grünwedel who was the first to suggest that this representation of the peacock was due to the fact that the peacock was the dynastic emblem of the Mauryas.

Summary. Now to sum up these various traditions regarding the origin and lineage of Chandrgupta with reference to their points of agreement and divergence. The Greek accounts agree with the *Purāṇas* in ascribing a disreputable origin not to Chandragupta but to the Nanda king. They describe the Nanda king as an illegitimate son of a barber, while the *Purāṇas* describe the Nandas as Śūdras. The Greek accounts further trace their low origin to their Śūdra father described as a handsome barber with whom the queen of Nanda fell in love, carried on illicit intercourse, and then contrived to get her royal husband out of her way by murder. The *Mudrārākshasa*, however, turns the table, proclaiming a noble lineage for the Nandas, and Chandragupta as a mere upstart of unknown family. The drama is also sometimes inconsistent in suggesting a Nanda origin for Chandragupta. Buddhist and Jain traditions are at one in declaring for him a noble birth.

It is interesting to note that the Greek accounts of Alexander's invasion of India mention an Indian tribe called the *Morieis* corresponding to the Moriyas.

Early Life. Much romance has gathered round the origin and early life of Chandragupta, because so little is known of them. Legend grows in obscurity. It is fond of making hero of a man who rises to greatness from lowly origin. The details of Chandragupta's early life we owe to Buddhist legends. The chief sources of these legends are the two works already mentioned, *viz.*, (1) the *Mahāvaṁsa Ṭīkā*, also known as *Vaṁsatthappakāsinī* (of about first half of the 10th century A.D.) and (2) the *Mahābodhivaṁsa* written by *Upatissa* (of about 2nd half of 10th century A.D.). Both these texts draw upon older sources known as the *Sīhalaṭṭhakathā* and the *Uttaravihāraṭṭhakathā*. The former is supposed to be the work of Thera Mahinda (Asoka's son) and his companion monks from Magadha, who were chosen for the Mission to Ceylon by the Head of the church. Asoka added to it laymen like Bodhigupta and Sumitra who were brothers of his first wife, Devī. The king of Ceylon, Devānāṁpriya Tishya, appointed both of them as chief writers on the Conquest of Ceylon by the Bodhi Tree (*Laṇkājaya-Mahālekhaka*). Their work, which is no longer extant, appears to have been partly incorporated into the *Uttaravihāraṭṭhakathā*. This work gives some details about Maurya history not contained in the *Sihalaṭṭhakathā*. These were probably supplied by the aforesaid historians from Magadha and incorporated into the work of the dissenting and heterodox Uttaravihārins or Dhammaruchikas (from information supplied by Mr. C. D. Chatterji).

According to these traditions, Chandragupta came of the Kshatriya clan of the Moriyas, kinsmen of the Śākyas. The chief of the migrant Moriyas was his father who was unfortunately killed in a border-fray, leaving his family destitute. His helpless widow escorted by her brothers escaped to the city called Pushpapura (=Kusumapura =Pāṭaliputra) where she gave birth to the child Chandragupta. For his safety, the orphan was deposited by his maternal uncles at a cow-pen where he was brought up as his own son by the cowherd who later sold him as a grown-up to a hunter by whom he was employed to tend cattle. The story goes that at the village common, the boy, Chandragupta, showed himself to be a born leader by inventing the game of playing the king (*Rājakīḷaṁ*) with his companions as his subordinates and even getting up a mock court at which he was practising administration of justice. It was at one of these rural royal games that Chandragupta was first seen by Chāṇakya. Chāṇakya, with his prophetic vision, at once discovered in that rustic foundling the promise and signs of royalty and straightway bought him of his foster-father by paying down 1000 *kārshāpaṇas* on the spot. Chandragupta must have been then a boy of only eight or nine years. Chāṇakya, who is described as a resident of the city of Taxila (*Takkasilā-nagara-vāsī*,) returned to his native city with the boy and had him educated for a period of 7 or 8 years at that famous seat of learning where all the 'sciences and arts' of the times were taught, as we know from the *Jātakas*. He gave him an all-round education both in the humanities, and also in the practical or technical arts (*bāhusachchābhāvañcha* ; *uggahitasippakañcha*).

Education at Taxila. The *Jātakas* tell us how the kings of those days sent their sons for education to Taxila, where there were "world-renowned" teachers. We read: "Youths of Kshatriya and Brāhman castes came from all India to be taught the arts by one of these teachers." Taxila was a seat of advanced studies and not elementary education. Its students are spoken of as being admitted there at the age of 16 or when they "come of age." Elderly students or householders also studied there as day-scholars, making their own arrangements for residence. We read of a teacher at Taxila whose school had only princes as pupils, "princes who were at that time in India to the number of 101." Among the subjects of study are mentioned the three Vedas and eighteen *Sippas* or Arts among which are mentioned Archery (*Issattha-sippa*), Hunting, Elephant Lore (*Hatthisutta*) which were appropriate for princes. Training was given in both theory and practice. Taxila was known for its special schools of Law, Medicine, and Military Science. We have also reference to its Military Academy counting 103 princes as its pupils. We are told how a pupil, after graduation in military science, received by way of a diploma a present from his teacher of his own " sword, a bow and an arrow, a coat of mail, and a diamond," and was asked by his teacher to take his place as the head of his school of 500 pupils, all seeking instruction in the military arts, as he was old and wanted to retire [See Chapter XIX of my *Ancient Indian Education* (Macmillans, London) for references].

Thus Chāṇakya could not do better for the education of his youthful protege than to place him at Taxila for the purpose. An eight years' education at its military school in the stimulating company of so many princely pupils must have made him a master of the military sciences and arts of the days and gave him the best possible preparation and equipment for the great task to which Chandragupta was consecrated by his guardian, Chāṇakya.

Incidentally, Chandragupta's early life and education at Taxila in a way prove the truth of Plutarch's interesting statement that Chandragupta, as a youth, had seen Alexander in the course of his campaigning in the Punjab. It was possible for a youth of that locality who must have sought an interview with the greatest military leader of the times for his own education as a military student.

And these details of Chandragupta's early life from Pali sources also confirm the truth of Justin's statement that he was " born in humble life."

CHAPTER II

CONQUESTS AND CHRONOLOGY

First Meeting of Chanakya and Chandragupta. We have already seen the circumstances under which Chāṇakya and Chandragupta met for the first time in their lives. That meeting was a most fateful meeting fraught with immense consequences not merely to their personal history, but also to the history of their country. For Chandragupta it proved to be the turning-point in his life. No longer was he to live the insecure life of a hunter in the obscurity of wilderness. He was now to live the cultured life of a citizen, receiving the highest possible education of the times at India's greatest seat of learning at far-off Taxila, and preparing for one of the biggest enterl prises in history. But before dealing with the details of his politica- career, it is necessary to know the details of the circumstances which led up to the fateful meeting of Chāṇakya and Chandragupta in the vicinity of far-off Pāṭaliputra.

Pataliputra as a centre of Learning. As related in the *Mahāvaṁsa Tīkā,* Chāṇakya came all the way from Taxila to Pāṭaliputra in pursuit of learning and disputation centred at that imperial capital (*vādaṁ pariyesanto Pupphapuraṁ gantvā*).

It is an extraordinary compliment paid to the status of Pāṭaliputra as the intellectual capital of India in those days when a scholar of encyclopaedic learning like Chāṇakya, himself the product of one of the greatest centres of learning like Takshaśilā, should seek to win fresh laurels for his learning at this far-off city in eastern India.

The fame of Pāṭaliputra as a centre of learning continued through the ages, outliving its political glory. Thus it is referred to in a work which is about a thousand years later, the classical work known as *Kāvyamīmāṁsā* by the poet Rājaśekhara who makes the following interesting statement: "There is a tradition (*śrūyate*) that Pāṭaliputra was the place which was the centre of examination of all makers of *Śāstras* (*Śāstrakāra-parīkshā*), the founders and exponents of different systems. Here were thus examined eminent creative geniuses and authors like Varsha and Upavarsha, Pāṇini and Piṅgala, and Vyādi. In later times, Vararuchi and Patañjali achieved fame as scholars by first passing their examination (*parīkshā*) at this city of learning."

It will be seen that Varsha was a most ancient author as one who was the teacher of Pāṇini himself (c. 500 B.C. or earlier). Upavarsha was his brother and a commentator of *Mīmāṁsā* and *Vedānta Sūtras*, from whom citations have been made even by the great Śaṅkarāchārya. Piṅgala, according to tradition, was Pāṇini's younger brother, the author of the *Chhanda-Śāstra*. Vyādi was the grammarian who came after Pāṇini and wrote on his system. Vararuchi and Patañjali were of course much later authors. It thus appears that Rājaśekhara has mentioned all these men of learning from Varsha to Vararuchi, Piṅgala to Patañjali, in a chronological order. All these hailing from different parts of the country emerged into eminence by taking their examination at Pāṭaliputra.

Ugrasena-Nanda. The then ruler of Magadha, known as merely Nanda in Sanskrit tradition, is named Dhana-Nanda in the Pali texts which further acquaint us with the names and some particulars of all the nine Nandas. We are told that all the nine Nandas, who were brothers, ruled one after another in accordance with seniority (*vuḍḍhapaṭipāṭiyā*). Dhana-Nanda was the youngest of them. The eldest brother is named Ugrasena-Nanda, the founder of the Nanda dynasty. His early life was quite romantic, like that of Chandragupta. Originally, he was from the frontiers (*pachchanta-vāsika*) and fell into the hands of robbers who carried him captive to a frontier province called Malaya (cf. Malaya in *Mudrārākshasa*) and won him over to the doctrine that pillage was preferable to tillage as a pursuit. He enlisted himself as one of the gangs of robbers together with his brothers and kinsmen and soon became their leader. They started raiding the kingdoms of the neighbourhood (*raṭṭhaṁ vilumpamāno vicharanto*) and, marching against the cities of the frontiers (*pachchanta nagaraṁ gantvā*), gave them the ultimatum : 'Either surrender your kingdom, or give battle (*rajjam vā dentu yuddhaṁ vā*).' Gradually they aimed at supreme sovereignty (*Mahāvaṁsa Ṭīkā* in Sinhalese text, read for me by Mr. C. D. Chatterji). A robber-king thus rose to be a king of kings.

But he achieved this position by nefarious means on which the Buddhist text is silent but other sources throw some light. Bāṇa's *Harshacharita*, a text of the seventh century A.D., records the story that Kākavarṇī Śaiśunāga was killed by a dagger thrust into his throat in the neighbourhood of his city' (Pāṭaliputra). He is called Kākavarṇa in the *Purāṇas* but Kālāsoka in the *Mahāvaṁsa* list of the kings preceding the Nandas. Very probably the incident of this assassination is related by Curtius when he states : "The father of Agrammes was a barber scarcely staving off hunger by his daily earnings, but who, from his being not uncomely in person, had gained the affections of the queen, and was by her influence advanced to too near a place in the confidence of the reigning monarch. Afterwards, however, he treacherously murdered his sovereign and then, under the pretence of acting as guardian to the royal children, usurped the supreme authority, and, having put the young princes to death, begot the present king." The form Agrammes is modified into *Xandramas* by Diodorus, and F. W. Thomas takes it to be the equivalent of *Chandramas*. He takes Agrammes to be Dhana-Nanda [*Cambridge History of India*, I. p. 469], taking Dhana-Nanda to be his nickname, and Chandramas as his personal name. 'The young princes' mentioned by Curtius as being murdered by Ugrasena-Nanda were most probably the ten sons of Kālāsoka-Kākavarṇī of the aforesaid *Mahāvaṁsa* list.

It is to be noted that Buddhist tradition does not impute any base origin to the Nandas and thus runs counter to the Brahminical and Jain traditions. The first Nanda in the Buddhist account simply overthrows by force the previous ruling dynasty of Magadha as the culmination of a previous career of violence, as described above. Another notable point of divergence between Buddhist and other traditions is that the Buddhist texts, while knowing of the *nine* Nandas, and even of the name of each Nanda, describes them as brothers. The *Mahāvaṁsa* states: "*Nava Nandā* (also *navabhātaro*) *tato āsuṁ*." The worst infamy which Buddhist tradition records against these Nandas is that they were originally outlaws and robbers. The *Mahābodhivaṁsa* describes the Nanda kings as *chorapubbas*,[1] "the dacoits of old."

Dhana-Nanda insults Chanakya. Be that as it may, when Chāṇakya came to Pāṭaliputra, he saw Dhana-Nanda as the reigning king. He was notorious for his avarice, the possessor of "riches to the amount of 80 *koṭis*," and given to "levying taxes even on skins, gums, trees and stones." He was called Dhana-Nanda by way of contempt, because he was "addicted to hoarding treasure" [*Mahāvaṁsa Ṭīkā*]. The *Kathāsaritsāgara* speaks of Nanda's "990 millions of gold pieces." He is stated to have buried all his treasure in a rock excavated in the bed of the river Ganges [*Ib.*]. The fame of his riches reached the far South. A Tamil poem refers to his wealth "which having accumulated first in Pāṭali hid itself in the floods of the Ganges" [Aiyangar's *Beginnings of South Indian History*, p. 89].

1. The Pali Text Society prints the word as "*c'orapubbā*" (=*ca orapubbā*) but admitted the above reading *corapubbā* (*chorapubbā*) as correct at the suggestion of Mr. C. D. Chatterji (11th Dec. 1929).

But Chāṇakya found him a changed man. Instead of any more hoarding of wealth, he was now bent upon spending it in charities which he organised through the machinery of an institution called *Dānaśālā* administered by a *Saṁgha* whose president was to be a Brāhman. The rule was that the President could make gifts amounting up to a crore of coins, while the juniormost member of the *Saṁgha* could give up to one lac. Chāṇakya came to be chosen as the president of this *Saṁgha*. But, as fate would have it, the king could not brook him for the ugliness of his features and manners and dismissed him from that office. Chāṇakya, incensed at this insult, cursed the king, threatened the ruin of his race, and escaped from his clutches in disguise as a naked Ājīvika ascetic. In his wanderings he chanced to come across the child Chandragupta under circumstances already related.

It may be noted that this story of the Buddhist text has its echo in the Sanskrit work, *Mudrārākshasa*, which mentions king Nanda expelling Chāṇakya publicly from the place of honour assigned to him in his court [*agrāsanatovakṛishṭavaśam* (I. 11)], whereupon Chāṇakya vowed that he would avenge himself on Nanda by encompassing the destruction of his whole family and progeny.

First task of Chandragupta : Overthrow of Greek rule. We now return to the history which followed Chāṇakya's fateful discovery of Chandragupta as the chosen instrument of his designs. We have seen with what patience Chāṇakya first undertook the preliminary task of giving Chandragupta the best possible upbringing and education spread over a period of eight years so as to equip him for the great schemes he had in view. The first of these was to surmount a difficulty that lay at his door. His youthful imagination was already fired by the spectacle of a foreign invasion of his fatherland in progress before his very eyes, the amount of resistance offered to it at different centres by small republican peoples of the Punjab, and the final passing away of his country under foreign Greek rule. Thus his immediate imperative task was the liberation of his country from the yoke of this subjection. He was inspired in this task by the teaching of his preceptor, Kauṭilya, who condemned foreign rule as an unmitigated evil. He condemns foreign rule (*Vairājya*) as the worst form of exploitation, where the conqueror, who subdues a country by violence (*parasyāchchhidya*), never counts it as his own dear country (*naitat mama iti manyamānaḥ*), oppresses it by overtaxation and exactions (*karshayati*), and drains it of its wealth (*apavāhayati*) [VIII 2.]. Details are wanting as to how he was able to organise measures, the ways and means for the accomplishment of that stupendous task in the atmosphere of depression created by the victory of Alexander and the breakdown of the national opposition. He had to fall back upon the remnants of that opposition, to fan into flame its dying embers, and to reorganise the military resources of the country in men and material for purposes of another national endeavour to strike a blow for its freedom.

Sources of Chandragupta's Army; the republican peoples who resisted Alexander. We learn from the *Mahāvaṁsa Ṭīkā* that on the completion of Chandragupta's education at Taxila, both Chāṇakya and Chandragupta set out for collecting recruits (*balaṁ saṁgaṇhitvā*) from different places (*tato tato balaṁ sannipātetvā*). Chāṇakya placed the army thus recruited under the command of Chandragupta (*Mahābalakāyaṁ saṅgahetvā taṁ tassa paṭipādesi*). Rhys Davids [*Buddhist India*, p. 267] points out that "it was from the Panjab that Chandragupta recruited the nucleus of the force with which he besieged and conquered Dhana-Nanda." Justin also states [XV. 4] that Chandragupta got together an army of local recruits whom he describes as "robbers." As pointed out by McCrindle [*Invasion of India by Alexander*, p. 406], the term 'robbers' indicated the republican peoples for which the Punjab was known in those days, the *Arāṭṭas* or *Arāshṭrakas*, "kingless" peoples, peoples not living under a *rāshṭra* or State, of which the usual normal type was a kingship. Baudhāyana, in his *Dharmasūtra* (*c.* 400 B. C.), describes the Punjab as the country of *Āraṭṭas* [I. 1, 2, 13-15]. The *Mahābhārata* [VIII. 44, 2070] calls the *Āraṭṭas* as *Pāñchanadas*, 'natives of the land of the five rivers', [*Ib.* 45, 2110] and olso *Vāhīkas*, 'people of the land of rivers,' comprising the Prasthalas, Madras, Gāndhāras, Khaśas, Vasātis, Sindhus, and Sauvīras.

It is also interesting to note that Kauṭilya mentions as the sources of recruitment for the army (1) the *Choras*, or *Pratirodhakas*, of the day, the robbers and outlaws, (2) the *Chora-gaṇas*, organised gangs of brigands, (3) the *Mlechchha* tribes like the Kirāta highlanders, (4) the *Āṭavikas*, the foresters, and (5) the Warrior clans called *Śastropajīviśreṇīs*, and that he counts the soldiery recruited from these clans as most heroic (*pravīra*) [VII. 10; 14; VIII. 14]. The Punjab in those days had abundance of this type of military material. Alexander himself had to deal with some of these peoples in his campaigns. As is shown below, it is possible to find out the Indian equivalents of their Greek names as recorded in the classical accounts of his invasion.

Republican peoples known to the '*Mahābhārata*.' The *Mahābhārata* mentions the following republican peoples of these regions, viz.

(1) *Yaudheyas* [II. 52 ; VII. 9] ; (2) *Kshudrakas* (II. 51 ; VI. 57] ; (3) *Mālavas* [II. 32 ; II 52] ; (4) *Vasātis* [II. 52 ; V. 30] ; (5) *Śibis* [II. 32 ; II. 52] ; (6) *Udumbaras* [II. 52] ; (7) *Prasthalas* [VIII. 44] ; (8) *Trigartas* [II. 52] ; (9) *Madras* [II. 52 ; VI. 61] ; (10) *Kekayas* [III 120] and (11) *Agreyas* [III. 254].

Republican peoples known to Pāṇini. Pāṇini's term for a republic is *Saṁgha* or *Gaṇa* [III. 3, 86]. Most of these republics took to the pursuit of arms and were known as *Āyudhajīvi-Saṁghas*, 'Warriors-communities.' They were of the *Vāhīka* country, 'the land of rivers,' another name for the Punjab [V. 3, 114]. As examples of these self-governing communities of warriors, Pāṇini mentions the following :

(1) *Kshudrakas* (Greek *Oxydrakai*), [IV. 2, 45].

(2) *Mālavas* (Greek *Malloi*) [*Ib.*].

(3) *Vṛikas*, also called *Vārkeṇya* [V. 3, 115], most probably corresponding to the people known as Hyrcanians (Śakas) mentioned as *Varkānaḥ* in the Behistun and as *Varkāḥ* in another old Persian inscription of Darius I.

(4) *Dāmani* and others (not identified) [V. 3, 116].

(5) Confederacy of the six *Trigartas* comprising (a) *Kauṇḍoparatha*, (b) *Dāṇḍaki*, (c) *Kaushṭaki*, (d) *Jālamāni*, (e) *Brāhmagupta* and (f) *Jānaki*.

(6) *Parśu*, associated with *Asura* and *Rakshas*, and probably of the country called *Pārśa* in the Behistun inscription of Darius I, the place of origin of the Achaemenians, whence the name Persia.

(7) *Yaudheyas*.

(8) *Sālvas* (Alwar and its surrounding country), a large confederacy comprising (a) *Udumbaras*, (b) *Tilakhalas*, (c) *Madrakāras*, (d) *Yugandharas*, (e) *Bhūliṅgas*, (f) *Śarandaṇḍas*, (g) *Budhas*, (h) *Ajakrandas* and (i) *Ajamīḍhas*, [IV. I, 173].

(9) *Bhargas*, mentioned in the *Gaṇa-pāṭha* along with (a) *Karushas*, (b) *Kekayas*, (c) *Kāśmīras*, (d) *Sālvas*, (e) *Susthalas*, (f) *Uraśas* (of Hazara District) and (g) *Kauravyas*, [IV. 1, 178].

(10) *Ambashṭhas* (Greek *Abastanoi*) who are associated in the *Mahābhārata* [II.52, 14-15] with the *Śibis*, *Kshudrakas*, *Mālavas* and other north-western tribes.

(11) *Hāstināyana* [VI. 4, 174] (Greek *Astanenoi*).

(12) *Prakaṇva* [VI. 1, 153], corresponding to modern Ferghana whose people called the *Parikanioi* correspond to *Prakaṇvāyanas* [Sten Konow, *Kharoshṭhī Inscriptions*, p. XVIII.].

(13) *Madras*, [IV. 2, 131].

(14) *Madhumantas* [IV. 2, 133; *Mbh.* Bhīshma P., IX. 53] corresponding to the *Mohmands*.

(15) *Āprītas* [IV. 2, 53], (Greek *Aparytai*, corresponding to the *Afridis*).

(16) *Vasāti* [*Ib.*] (Greek *Ossadioi*).

(17) *Sibis* [IV. 3, 112] (Creek *Sibioi*).

(18) *Āśvāyana* [IV. 1, 110] and *Āśvakāyana* [*Ib.* 99) corresponding to Greek *Aspasii* and *Assakenoi* whose stronghold was Massaga (=*Maśakāvatī*).

It is interesting to note that the city called Aornos by the Greeks corresponds to the term *Varaṇā* used by Pāṇini [IV. 2, 82].

In the above list, the republican peoples outside the Punjab and the sphere of Chandragupta's work are omitted.

It will be seen from the above list that in Pāṇini's time there were both individual republics functioning by themselves and confederacies of such republics such as the *Trigarta shashṭha*, or the *Sālvas* [V. S. Agrawala's *Pāṇini as a Source of History* to be published shortly.]

As Arrian tells us [IV. 21], a large part of the Punjab was then held by these "independent Indian tribes" whom Curtius [IX. 4] describes as "fierce nations" ready to resist Alexander "with their blood". The kingdom which was restored by Alexander to his old enemy, king Poros (=Paurava), comprised territories held by "fifteen republican peoples owning 5000 considerable cities and villages without number" [Plutarch, *Lives.* lx].

How they fought Alexander : their military resources. The military potentialities and heroism of these 'independent' peoples of the Punjab were brought to light by Alexander's invasion and must have been observed by youthful Chandragupta. The story of their resistance against Alexander's campaigns is not less inspiring than the story of Alexander's victories. The Indian opposition to Alexander which was offered to him from different centres may be appraised and assessed in the light of the facts and figures recorded by the Greeks themselves.

Alexander had its first taste from the tribal chief whom the Greeks call Astes corresponding to Sanskrit *Hastin*, the chief of the people known by the Indian name of *Hāstināyana* [Pāṇini, VI. 4, 174]. Greek *Astakenoi* or *Astanenoi*, with his capital at Peukelaotis or Pushkalāvatī. This heroic chief stood the Greek siege of his walled town for full thirty days till he fell fighting.

Similarly, the *Āśvāyanas* and *Āśvakāyanas* fought the invader to a man, as will be evident from the fact that as many as 40,000 of them were taken as captives. Their economic prosperity may also be noted from the fact that as many as 230,000 oxen fell into the hands of Alexander.

The *Āśvakāyanas* gave the battle to Alexander with an army of 30,000 cavalry, 38,000 infantry, and 30 elephants, aided by 7,000 mercenaries from the plains, all garrisoned in their fortified capital called Massaga [Sanskrit *Maśaka*, which stood on the banks of the river called Maśakāvatī in the *Kāśikā* comment on Pāṇini (IV. 2, 85; VI. 3, 119)], led by the heroic Queen Cleophis (= Sanskrit *Kṛipā* ?), "resolved to defend their country to the last extremity." Even their women took part in the defence along with the Queen. Even their mercenaries, at first vacillating, caught their spirit and preferred "a glorious death to a life with dishonour" [McCrindle's *Invasion*, pp. 194 (Curtius), 270 (Diodorus)]. Their spirit infected the neighbouring hill-country called Abhisāra, which also joined them in their defence.

The free cities of the region also followed suit, such as Aornos, Bazira, Ora or Dyrta, each of which surrendered after a protracted siege.

The Indian military strength was seen at its highest in the army of King Poros (Paurava) who was Alexander's most formidable enemy whom he opposed with an army estimated by Arrian at 30,000 foot, 4,000 horse, 300 chariots, and 200 elephants. Even after his defeat, Alexander had to seek his alliance.

The Agalassoi fought Alexander with an army of 40,000 foot and 3,000 horse. We are told that in one of their towns, the citizens numbering about 20,000 cast themselves into the flames, along with their wives and children, rather than submitting as prisoners to the enemy.

Next, Alexander had to meet the opposition organised by a confederacy of the autonomous peoples, such as the Mālavas and the Kshudrakas, whose allied strength was made up of 90,000 foot, 10,000 horse, and above 900 chariots. Even their Brāhmans left the pen for the sword, and died fighting, " with few taken as prisoners."

The Kaṭhas were another heroic people who " enjoyed the highest reputation for courage" [Arrian, V. 22, 2]. We are told that their casualties alone amounted to 17,000 killed and 70,000 captives.

The Mālavas by themselves defended the passage of a river with 50,000 men.

The Ambashṭhas had an army of 60,000 foot 6,000 horse, and 500 chariots.

In the campaigns of the lower Indus, the number of killed alone amounted to 80,000. In this region, it was the Brāhmans who took the lead and created the spirit of resistance and war fever, and cheerfully sacrificed their lives in the defence of their *Dharma* [Plutarch, *Lives*, lix ; *Cambridge History*, I. p. 378].

Causes of their defeat. It may be noted that all these fairly large armies were recruited from small republican States. The number of the army was very large in proportion to the number of the total population of the State concerned. These republican peoples must have fought to a man, and mobilised their entire man-power in defence of their freedom in a sheer spirit of patriotism. Even their women fought with the men. If their heroic fight in the defence of their liberties against a supreme military leader like Alexander had failed for the time being, it was because it lacked leadership, organisation, unity of direction, and pooling of resources. The defence was far too localised and isolated at different centres. It was not organised into a national defence. Alexander was thus able to deal with the defence piecemeal, to proceed against each State separately, and to subdue it easily. The multiplicity of States prevented a united front against a common enemy and caused the collapse of opposition at individual and isolated centres. Division was fatal to defence. Some kind of national opposition was organised for once by the confederacy of the Kshudrakas and Mālavas who united their military resources in a powerful allied army. Such a federal army was known even in the days of Pāṇini who calls it 'the Kshaudraka-Mālavī-senā.' But these defects and deficiencies of the Indian military situation were soon to be removed by a great leader like Chandragupta with his superior power of organisation.

It was left to the genius of Chāṇakya and Chandragupta to exploit and utilise once again the magnificent military material and resources, potentialities and possibilities, available in such abundance all over the Punjab among her republican peoples and States and her general population. It was easy for them to produce out of this material, the unconquered spirit of resistance in the people, a well-organised army to fight freedom's battle and to win it.

Other recruits for Chandragupta's Army. But Chandragupta did not confine his army to the mere local recruits, if we may believe in the legends about it. For instance, the *Mudrārākshasa* mentions an alliance which Chāṇakya had arranged with a Himalayan chief named Parvataka or Parvateśa. The Jain text, *Pariśishṭaparvan*, also refers to this Himalayan alliance, stating that "Chāṇakya went to Himavatkūṭa and entered into alliance with Parvataka, the king of that region." Buddhist accounts also mention a Parvata as a close associate of Chāṇakya. Thus three traditions record this alliance. F. W. Thomas has gone further in suggesting (*Camb. Hist. of India*, Vol. I p. 471), that this Parvataka was perhaps the same person as king Poros of the Greeks. The suggestion is quite plausible, considering what a large place Poros had filled in the politics of his country in his time, so that no adventure in that region could be undertaken without enlisting his support.

The *Mudrārākshasa* gives us the further information that his Himalayan alliance gave Chandragupta a composite army recruited from a variety of peoples. Among these are mentioned the following: Śakas, Yavanas (probably Greeks), Kirātas, Kāmbojas, Pārasikas, Bahlīkas [II. 12]. Chandragupta was opposed by a coalition of 5 kings, viz, Chitravarmā of Kulūta, Simhanāda of Malaya, Pushkarāksha of Kāśmīra, the Saindhava prince, Sindhusheṇa, and Meghākhya, the king of the Pārasīkas, who joined with a large force of cavalry (*prithuturagabalaḥ*) [I. 20]. The army of Malayaketu comprised recruits from the following peoples: Khaśa, Māgadha, Gāndhāra, Yavana, Śaka, Chedi, and Hūṇa [V. II]. Thus these various peoples, mostly from the Punjab and the frontier Highlands, were involved in the great war between Chandragupta and his enemies in Magadha. This list unfortunately affects the value of *Mudrārākshasa* as a source of history. Some of the peoples named in it such as the Śakas or the Hūnas appear in Indian history much later than the time of Chandragupta.

Insecurity of Greek Rule. But apart from the military strength which Chandragupta was able to mobilise for his mission, it was materially helped by the internal conditions of the country and other factors which did not augur well for the future of Greek rule in India. Even from the very beginning, the course of Alexander's invasion did not run smooth. It appeared to be smooth only on the surface. Its difficulties lay deeper. Alexander was not sure of his rear. It was threatened by rebellions both among Greeks and Indians. The prospects of his enterprise did not appeal as much to his followers as to him personally. Alexander's policy was to plant colonies of Greek veterans at suitable centres, the new eastern cities, to mark the progress of his conquests, and to secure its fruits [Arrian, V. 27, 5]. Such colonies were set up first in Bactria and Sogdiana, but it was against the will of the colonists who were not reconciled to this exile. They were always longing for opportunity to desert.

When Alexander was fighting with the distant Mālavas and received a wound, a rumour of his death spread far and wide, and at once these Greek colonists numbering 3,000 left for home [Diodorus, XVII. 99]. Alexander himself thought of these colonies as penal settlements to which the Greeks convicted of disloyalty were committed [Justin, XII. 5, 8, 13].

The Greek Satrapies. Nor was the attitude of the Indians, who were subdued, more favourable. Their spirit of revolt was not subdued. The administrative arrangements which Alexander made to secure his conquests betray his own sense of their insecurity. He divided Greek India into six Satrapies, three on the west side of the Indus, and three on the east. The three western Satraps were Greeks, but not the eastern Satraps who were all Indians. Of the three western Satraps, Peithon was posted as governor of Sind. Nicanor was placed in charge of the province called 'India-west-of-the Indus'. It comprised lower Kabul valley and the hill tracts up to the Hindukush, with its capital at Pushkalāvatī (Charsadda). The governor had at his disposal a Macedonian garrison under commandant Philip. Higher up, Oxyartes was appointed governor of the province of Paropanisadae (Kabul valley) with its capital at the new city called 'Alexandria under the Caucasus'. At first, Alexander tried Persian Satraps, but they failed. As Curtius informs us [IX. 8], "there were charges of extortion and tyranny proved against the Persian Satrap, Tyriespes, by the people of the Paropanisadae." This was about 326 B. C. Conditions were sought to be stabilised by Alexander appointing as Satrap his own father-in-law, Oxyartes, another Iranian noble.

Alexander could not venture to post Greek governors to the east of the Indus. Here the three Satrapies were placed under Indian kings : Āmbhi, king of Taxila, ruling from the Indus to the Hydaspes; Poros (Paurava) ruling from the Hydaspes to the Hyphasis ; and the king of Abhisāra country (Kashmir) ruling over the remainder.

Indian Unrest : Murder of Satrap Nicanor. The position of the Greek governors to the west of the Indus rapidly became precarious. First, Kandahar raised the standard of rebellion at the instigation of an Indian chief whom the Greeks called Samaxus or Damaraxus. Next came the turn of the Āśvāyanas who dispatched the Greek Satrap, Nicanor, planted in their midst [Arrian, V. 20, 7]. The Āśvakāyanas made the position of their Greek governor very unsafe. It was the traitor of an Indian, Sisikottus, or Śaśīgupta, the Indian agent of Greek Imperialism. Alexander sent him help from his westernmost Satrapy, as also further help under Philip from Taxila.

Decline of Recruits and Morale. All this trouble was brewing in 326 B.C., when Alexander was busy in the interior in the thick of his campaigns. His supply of men was failing as he was advancing farther and farther. His progress was brought to a standstill on the banks of the Chenab till the situation was saved by the arrival of Thracian reinforcements from distant Iran. But the Beas proved the limit of his advance. It was because the limit of endurance was reached by his followers. The situation was thus brought home to him by Koinos as their spokesman : "From our ranks you sent away home from Baktra the Thessalians as soon as you saw they have no stomach for further toils .. . Of the other Greeks, some have been settled in the cities founded by you where all of them are not willing residents ; others still share our toils and dangers. They and the Macedonian army have lost some of their numbers in the fields of battle ; others have been disabled by wounds ; others have been left behind in different parts of Asia, but the majority have perished by disease. A few only out of many survive, and these few possess no longer the same bodily strength as before, while their spirits are still more depressed. You see yourself how many Macedonians and Greeks started with you and how few of us are left."

Inherent Defect of Alexander's Scheme. These words expose the inherent difficulty in the way of Alexander's ambitious scheme materialising. It was impossible to build up an empire which could not command its supplies and the support of its own people.

The Indian popular opinion on the situation was cleverly conveyed to Alexander by an Indian ascetic. Taking a piece of dry hide, he placed it on the ground and asked Alexander to tread on it. As he placed his foot on one of its ends, the other ends flew up. It was difficult to keep the hide flat. Alexander was thus shown a visible image of what his strange enterprise meant, the uncertain and unstable consequences of campaigns carried on in countries too far from "the centre of his dominion" [McCrindle's *Invasion*, p. 315]. The fact was that the Indians do not seem to have taken Alexander's invasion very seriously. It was like a spectacular march through the country. The consolidation of conquests in distant countries depended on communications which could be ensured. The Indian attitude is truly expressed in the poet's words :

"The East bowed low before the blast
In patient, deep disdain ;
She let the legions thunder past,
And plunged in thought again."

—*Mathew Arnold.*

Murder of Philip. To return to the fate of the Greek Satrapies, on the assassination of governor Nicanor by the Indian "mutineers", Commandant Philip was deputed by Alexander to take his place. Philip was the most experienced Greek administrator in India. He started as Alexander's agent at Taxila to keep watch over the activities of the powerful Indian chief, Paurava. Alexander depended upon Philip to guard the rear of his advance down the Hydaspes. Alexander later deputed him to take charge of the territories of the free peoples, the Mālavas, and the Kshudrakas, as they were conquered by Alexander, and these stretched as far south as the confluence of the Indus and the Chenab. He was now put in charge of the most important province of Greek India which was like the gateway to India. Philip very soon left his new headquarters to see Alexander off on his return journey down the Hydaspes. But little did he know that his own days were numbered ! He was assassinated on his return.

A Blow to Greek Rule. According to Arrian [VI. 27, 2], Philip fell a victim to jealousy between the Greeks and Macedonians. But such a grave incident was due to deeper causes, to popular discontent with foreign rule. The murder of a Greek official of commanding position like Philip, in whom Greek rule was embodied and represented at its best, was really a fatal blow struck at that rule. He was the pillar of Greek Imperialism in India. His assassination took place in 325 B.C. when Alexander was in a position to retrace his steps to avenge it, as he had not gone even as far as Carmania. But he could not do so. The act was a challenge to Alexander's authority. But it was beyond his power to answer it. Alexander was retreating from India, with Greek rule retreating with him. The only remedy that he could think of was to seek the good offices of his Indian ally, the king of Taxila, to whom he sent despatches asking him kindly "to assume the administration of the province previously governed by Philippus until he could send a Satrap to govern it" [Arrian, VI. 27]. Such a Satrap was never sent. Eventually Alexander had to trust his Indian ally with that charge. This meant that the Indian king was helped to extend his authority beyond the Indus and the frontiers up to the Kabul valley and the Hindukush. A Thracian named Eudamus was now left as the sole Greek agent in India, who, under the Indian king, was placed in charge of the military garrison at Pushkalāvatī and also of the "command of the scattered bodies of Greek and Macedonian troops, with authority over the various colonists of Hellenic nationality" settled in that region [*Cambridge History*, I. p. 429].

Collapse of Greek Rule after Alexander's death in 323 B.C. On the top of this took place the death of Alexander[1] himself (without issue) in 323 B.C. in distant Babylon, followed by confusion in his own empire. The empire could not hold together. His generals immediately met and decided on its division among themselves. A second partition of the empire took place in 321 B. C. at Triparadisus, in which no part of India to the east of the Indus was included as a part of that empire. The Greek governor of Sind, Peithon, was now removed, and placed in charge of the province between the Indus and the Paropanisus. Eudamus was the solitary Greek agent lingering on in India, but he had no official position in the empire and is ignored in its partitions. He probably set himself up as the leader of the Hellenic 'outlanders' left in the valleys of the Indus and the Hydaspes, but he, too, left India in 317 B. C. to help his chief, Eumenes, against Antigonos, with a small force of infantry and cavalry and of 120 elephants which he had secured by slaying treacherously an Indian chief (supposed to be Poros) who was his trusted colleague. Poor Eudamus met his doom at the hands of Antigonos [Diodorus, XIX. 44, 1]. Peithon also left his province and joined the fray and met the same fate. He fell fighting by the side of Demetrius at the battle of Gaza [I *b*. 85, 2]. There was no more Greek to take place of either in India.

Chandragupta as Leader of Revolution. The Greek withdrawal from India was not an automatic process. It was forced by a revolution, a war of independence declared by Chandragupta as its leader. The assassinations of the Greek governors are not to be looked upon as mere accidents or isolated events. They were the preliminary incidents of a planned scheme of attack against Greek rule. The two years, 325 B. C. 323 B.C., that intervened between

---

1. The name Alexander passed immediately into Indian literature in various forms. Asoka in his inscriptions uses the forms *Alikasudara* (Shahbazgarhi Rock Edict XIII) and *Alikyasudala* (Kālsi text) Alexandria is transformed into *Alasanda* in *Milindapañho*. Sylvan Levi reads a definite, though solitary, reference in Sanskrit Literature to Alexander the Great himself in a passage in Bāṇa's *Harshacharita* stating that "Alasa-Chanḍakosa having conquered the earth did not penetrate into *Strīrājya* or the Kingdom of women." Alexander is here meant because Greek tradition mentions his conquest of a Kingdom of Amazons which he abstained from entering as special favour [*Memorial Sylvain Levi*, p. 414 (in French)].

According to Weber [*Berlin S. B*, 1890, p. 903], "If Indian literature remembered Alexander at all, it was only in the form of a bogey called *Skanda*, used to frighten naughty children" [Tarn, *The Greeks in Bactria and India*, p. 168].

the death of Philip and that of Philip's master were busy years for those who were planning India's freedom. What was then happening may be gathered from the following words of Justin [XV. 4], our only source of evidence for this fateful episode in India's history : "India, after the death of Alexander, had shaken, as it were, the yoke of servitude from its neck and put his governors to death. The author of this liberation was Sandrocottus. This man was of humble origin but was stimulated to aspire to regal power by supernatural encouragement; for, having offended Alexander (*Alexandrum* which some scholars replace by the name *Nandrum* or Nanda) by his boldness of speech, and orders being given to kill him, he saved himself by swiftness of foot; and, while he was lying asleep, after his fatigue, a lion of great size, having come up to him, licked off with his tongue the sweat that was running from him, and after gently waking him, left him. Being first prompted by this prodigy to conceive hopes of royal dignity, he drew together a band of robbers and instigated the Indians to overthrow the existing (Greek) government. Sometimes after, as he was going to war with the generals of Alexander, a wild elephant of great bulk presented itself before him of its own accord and, as tamed down to gentleness, took him on his back and became his guide in the war and conspicuous in fields of battle. Sandrocottus, having thus acquired a throne, was in possession of India when Seleucus was laying the foundations of his future greatness". Stripped of its miraculous elements, the passage is a record of important history. It declares definitely that Chandragupta was the hero of this Indian war of independence. It also exhibits Chandragupta's plan of action which was first to dispose of what may be called the tall poppies of Greek India, its provincial governors who were Alexander's generals. We have already seen how this plan was given effect to by the assassination of the two most important Greek Satraps, Nicanor and Philip. It may be taken for granted that the removal of these two Greek governors practically meant the overthrow of Greek rule in India. Alexander when living was unable to take any effective steps against this defiance of his authority, and, after his death in 323 B.C., there was disruption in his empire, and India was left alone by the generals who partitioned the empire. Thus it may be assumed that the death of Alexander meant the death of Greek rule in India. We have already seen how the provisions of the second partition of Alexander's empire in 321 B.C. practically point to the Greek recognition of the independence of India which was achieved by Chandragupta about 323 B.C., and, certainly, before 321 B.C.

If may be further noted that even if the reading *Alexander* is taken for the word *Nandrum* in the above passage of Justin, it will be quite in accord with the probabilities of the situation. The hero of Indian independence must have impressed Alexander with the promise of his future and roused his suspicion and enmity. This only added a private cause to the national cause of Chandragupta's hostility to Greek rule.

War against Nanda : Stories of its strategy. With the first part of his mission in life thus achieved in liberating the Punjab from foreign rule, he now turned to its second part, the liberation of the other parts of the country from the tyranny of its rulers, the hated Nandas. Unfortunately, there is not much evidence available on this important event of Chandragupta's conquest of Magadha. There is, however, evidence to show that the event created a widespread sensation and roused popular interest. It passed into folk lore and tradition. It seems that, after recruiting their army locally in the Punjab in the manner described above, Chāṇakya and Chandragupta started by invading the countries on the frontiers (*āntojanapadaṁ pavisitvā*) and plundering their villages (*gāmaghātādikammaṁ*) in their desire for sovereignty (*rajjaṁ ichchhanto*). Chandragupta's movement was from the frontier to the interior of India, towards Magadha and Pāṭaliputra, but he first made mistakes in strategy. The story is thus related : "In one of these villages a woman [by whose hearth Chandragupta's spy had taken refuge] baked a *chapathy* and gave it to her child. He, leaving the edges, ate only the centre, and, throwing the edges away, asked for another cake. Then she said, 'This boy's conduct is like Chandagutta's attack on the kingdom.' The boy said, 'Why mother, what am I doing, and what has Chandagutta done?' 'Thou, my dear,' said she, 'throwing away the outside of the cake, eatest the middle only. So Chandragutta, in his ambition to be a monarch, without beginning from the frontiers, and taking the towns in order as he passed, has invaded the heart of the country .. and his army is surrounded and destroyed. That was his folly " [*Mahāvaṁsa Ṭīkā*, p. 123 ; Appendix 1]. Next, Chandragupta tried another method. He commenced operations from the frontiers (*puchchantato paṭṭhāya*) and conquered many *rāshṭras* and *janapadas*, States and peoples, on the way ; but his mistake was not to post garrisons to hold the conquests. The result was that the people left in the rear of his advance were free to combine, to encircle his army, and defeat his designs. Then the proper strategy dawned on him. He had garrisons stationed at the *rāshṭras* and *janapadas* as they were conquered (*uggahitanayā balaṁ saṁvidhāya*) and, crossing the frontiers of

Magadha with his victorious army, besieged Pāṭaliputra and killed Dhana-Nanda (Appendix I).

A similar comment on strategy is also contained in the Jain work, *Pariśishṭaparvan*, which states: "Like a child burning his finger which he greedily puts in the middle of the dish, instead of eating from the outer part which was cool, Chāṇakya had been defeated, because he had not secured the surrounding country before attacking the stronghold of the enemy. Profiting by this advice, Chāṇakya went to Himavatkūṭa and entered into alliance with Parvataka the king of that place... They opened the campaign by reducing the provinces" [VIII. 291-301]. The same text further relates that at the very opening of this campaign, Chāṇakya and Chandragupta suffered a reverse by failing to reduce a town, until Chāṇakya reduced it by a ruse, throwing its defenders off their guard. Then they devastated the country (*Nandadeśam*), besieged Pāṭaliputra, and forced Nanda to capitulate, with his reduced wealth (*kshīṇa-kośā*), army (*bala*), capacity (*dhīḥ*), and prowess (*vikrama*) [*Ib.* 301-313]. Nanda, however, was spared his life and permitted by Chāṇakya to leave Pāṭaliputra with his two wives and one daughter and as much luggage as he could carry off in a single chariot [*Ib.* 301-317].

These stories, however, bring out the fundamental fact of Indian history through the ages that all movements of conquest in India have been from the frontier to the interior, from the north to the south, from the highlands to the plains. It is only in the case of an invading naval Power like the British that its movement has followed a different direction, from the sea upwards into the inland.

Power of Nanda. The stories also bring out the probable fact that the conquest of Nanda's empire was not an easy undertaking, but the result of several attempts. It was because that empire was possessed of immense power and resources. Curtius estimates its military strength at 200,000 infantry, 20,000 cavalry, 2,000 four-horsed chariots, and 3,000 elephants. The empire was also very wide in extent. It extended as far as the Punjab. It is stated that when Alexander invaded his country which lay between the Chenab and the Ravi, the second Poros escaped for shelter into the adjoining territory of the Nanda king [McCrindle's *Invasion*, p. 273]. We have already seen how the Nanda king by his conquests made himself the supreme sovereign (*ekarāṭ*) of numerous States which he brought together under the umbrella of his sole authority (*eka-, chchhatra*). These States are described to be those of the Aikshvākus

Pañchālas, Kāśis, Haihayas, Kaliṅgas, Aśmakas, Kurus, Maithilas, Śūrasenas, and Vītihotras. All these Kshatriya dynasties were "uprooted," as the *Purāṇas* tell us. He is known to the Greeks as the ruler of peoples called the Gangaridae and the Prasii, i e., the peoples of the Ganges valley, and the Prāchyas or 'easterners', peoples living to the east of the "Middle country," such as the Pañchālas, Śūrasenas, Kosalas, and the like. Towards the south also the Nanda king extended his sovereignty by his conquest of Kalinga, as recorded in the Hāthīgumpha inscription of Khāravela. It mentions 'Nanda-Rāja' as being associated with an old aqueduct, and as having carried away to Magadha as trophies the statue (or foot-prints) of the first Jina and treasures of the royal house. Nanda rule is also stated to have extended up to the province of Kuntala in the north of Mysore in some Mysore Inscriptions [Rice, *Mysore and Coorg from Inscriptions*, p. 3]. But these inscriptions are as late as twelfth century and cannot be considered as reliable evidence, failing earlier evidence on the subject. We have also seen how, by his grinding taxation, he made himself master of untold wealth which he hoarded in subterranean chambers.

His lack of popularity. Nanda had thus enough of power and pelf. But he lacked popularity. Chandragupta himself, as we have seen, reported to Alexander that he was "hated by his subjects" and Alexander had this report confirmed by the Indian kings Poros (Paurava) and Phegelas (Bhagalā). His unpopularity is due as much to the original sin of his ancestor as mentioned above as to his tyrannical rule and exactions. Thus, his power was tottering to its fall. It was not broad-based upon the people's will. Thus the moral factor helped Chandragupta in his fight against Nanda more than the military factor.

Casualties. The details of the actual battle between Chandragupta and Nanda are not known. The Jain work *Pariśishṭaparvan* [VIII. 253-54] contains a verse stating that 'Chāṇakya recruited for Chandragupta an army by means of wealth hidden underground for the purpose of uprooting Nanda.' "It has been conjectured that he employed Greek mercenaries in his struggle with Nanda" [*Cambridge History*, I. p. 435]. That it was a bloody battle between the two is indicated in exaggerated terms in a passage in the *Milindapañho*, [*SBE*, XXVI. p. 147] stating that "100 koṭis of soldiers, 10,000 elephants, 1 lac of horses and 5,000 charioteers" were killed in action and that Bhaddaśāla was the commander of Nanda's army. We have already seen the version of the event given in the *Mudrārākshasa* which begins with Chāṇakya's statement that he has already killed all the Nine Nandas and will not spare the surviving representative of the Nanda family, the old man, Sarvārthasiddhi, who, unable to stand the siege of his city Kusumapura, betook himself to the forest. Though living there as a hermit, he was done to death under orders of Chāṇakya who was out to uproot the last offshoot of the Nanda family.

Defeat of Seleucos, 304 B. C.: Extension of Empire up to Persia. Chandragupta did not merely supplant the Nanda king in the sovereignty of Magadha. He made himself at once the sovereign of an empire which was much larger than that of Nanda, for it included the land of the five rivers up to the Indus. This empire also extended farther by his later conquests. His subsequent career may be gathered from the following statement of Plutarch [*Lives*, Chap. LXII]: "Not long afterwards, Androcottos, who had at that time mounted the throne, presented Seleukos with 500 elephants and overran and subdued the whole of India with an army of 600,000." "The throne" here is the throne of Magadha which he had won by defeating the Nanda king. The present to Seleukos was the result of a war between the two. It would appear that in the struggle for power which ensued among the generals of Alexander after his death, Seleukos won for himself a secure position as the ruler of Babylon by about 311 B C. and felt free to devote himself to the consolidation of his authority in the distant provinces. Bactria was not subdued without hard fighting. And by about 305 or 304 B. C. at the latest, he planned for a recovery of the Indian conquests of Alexander. Taking the route along the Kabul river, he crossed the Indus [Appian, *Syr.* 55]. But the expedition proved abortive and ended in an alliance. It was because he had to confront a new India, strong and united, under Chandragupta in command of a formidable army, and felt that discretion was the better part of valour. By the terms of the treaty, Seleukos ceded to Chandragupta the Satrapies of Arachosia[1] (Kandahar) and the Paropanisadae (Kabul), together

1. It is interesting to note the original old Iranian forms of these names as used in the Behistun and other inscriptions of the Achaemenian emperor Darius I (521-485 B. C.), as these names correspond closely to Sanskrit names. Thus Achaemenes (father of Teispes)=*Hakhāmani*, Darius—*Dārayavau* (Sanskrit *Dhārayadvasu*, holding, possessing goods); Cyrus=*Kuru*; Xerxes=*Kshayarsha*; Arachosia=*Harauvatī*=Sanskrit *Sarasvatī*; Vedic name of a river in S. W. Afghanistan, tributary of the river called *Haetumañt* in Avesta=classical Hermandus=modern Helmand.

Arachosia was the land of black grapes called *hārahūrā*, whence the wine called *Hārahūraka* mentioned by Kautilya (as will be seen below), just

with portions of Aria (Herat) and Gedrosia (Baluchistan). Thus Chandragupta was able to add another glorious feather to his cap. He extended his empire beyond the frontiers of India up to the borders of Persia. That is why it was possible for his grandson Asoka to declare in two of his Rock Edicts [II and XIII] that the Syrian emperor, Antiochus [*Aṁtiyako Yona-rājā*], was his "immediate" neighbour, one of his "frontagers" (an *Anta* or a *Pratyanta* king). Chandragupta on his part cemented this alliance by making a present to Seleukos of 500 war-elephants. This gift was of great value to Seleukos who was at that time very much worried by a call for help from his friends, the confederate kings Cassander, Lysimachus, and Ptolemy, against their common adversary, Antigonus. The elephants arrived in time at the battle-field of Iptus to turn the scale of victory against Antigonus. The present of Indian elephants by Chandragupta to Seleukos was followed by a demand for them in western wars. Pyrrhos transported these elephants from Epiros to Italy in 281 B. C. Hasdrubal in 251 B. C, used at Panormus elephants driven by 'Indians'. So did Hannibal and Hasdrubal during the second Punic war with Rome, and, at the battle of Raphia, Ptolemy's Libyan elephants were no match for the Indian elephants of Antiochos [Warmington, *Commerce between Roman Empire and India*, p. 151].

The present of elephants was followed by other expressions of friendly relations between the two kings. There is a suggestion made by Appian [*Syr*. 55] that there was a marriage alliance between the two kings so that Seleukos became either the father-in-law or the son-in-law of Chandragupta. It is more likely that, as Strabo suggests [XV. 724], "there was a convention establishing a *jus connubii* between the two royal families. In that land of caste, a *jus connubii* between the two peoples is unthinkable." [*Cambridge History*, I. p. 431]. That Chandragupta's relations with Seleukos continued to be very friendly is indicated by the story related by Athenaeus that he sent to Seleukos a present of some Indian drugs [*Ib*. p. 432],

---

as the green grapes of Kapiśā, Northern Afghanistan, yielded the wine called *Kāpiśāyana*.

Paropanisadae is the Greek equivalent of Babylonian *Parruparaesana*= Old Persian *Gandāra*=Sanskrit *Gandhāra* with its capital at Pushkalāvatī.

Aria in Old Persian=*Haraiva* from *Harayū* or *Sarayū*, the name of the river on which Herat stands. Haraiva is to be equated with Sanskrit Sārava derived from Sarayū mentioned by Pānini [VI. 4. 174].

India=Old Persian *Hidauv* from *Sindhu*. *Hidauv* is locative of *Hidu* [V. S. Agrawala's *Place-names in the Inscriptions of Darius* in *UPHSJ*, 1940].

while Seleukos further confirmed this friendship by sending Megasthenes as an ambassador to the Mauryan court. He had been serving as his ambassador at the court of Sibyrtius, Satrap of Arachosia. According to Arrian, Megasthenes resided for some time even at the court of Poros [V. 220], but the original is translated differently by Schwanbeck. At any rate, he must have come to live at Pāṭaliputra somewhere between 304 and 299 B.C., the date of Chandragupta's death. Thus he was able to see Mauryan India as a well-organized State under Chandragupta at the height of his power in the last days of his life.

Friendly relations were continued between India and the West after these two kings. Chandragupta's son, Bindusāra, asked the son of Seleukos, Antiochos I, to get him sweet wine, figs, and a philosopher. Antiochos I sent as his ambassador to Bindusāra Daimachus of Plataea. Pliny [*Natural History*, VI. 58] mentions Dionysius as the ambassador despatched to India by Ptolemy Philadelphus (King of Egypt, 285-247, B.B.). The Indian king to whom Dionysius was despatched must have been either Bindusāra or his son Asoka who in his Rock Edict XIII refers to him as one of the five foreign kings to whom he despatched his own Welfare Missions.

We may note in this connection that Megasthenes states that since his time "many writers (Greek writers) no longer give the river Indus as the Western boundary of India but include within it four Satrapies," as named above [Frag. LVI quoted by Pliny].

Conquest of the South. Having now extended his empire beyond the borders of India, Chandragupta next thought of extending the empire beyond the barrier of the Vindhyas to the South. In the passage cited above from Plutarch, it is stated that "he overran and subdued the whole of India with an army of 600,000." The details of this all-India conquest are lacking, but there is reliable evidence for it in the inscriptions of Asoka. In the first place, Asoka's rule in the South is declared by his inscriptions at Siddapura, Brahmagiri, and Jatinga-Rameśvara hill in the Chitaldroog District of Mysore, the Govīmaṭh and Pālkīguṇdu Inscriptions in the Kopbal Taluk, the Maski Inscription in the Deccan in the Nizam's Dominion, and the Gooty Inscription in the Kurnool District. Secondly, Asoka himself indicates the southern limits of his empire by mentioning as his "frontagers" or immediate neighbours, peoples like the Cholas and Pāṇḍyas, Satyaputras and Keralaputras [Rock Edicts II, XIII]. Thirdly, he himself informs us in his Rock Edict XIII that his own conquest was only that of Kalinga, and further that even this conquest was the cause of much pain and repentance to him, because it had to be achieved by so much violence and bloodshed, resulting in "150,000 captives (*apavuḍhe*), 100,000 killed (*hate*), and many times that number dead from the wounds received (*muṭe*)". He felt so deeply his personal responsibility for this colossal carnage and suffering that he at once foreswore such bloody conquests for the future, and declared for *Dharma-vijaya* (Moral Conquest) as his imperial policy, abolishing the previous imperial policy of aggression and annexation. He stood now for a thorough-going creed of Non-Violence or *Ahiṁsā*. Thus the conquest of the South was not the work of Asoka. Nor was it that of his father, Bindusāra, failing definite evidence as against the statement of Plutarch attributing it to Chandragupta. No doubt, Bindusāra was not a pacifist like Asoka. This is indicated by his very title, *Amitraghātā* ('slayer of foes'), and this title may have been earned by him by some of his conquests. A vague hint of these is given by the author of *Ārya-Mañjuśrī Mūla-Kalpa*, Hemachandra, and Tārānātha, who state that that apostle of violence, Chāṇakya, had outlived Chandragupta, and continued as a minister of Bindusāra, as "one of his great lords". Tārānātha states : "Chāṇakya accomplished the destruction of the nobles and kings of sixteen towns and made Bindusāra master of all the territory between the eastern and western sea". This is taken by some scholars to indicate Bindusāra's conqnest of the Deccan. It is, however, forgotten that a more authentic document, Rudradāman's inscription, describes Surāshṭra as a province of Chandragupta's empire which thus had extended from the western to the eastern sea. At the same time, we have somewhat discouraging evidence against Bindusāra's capacity as a conqueror that his north-western province of Taxila had revolted during his reign so that he had to depute his worthy son, Asoka, to quell the revolt. It may be presumed that the mere maintenance of the vast empire which was bequeathed to him by this father was too heavy a burden for a man of his easy-going disposition whose delight in life was "figs and raisin wine", for which he indented upon his friend, the Greek king, Antiochos. He can hardly be credited with any additions to the empire by his own conquests.

Sravana Belgola Traditions. We may also consider the implications of the unanimous Jain tradition that Chandragupta in his old age abdicated and followed the Jain saint Bhadrabāhu as his teacher. Both teacher and pupil then travelled towards the South and settled down at a place known as Sravana Belgola. The tradition is recorded with minor variations in a number of documents, both literary and epigraphic. The literary documents are (1) *Bṛihatkathā*

Kośa by Harisheṇa, dated in 931 A. D. (2) *Bhadrabāhu-Charita* by Ratnanandi of about 1450 A. D. (the Kannada work, *Munivaṁsābhyudaya* of c. 1680 A. D. and (4) the Kannada work, *Rājāvalīkathe*. All these works agree as to the main facts. Bhadrabāhu in consequence of a severe famine in Bihar led a migration of the Jains towards the South. Chandragupta, "the king of Pāṭaliputra," [*Rājāvalīkathe*] abdicated the throne in favour of his son and followed Bhadrabāhu as his disciple. He became his chief disciple, attended him at his death at Sravana (Śramaṇa) Belgola where he lived on as an ascetic for some years till he died of starvation according to Jain practice.

This tradition has been recorded in local inscriptions and monuments. The oldest inscription of about 600 A.D. associated "the pair (*yugma*), Bhadrabāhu along with Chandragupta *Muni*." Two inscriptions of about 900 A.D. on the Kāverī near Seringapatam describe the summit of a hill called Chandragiri as marked by the footprints of Bhadrabāhu and Chandragupta *munipati*. A Sravana Belgola inscription of 1129 mentions Bhadrabāhu 'Śrutakevalī,' and Chandragupta who acquired such merit that he was worshipped by the forest deities. Another inscription of 1163 similarly couples and describes them. A third inscription of the year 1432 speaks of Yatīndra Bhadrabāhu, and his disciple, Chandragupta, the fame of whose penance spread into other words.

To add to this striking and uniform epigraphic evidence, we have significant monumental evidence. A smaller hill at Sravana Belgola is called *Chandragiri*, because Chandragupta lived and performed his penance there. On the same hill is a cave named after *Bhadrabāhu*, as well as an ancient temple called *Chandragupta-Basti*, because it was erected by Chandragupta. Moreover, the facade of this *basti* or temple which is in the form of a perforated screen, contains 90 sculptured scenes depicting events in the lives of Bhadrabāhu and Chandragupta.

Jain Tradition. It is also to be noted that this Jain migration is the initial fact of the Digambara tradition. The Jain community was undivided for long. It was only with Bhadrabāhu that the Digambaras separated from the Śvetāmbaras.

Vincent Smith pertinently points out that it is Jain tradition alone which explains Chandragupta's unexpected exit from the throne at a time when he was comparatively young and at the height of his power. As he says, "the only direct evidence throwing light on the manner in which the eventful reign of Chandragupta Maurya came to an end is that of tradition. His abdication is an adequate explanation of his disappearance at such an early age (when he must have been under fifty)."

There is also no evidence to disprove the fact taken for granted without the need of any argument or demonstration by all Jain writers that Chandragupta became a convert to their religion. The atmosphere of Jainism had already penetrated into Pāṭaliputra, as we have already seen, in the time of the Nandas who had Jain leanings and Jain ministers [*Hindu Civilisation*, p. 277]. In the *Mudrārākshasa*, also, we find an acknowledgment of this fact in the prominent position it gives to the Jains at the court of Pāṭaliputra and the employment by Chāṇakya himself, an uncompromising champion of Brahminism, of a Jain as one of his chief emissaries Jain influence was already predominant at the royal court [Rice, *Mysore and Coorg from Inscriptions*, pp. 3-9 ; *Ep. Carn.*, II. pp. 35-43 (Inscriptions at Sravana Belgola)].

If, therefore, it is taken as a fact that Chandragupta spent the last days of his life at Sravana Belgola, it is not unreasonable to assume that he settled down at a place within the limits of his empire and a place so close to Asoka's inscriptions.[1]

Tamil Tradition. Further, the Maurya invasion of the South is also recorded in Tamil tradition. There are four references to it in Tamil works, three in *Ahanānūru* and the fourth in *Puranānūru*. These speak of the *Moriyas* cutting their way through the rocks with their chariots, "their army of horses and elephants", to subdue the king of Mohūr who had refused to submit. In this expedition, they

1. It may be noted that Fleet [*IA*, XXI. p. 156] did not believe in this tradition and considered Bhadrabāhu of Inscription No. 1 as Bhadrabāhu II mentioned in *Sarasvatī Gachchha Paṭṭāvalī* as becoming Pontiff in 53 B. C., with his disciple Guptigupta succeeding him as Pontiff in 31 B. C. In his opinion, this Guptigupta has been confused with Chandragupta.

Dr. Hoernle, however (*Ib.*, pp. 59-60], after a critical study of all the Jain *Paṭṭāvalīs*, believes in the tradition and records his conclusion thus : "Before Bhadrabāhu, the Jain community was undivided. With him the Digambaras separated from the Śvetāmbaras. The question is, who this Bhadrabāhu was. The Śvetāmbara *paṭṭāvalīs* know only *one* Bhadrabāhu who, from the dates assigned to him by the Śvetāmbaras and Digambaras alike, must be identical with Bhadrabāhu I of the Digambaras. Considering the varying and contradictory character of the Digambara tradition, the probability is that the inception of the great separation took place under Bhadrabāhu I who died 162 A. V., according to the Digambaras, or 179 A. V , according to the Śvetāmbaras (both dates being within the reign of Chandragupta). The Digambara separation originally took place as a result of the migration southwards under Bhadrabāhu in consequence of a severe famine in Bihar, the original home of the undivided Jain community."

were helped by their local allies, the *Kośar*, who "routed the enemies' forces on the field of battle" and the *Vaḍukar* fighting with "their swift-flying arrows". Some think that the *Moriyas* of these passages may refer to the latter day Mauryas of Koṅkān who emerge in history in the fifth century A.D., but there is in one passage a reference to "the untold wealth of the Nandas," showing by its context that it is the imperial Mauryas, the successors of the Nandas, who are thought of in these Tamil works. We have already cited the reference made by *Māmulanār*, a Śangam poet, to the hoarded wealth of the Nandas "swept away and submerged later on by the floods of the Ganges". Thus Tamil tradition is quite familiar with the Nandas and the imperial Mauryas coming after them [S. K. Aiyangar, *Beginnings of South Indian History*, pp. 69, 81, 103; V. R. Ramachandra Dikshitar, *Mauryan Polity*, pp. 58 ff.].

Conquest of Western India. Along with all this general evidence pointing to the extension of Chandragupta's empire to the South, we have a piece of definite evidence proving that Western India formed part of his empire. It was not so in the time of his predecessor, Nanda, who was known to the Greeks as the king of the Gangaridae and the Prasii, of the Ganges Valley and eastern India. The Girnar Rock Inscription of Rudradāman of 150 A.D. describes how the lake (*taḍāga*) Sudarśana was created on Mount Ūrjayat by the construction of a dam (*setu*) across the rivers flowing down the hill, such as Suvarṇasikatā, Palāśinī, and others. The dam rivalled the rock with its joints well cemented against leakage (*niḥsandhibaddha-dṛiḍha — sarvapātikatvāt — parvata — pāda-pratispardhi-suślishṭabandham*). It was constructed by the provincial governor (*Rāshṭriya*) of King Chandragupta Maurya. He is named Vaiśya Pushyagupta. The reservoir was lavishly provided with conduits (*praṇālībhiralaṁkṛitam*) in the time of Asoka Maurya by the Yavana (Greek) Rāja Tushāspha appointed to that province. The province is described as the province of Ānarta and Surāshṭra. Thus Western India was so efficiently governed as a province of Chandragupta Maurya's empire that even its irrigation facilities were provided by the construction of costly and difficult works like a reservoir for the storage of water, fitted with sluices and channels for its distribution among the cultivated fields below.

It is also interesting to note in this connection that the Pāli work *Petavatthu* and its commentary, *Paramatthadīpanī*, mention a ruler of Suraṭṭha (Surāshṭra) named Piṅgala who ascended the throne in the sixteenth regnal year of Bindusāra (283 B. C.). He had a *senāpati* or a general named Nandaka who converted him to a new doctrine, a sort of atheism called (*Natthika-diṭṭhi*). Fired with his zeal for his new faith, he was bold enough to leave for Pāṭaliputra with a large retinue to convert to his creed the emperor Dharmāśoka (*Piṅgalo rājā Dhammāsokassa rañño ovādaṁ dātum gato*) but remained himself to be converted to the emperor's creed of Buddhism [B. C. Law, *Buddhist Conception of Spirits*, p. 72 f ; C. D. Chatterji in *D. R. Bhandarkar Volume*, pp. 329-340.]

We have in these texts remarkable evidence of the continuity of administrative history for the Province of Surāshṭra during the reigns of three Maurya emperors, Chandragupta, Bindusāra, and Asoka.

Some light is thrown on the severity of Chandragupta's penal code as shaped by his minister, Chāṇakya, by the case of a learned Brahman scholar named Subandhu being condemned to servitude for life with his young son in his teens wandering away homeless to escape a similar fate. The sin of Subandhu was his astute political wisdom [*Ibid.*].

We may consider the constitutional significance of these references to Surāshṭra. We have three descriptions of its constitutional status which it is difficult to reconcile with each other. These are : (1) Surāshṭra as a province of the Maurya empire under an imperial official as its Governor ; (2) Surāshṭra under a chief as a feudatory of the Maurya emperor ; and (3) Surāshṭra as a *Saṁgha* or a republic. The third description is attributed to Kauṭilya, but not quite accurately. Kauṭilya does not describe Surāshṭra as a full-fledged republic, but only refers to certain sections of its population as belonging to self-governing corporations or *Śreṇīs*. These *Śreṇīs* were formed by the Kshatriyas and Vaiśyas of Surāshṭra and were either economic or military guilds, devoting themselves either to *Vārtā* (agriculture, cattle-rearing, and trade) or to the profession of arms as means of livelihood (*Surāshṭra-Kshatriyaśreṇyādayo vārtā-śastropajīvinaḥ*) [VII. 1]. Thus Surāshṭra under this description may still be a kingdom. The two other points to settle about its constitutional position are (1) whether it was a local chiefship and a feudatory State under the Maurya emperor or (2) whether it was completely annexed by Chandragupta Maurya to his empire and created a governorship under him. The second point is established beyond doubt by Rudradāman's Inscription which has greater evidential value than tradition and literary text. The first point can be reconciled with the second only on the supposition that, as in modern India, an imperial province may accommodate its hereditary ruling princes figuring as feudatories acknowledging the paramount sovereignty of the emperor. It is thus that Piṅgala as a local chief of Surāshṭra was out to pay homage to Asoka.

That the Maurya conquest of Western India extended beyond the province of Surāshṭra farther south is indicated by the location of Asoka's inscriptions at Sopara in the district now called Thana in the Bombay Presidency. The conquest of this part of India (which may be identified with Konkan) was not claimed by Asoka. It must have been the work of Chandragupta Maurya who, as we have seen, had already established his authority over the neighbouring region of Surāshṭra. The province of which Sopara or Śūrpāraka was the capital must have formed part of Maurya empire for some time to lead Asoka to locate his edicts at its capital.

Chronology. We may now consider the chronology of Chandragupta's reign. We have already seen that the first exploit of Chandragupta was the overthrow of the Greek rule which was established in India as a result of Alexander's victorious campaigns. But it was short-lived. Two events marked its rapid fall. The first was the murder of the most powerful Greek governor in the person of Philip in 325 B. C. followed by his place being taken by an Indian. The second event was the death of Alexander himself in 323 B.C. The first signal of the Indian battle for freedom was the murder of the Greek Satrap, Nicanor, by the Āśvāyanas in 326 B. C. As has been already related, the battle was won shortly after Alexander's death in 323 B. C. In 321 B. C., at the second partition of Alexander's empire, its easternmost Satrapy was the Trans-Indus Satrapy of Paropanisus. India proper was not counted as a part of that empire. An attempt to reconquer it only ended in the expansion of Chandragupta's empire to the trans-Indus provinces up to the borders of Persia. We may, therefore, take it for granted that between 323 and 321 B.C., Chandragupta made himself the ruler of the Punjab and Emperor of Magadha. We may take 322 B. C. as the date of his accession to sovereignty and of inaguration of the Maurya Dynasty.

We have other data to confirm this date. If we believe in the reckonings of reigns given in the *Purāṇas*, we shall see that Chandragupta's reign was one of 24 years and hence ended in 298 B.C., and that his son, Bindusāra, reigned for 25 years, i.e., up to 273 B.C. The date of Asoka's accession to sovereignty is thus to be taken as 273 B.C., a date which is supported by the unimpeachable data of Asoka's inscriptions. The *Mahāvaṁsa* distinguishes between Asoka's accession to throne and his coronation, and places an interval of 4 years between them [V. 22]. This makes 269 B.C.

as the date of his coronation. His inscriptions again date from his coronation. His Rock Edict XIII is dated 13 years after his coronation. So its date should be 256 B.C. if the date 269 B.C. of his coronation is correct. It is correct, because it is proved by the well-known chronological data of Rock Edict XIII itself. Rock Edict XIII is a document of unique chronological importance in Indian History. Aśoka in this Edict mentions the five most important Greek kings with all of whom he had friendly dealings through his Welfare Missions. The date of his references to them must, therefore, be at the latest the date up to which they were all alive and were known to be so to Asoka, and may be taken one year earlier, when all were hale and hearty.

The duration of the reigns of three of these kings is known with certainty, viz., those of

(1) *Aṁtiyoka*, i.e., Antiochus II Theos, king of Babylon and Persia, 261-246 B. C.

(2) *Turamaya*, i.e., Ptolemaeus II Philadelphos, king of Egypt, 285-247 B. C.

(3) *Aṁtikini*, i.e., Antigonus Gonatas, king of Macedonia, 277-240 B.C.

The uncertainty is as regards :

(4) *Maka*, i.e., Magas, king of Cyrene, whose date may be taken to be that proposed by both Beloch and Geyer, viz., 300-250 B. C.

(5) *Alikasudara*, whose identity and duration of reign are the subject of controversy. He may be either Alexander of Epirus or Alexander of Corinth. Of the two Alexanders, Alexander of Epirus was by far the more important personality worthy of Asoka's attention, the son of the famous Pyrrhus of Epirus, and the rival of Antigonus Gonatas of Macedonia. Alexander of Corinth was almost like a local king who ended as a "tyrant over a town and an island, without military glory or a famous lineage." There were several kings of Asia Minor of equal and higher status whom Asoka should have mentioned such as Eumenes of Pergamon (262-240 B. C.) or, nearer home, Diodotus of Bactria. It is known that Alexander of Epirus, the true subject of Asoka's reference, had lived up to 255 B.C.

Considering the dates of the reigns of all these five kings, we find 255 B.C. as the date up to which all were alive. From this follows that the date of Asoka's reference to them in Rock Edict XIII must be before 255 B. C. Professor P. H. L. Eggermont of the Hague, Holland (who honoured me by posting to me his learned paper on 'The Date of Asoka's Rock Edict XIII' on 30th April,

1940, a few days before Holland itself was submerged by German invasion) has very well shown by skilful calculations that the news of the death of one of these Greek kings could not take more than 4 or 5 months to reach Asoka at Pāṭaliputra, and so we need not allow for an interval of one year for it, as I had done in my *Asoka*. He has also after a good deal of discussion established the dates of the two kings, Alexander of Epirus and Magas of Cyrene. The former lived up to 255 B.C. and the latter up to 250 B.C. according to his findings which are followed here. If, therefore, Rock Edict XIII is dated at 256 B.C. since it was in the 13th year of Asoka's coronation, the date of his coronation was 269 B.C., the very date which is led up to by the assumed date of 322 B.C. for Chandragupta's accession to sovereignty and the duration of his reign and that of his successor, as reckoned in the *Purāṇas*. We have thus here a remarkable convergence of chronological conclusions derived from sources as different and foreign and Indian works, Brahminical texts and Buddhist inscriptions, and this convergence proves their truth.

CHAPTER III

ADMINISTRATION : IDEALS : DIVISIONS

Indian Ideals of Polity. The governance of such a vast empire which stretched from Persia to Mysore was a formidable undertaking. It was specially so in olden times, in pre-mechanical ages lacking the means of speedy communication and quick transport between the different and distant parts of a large empire. News would take months to travel from Paropanisus to Pāṭaliputra. This initial difficulty of administration led John Stuart Mill to doubt the existence of large empires in ancient times, "because the machinery of authority was not perfect enough to carry orders into effect at a great distance from the person of the ruler, nor did there exist the means of making the people pay an amount of taxes sufficient for keeping up the force necessary to compel obedience throughout a large territory."

These natural difficulties, however gave way before human ingenuity. A suitable system of administration could cope with them. The difficulties are formidable for a system of centralized authority. It is not so where government is not carried on from one centre but from many centres. Decentralisation of authority solved the problem of government for large empires in ancient times. It divided up the empire into a number of provincial governments and local administrations in which sovereignty could make its presence and power felt. The area of each such government was conveniently sized.

Rural Republics. Ancient India was built upon the basis of decentralisation on principle. It did not believe in centralisation of authority, resulting in a system of over-government of the people. It believed in the self-government in the group, in the extension of self-government from the sovereign at the top through all grades and strata of society down to the lowest classes in the villages. Every village was self-governing. There were also unions of villages as self-governing federations. Ancient India was thus built up as a vast rural democracy. Society was functioning apart from the State proper as a separate entity in defined spheres of self-government. Rural politics was independent of state-politics and of the vicissitudes of political fortune affecting the State or the Sovereign at the top. India owes the preservation of her culture to her self-governing villages or rural republics in which it was centred through the long course of her history which has seen so many political revolutions and changes of sovereignty. The position is very well summed up in the words of Sir Charles Metcalfe giving evidence before a Select Committee of the House of Commons [Report, 1832, Vol. III, App. 84, p. 331] : "The Indian village communities are little republics, having nearly everything they can want within themselves, and almost independent of any foreign relations. They seem to last where nothing else lasts. Dynasty after Dynasty tumbles down ; revolution succeeds to revolution . . .. but the village community remains the same...... This union of the village communities, each one forming a separate little State in itself, has, I conceive, contributed more than any other cause to the preservation of the peoples of India, through all the revolutions and changes which they have suffered, and is in a high degree conducive to their happiness, and to the enjoyment of a great portion of freedom and independence."

The aloofness of the Indian village from high politics at the centre attracted the attention of Megasthenes who has described how the bulk of India's population who were living on land as agriculturists were exempted from military service and were often found freely working, out in the fields, even in sight of a battle raging close by. He says : "Whereas among other nations it is usual, in the contests of war, to ravage the soil, and thus to reduce it to an uncultivated waste, among the Indians, on the contrary, by whom husbandmen are regarded as a class that is sacred and inviolable, the tillers of soil, even when battle is raging in their neighbourhood, are undisturbed by any sense of danger, for the combatants on either side in waging the conflict make a carnage of each other, but allow those engaged in husbandry to remain quite unmolested. Besides, they neither ravage an enemy's land with fire, nor cut down its trees." And again : "The Husbandmen appear to be far more numerous than the others. Being moreover exempted from fighting and other public services, they devote the whole of their time to tillage ; nor would an enemy coming upon a husbandman at work on his land do him any harm, for men of their class, being regarded as public benefactors, are protected from all injury The land thus remaining undamaged, and producing heavy crops, supplies the inhabitants with all that is requisite to make life very enjoyable. The husbandmen themselves, with their wives and children, live in the country, and entirely avoid going into town either to take part in its tumults or for any other purpose"

[Frag. I, XXXIII]. These rural retreats of democracy kept the culture of the country in tact and free from all political disturbances.

Dharma as Sovereign. There was, however, a deeper political philosophy which moulded Indian polity to this form. Hindu thought counts *Dharma* as the true Sovereign of the State, as the Rule of Law. The king is the executive called the *Daṇḍa* to uphold and enforce the decrees of *Dharma* as the spiritual sovereign. Thus the king or the temporal sovereign is not the source of Law in the Hindu State. The sources of Law are above and beyond him. They are not his creation. He has only to see to their observance.

Sources of Law. The sources of Law are stated by Manu to be (1) *Veda* or *Śruti* (2) *Smṛiti* or Dharma-Śāstra (3) *Śīla* or code of conduct enjoined by the Śāstras (4) *Āchāra* or the manners and customs of holy men.

It was provided that doubtful points of Dharma arising out of these primary sources of Law were to be decided by a body of legal experts called *Śishṭas*, 'well versed in sacred lore and disciplined in correct conduct.' This body was called *Parishad.* Thus legislation was considered too important for the State and for the common weal to be left to party politics or the opinions and fancies of its individual leaders. John Stuart Mill recommended the creation of a Standing Legal Commission to guide legislation by Parliament.

Varnasrama-Dharma. It is, however, to be noted that the Dharma for which the Hindu State stood was what is known as *Varnāśrama-Dharma.* It was the law that regulated the occupations of different castes of people, and duties of life depending on its different stages called Āśramas. The Hindu scheme of life determines its duties normally in accordance with caste, i.e., birth and heredity, and also with age. Kauṭilya ln his *Arthaśāstra* presents this scheme as follows.

Each *Varṇa* or caste, and each *Āśrama,* is to follow its *Svadharma,* its own Dharma, to which one must be true.

Duties of different castes. The duties of *Brāhmaṇa* are : (1) Learning (*Adhyayanam*), (2) Teaching (*Adhyāpanam*), (3) Worship (*Yajanam*), (4) Conducting Worship (*Yājanam*), (5) Making gifts (*Dāna*), (6) Receiving gifts (*Pratigraha*).

The *Kshatriya* is to observe (1), (3), and (5) of the above list, and to follow in addition the two following special duties, viz., (a) The pursuit of arms (*Śastrājīva*); (b) Defence of his country (*Bhūtarakshaṇam,* protection of all living beings).

The *Vaiśya* is to observe (1), (3), and (5) but is to follow the special occupations named (a) Agriculture, (b) Cattle-rearing and (c) Trade.

The *Śūdra's* duties are specified to be (1) Service of the first three castes, "the twice-born"; (2) Agriculture, Cattle-rearing and Trade (*Vārttā*); (3) Craftsmanship (*Kārukarma*); and (4) Minstrelsy (*Kūśīlavakarma*).

Duties of different *Āśramas*. There are pointed out the four Ages of Life called the *Āśramas*, viz., those of (1) *Brahmachārī* (student) (2) *Gṛihastha* (the married state) (3) *Vānaprastha* (dweller in forest) (4) *Parivrājaka* (wandering ascetic).

The duties of the Brahmachārī are stated to be (1) study of the Vedas (*Svādhyāya*), (2) worship and offering to fire (*Agnikāryābhishekau*), (3) practice of begging (*Bhaikshyavratatvam*), (4) following the teacher unto death.

The duties of the house-holder are stated to be

(1) earning livelihood by the pusuit of prescribed occupations (*svakarmājīva*);

(2) marrying into families of equal status but different *gotras*;

(3) offering food to gods, ancestors, guests, and paid servants, and appropriation of what remains to himself (*śeshabhojanam*).

The house-holder, who leaves his home for the forest, has to observe the following duties, viz., (1) Continence (*Brahmacharya*) (2) Sleeping on bare earth (3) Wearing long hair and deer skin (4) Offering worship and oblations to fire (5) Worship of gods, ancestors, and guests (6) Eating what is grown in the forest.

The ascetic (*Parivrājaka*) has to observe the following injunctions: (1) Control of senses (2) Abstention from all scheming (*Anārambha*) (3) Renouncing all possessions (*Nishkiñchanatvam*) (4) Life of solitude (*Saṅgatyāga*) (5) Begging in different places (so as not to get attached to any) (6) Living in forest (7) Purity of body and heart.

The following duties are compulsory for all, viz, (1) Non-violence (*Ahiṁsā*) (2) Truthfulness (*Satyam*) (3) Purity (*Śaucham*) (4) Freedom from jealousy (*Anasūyā*) (5) Freedom from cruelty (6) Tolerance (*Kshamā*).

It was the supreme duty of the State or the Sovereign to uphold this social order or system which was taken to be the best system for ensuring the stability of society and the development of personality or the self-fulfilment of the individual as the supreme objective of the State itself.

The King as *Daṇḍa* or Upholder of Dharma. The *Aitareya Brāhmaṇa* [VIII. 26] describes the king as the Defender of *Dharma* (*Dharmasya goptā*). The *Śatapatha Brāhmaṇa* [XIV. 4, 2, 23] states that the *Daṇḍa* or the king is necessary to maintain *Dharma* or those "principles of justice by which the strong are prevented from eating up the weak" (*abalīyān balīyāṁsa mā śaṁsate dharmeṇa yathā*). The *Mahābhārata* [*Śānti P.* chh. 67, 122] points out that without *Daṇḍa*, Society will be in a state of nature described as *Mātsya-Nyāya* in which "people devour one another like fish or dog (*parasparaṁ bhakshayanto matsyā iva jale kriśān| parasparaṁ vilumpanti sārameyā yathāmisham* ||). This doctrine is thus stated by Kauṭilya: "Where there is no *Daṇḍa-dhara* or the sovereign wielding the sceptre of justice, the strong eat up the weak, as it is among fish. But, protected by the king, the weak become strong (*apranīto hi mātsyanyāyamudbhāvayati* | *Balīyānabalaṁ hi grasate daṇḍadharābhāve*| *Tenaguptaḥ prabhavati* ||) [I. 4]. Kauṭilya further states that the king who upholds *Dharma* "will attain happiness both here and hereafter" (*pretya cheha cha nandati* [I. 3]. It is also to be noted that subject to *Dharma* or the Law and Constitution of the realm, the Sovereign had supreme power in the State as its Head (*Kūṭasthānīyo hi svāmīti*) [VIII. 1]. Kauṭilya further points out [III. 1] that the king who governs (*anuśāsat*) in accordance with *Dharma* (*satye sthitaḥ Dharmaḥ*, 'established in truth'), *Vyavahāra* (Evidence or established laws), *Saṁsthā* (Custom, *lokāchāra*) and *Nyāya* (Justice or Reason) will be the conqueror of the whole earth up to the seas (*Chaturantaṁ mahīṁ jayet*). Kauṭilya also holds [IV. 13] that if the king exercises his power in an unlawful manner, he will be himself punishable (*adaṇḍyadaṇḍane rājño daṇḍastriṁśatguṇombhasi*, 'the king penalising an innocent person is to pay as penalty thirty times its amount). By paying the penalty, he will purify himself of the sin of injustice' (*tena tat pūyate pāpaṁ rājño daṇḍūpachārajam*). This is driving the theory up to its limit, but it is only to emphasise the fundamental position that *Dharma* is the ultimate Sovereign to whom the king also is subject. The Law or Rule is the ruler of men.

It was for the fulfilment of this lofty mission prescribed for kings that Chandragupta himself was called to the throne by Chāṇakya when he found that it was jeopardised under the Śūdra rule of the Nandas.

Custom as Law. It will also be seen that one of the established sources of Law is defined to be what is called *Āchāra* which Kauṭilya calls *Charitra* or *Saṁsthā*, the manners and customs of the country. These, however, vary with different families, castes, corporations, and regions, and these several groups were empowered to legislate for themselves. Accordingly, Manu says [VIII, 41, 46] that it is the Sovereign's duty to recognize and enforce the laws laid down for themselves by these several self-governing groups, such as *Kula* (family), *Jāti* (caste), *Śreṇī* (guild), and *Janapada* (region). Gautama [II. 2, 20, 21] goes farther and grants powers of legislation to the *Vargas* or Guilds (*Śreṇīs*) of cultivators, traders, herdsmen and artisans, thus granting self-government to Industry. As an instance of regional or local law which is to be recognised by the king, the commentator on Manu cites the South Indian custom of 'marrying the daughter of the maternal uncle.'

In this way, democracy descends to the villages and the lowest strata of social structure and operated as the most potent agency of uplifting the masses. Thus ancient Hindu monarchy was a limited monarchy under the very conception of the State. The self-governing groups upon which the State was founded formed a vast subterranean democracy limiting the absolutism of the sovereign at the top.

The Mauryan empire had to fit itself into this traditional framework of administration. The problem of imperial government was already solved in the very scheme of indigenous polity. The emperor had only to operate the existing administrative machinery.

Administrative Divisions. The Mauryan empire was divided into a number of Viceroyalties and Provinces and each of these was of the time-honoured and standardised pattern of the Hindu State, comprising the ruler or governor at the top, the Council of Ministers called *Mantriparishad,* Heads of Departments called *Adhyakshas,* the Civil Service represented by a hierarchy of officers in different grades of jurisdiction, and self-governing village communities at the foundation of the structure.

There is not much evidence available as regards the provinces of the Empire under Chandragupta Maurya. But we have some evidence for the time of his grandson, Asoka, by whom the institutions of his predecessors were continued except where they were reformed, or in the case of innovations which Asoka himself specifies in his inscriptions. None of the provinces indicated in his inscriptions is claimed by Asoka to be his own creation.

Viceroyalties. His inscriptions speak of at least four Viceroyalties with their headquarters at (1) Taxila (2) Ujjain (3) Tosali and (4) Suvarṇagiri.

The Viceroyalties were recruited from the princes of blood royal called *Kumāras* or *Āryaputras* in Asoka's inscriptions. Asoka served as his father's Viceroy at Ujjain, and again at Taxila, where he replaced his elder brother, Prince Susīma. Prince Kuṇāla, Asoka's son, served as his Viceroy at Taxila. Asoka also appointed his brother, Prince Tissa, as deputy king, *Uparāja*, to act for him at headquarters. The heir-apparent was known as the *Yuvarāja*.

Kauṭilya [XII. 2] provides for emergency which may cause the king's absence from the country, in which case an officer will take his place thus rendered vacant (*śūnya*) and will be appropriately called *Śūnya-Pāla*, a sort of a Deputy-king like Asoka's *Uparāja*.

Of the above Viceroyalties, Taxila was the capital of the newly-acquired North Western Frontier Province of Chandragupta's empire, and Ujjain of the Central Provinces then known as *Avantirāshṭra*, [*Mahāvaṁsa*, XIII, 8].

Suvarṇagiri was the capital of the southern province. Tosali was the capital of Kalinga, but it was not a part of Maurya empire under Chandragupta.

It may be noted that the traditional names of five Provinces into which India was divided are mentioned in the *Purāṇas* as

(1) *Udīchya* (Northern India) or Uttarāpatha.

(2) *Madhya-deśa* (Central India).

(3) *Prāchya* (Eastern India).

(4) *Aparānta* (Western India) and

(5) *Dakshiṇāpatha* (Deccan and South India).

Like the king, the Viceroy had his Council of Ministers known as *Mahāmātras*. Like him, he also could appoint special Ministers (*Mahāmātras*) for purposes of inspection of judicial administration [See my *Asoka* (Macmillan) p. 52].

Governorships. Side by side with these Viceroyalties under the Princes, there were also the Provinces under Governors. Seats of such governorships are mentioned in Asoka's inscriptions, such as Isila, and Samāpā in the South, and Kauśāmbī in modern U. P. near Allahabad. The Governors were called *Prādeśika-Mahāmātras*, and also *Rājūkas*, "set over hundreds of thousands of souls" and possessed of wide powers of government [*Ib.*]. The later inscription of Rudradāman of 150 A.D., however, calls the provincial Governor a *Rāshṭriya*. As we have seen, we owe to this inscription the important information that the Western Province of Chandragupta's empire was known as Ānarta and Surāshṭra, of which the capital was Girinagara and the Governor was Vaiśya Pushyagupta. Kauṭilya [II. 16; IX. 3] uses the term *Rāshṭra-Mukhya* or *Rāshṭra-pāla* [V. 1] or *Īśvara* [II. 10] for the provincial Governor.

CHAPTER IV

THE KING

The King : His Education. A large part of administrative work devolved upon the king. He had to go through a course of education to fit him for the work. We have already seen how Chandragupta was specially fortunate in having as his preceptor a scholar of encyclopaedic learning like Chāṇakya who gave him the best possible education then available in the country for a period of as many as 8 years at Taxila. Kauṭilya [I. 5] indicates the contents of the education prescribed for princes. The first requisite of education is stated to be Discipline (*Vinaya*) comprising the following qualities: (1) Desire for learning (*Śuśrūshā*) (2) Cultivation of the truth learnt (*Śravaṇam*) (3) Grasping what is learnt (*Grahaṇam*) (4) Retaining what is grasped (*Dhāraṇam*) (5) Knowledge of ways and means of achieving the truth learnt (*Vijñānam*) (6) Inference (*Ūha*) (7) Deliberation.

" Treatment can subdue only the material that is fit for it and not unfit." (*Kriyā hi dravyaṁ vinayati nādravyam*).

Education is also to comprise both study and practice. It is not merely theoretical.

The prince is to start with a knowledge of Arithmetic (*Saṁkhyā*) and writing (*Lipi*) and then to study (a) the three Vedas; (b) Philosophy under teachers; (c) the different departments of economic life (*Vārttā*) under experienced administrators (*adhyakshas*); and (d) the Science of Polity under teachers well-versed in its principles and practices (*Vaktṛiprayoktṛibhyaḥ*). The prince is to observe continence, practise *Brahmacharya* up to the age of 16 when he is to marry.

He must achieve complete control of his passions and recall the ruin brought on themselves by the greatest kings by their indulgence in passions [*Ib.* I. 6] and the prosperity of those known for their self-control, [*Ib.*].

Even after marriage and education, he must always cultivate the association of the elders in knowledge (*Vidyā-vṛiddha-saṁyoga*) as a means of increasing his knowledge.

In the forenoons, he is to undergo military training in fighting with the forces of elephants, horses, chariots, and infantry.

The afternoons he is to devote to the study of History including (1) *Purāṇa* (2) *Itivṛitta* (past history) such as *Rāmāyaṇa* and *Mahābhārata* (3) *Ākhyāyikā* (tales of gods and great men) (4) *Udāharaṇa* (anecdotes and biographies, or, according to one commentator, *Nyāya*, *Mīmāṁsā*, and *Upanyāsa-śāstra* or works of fiction) (5) *Dharma-Śāstra*, Law-books like Manu and (6) *Artha-śāstra*.

He is to devote his leisure hours to the acquisition of new knowledge and assimilation of what is learnt.

Thus educated and disciplined, the king becomes invincible.

He must never be off his guard, but should always be up and doing (*Utthānaṁ kurvīta*) [*Ib.* 19].

Time-Table of Duties. The time-table of the king's daily duties has been drawn up in accordance with the administrative work he has to take upon himself.

The day and night are each divided into eight parts by sun-dial or water clock. Thus each such part (*nālikā*) was of one hour and a half. The king's time is so full up and charged with duties that it is the subject of humorous comment in literature. Daṇḍin, in his *Daśakumāracharita* [II. 8], sneers at Kauṭilya's schedule of royal duties which would make royalty itself an unbearable burden.

Taking the day and night of equal duration, and counting in terms of hours the sixteen portions into which day and night are divided, the king's time-table may be thus worked out :

1-30 – 3 A.M.—Rise from sleep by the sound of music or trumpets (*Tūrya-ghosha*) ; pondering over injunctions of religion (*Śāstram*) and duties for the morrow.

3—4·30 A.M.—Determination of policy and plans and despatch of his secret emissaries in accordance therewith.

4-30 – 6 A.M.—Company of the sacrificial priest, the preceptor, and the domestic chaplain and receiving their benedictions (*svastyayana*) ; interviewing the physician, kitchen officials and astrologers.

6 – 7-30 A.M.—Attendence at the Hall of Audience (*Upasthāna*) and receiving there the reports of his military and financial advisers.

7-30 – 9 A.M.—Continued attendence at the Hall of Audience (*Upasthāna*) where he is to attend to the affairs of the people, urban and rural, giving free access to them.

9—10·30 A.M.— Bath, Meals, and study of religious texts.

10-30 A.M. – 12 Noon —Receiving the surplus of gold cash left over from the previous day (*hiraṇyapratigrahaṁ gatadivasotthita-dhanasvīkāram*) ; attending to the heads of Departments and assigning duties to them (*Adhyakshān kurvīta kāryaviśesheshu niyuñjīta.*)

12—1-30 P.M.—Correspondence by letter with the Council of Ministers ; settlement of plans of espionage with the Informers.

1-30—3 P.M.--Recreation and Rest and pondering over his Policy.

3—4-30 P.M.—Review of his Army, Cavalry, Elephants and Arsenal.

4-30—6 P.M.—Consultation with the Commander-in-chief as to his military strength ; Evening Prayers.

6—7-30 P.M.—Interviews with secret emissaries.

7-30—9 P.M.—Second bath and meal followed by religious meditation.

9—10-30 P.M.—Retirement for rest to the sound of music.

10-30 P.M.—1-30 A.M.—Sleep.

This completes the round of duties prescribed for the king.

It was a sort of a standard set for him. He was empowered to alter the time-table, "its divisions of night and day, and discharge his duties in accordance with his capacity."

'Upasthana' and Agnyagara. It will be seen from the above time-table that the king's hours of retirement and rest from public work were from 9 P.M. to 4-30 A.M., after which followed his round of daily administrative duties of different kinds. The most important of these was his daily Darbar in the Hall of Audience where he usually spends three hours in the morning from 6 A.M., personally disposing of the suits of petitioners who are given free access to him. It is pointed out that the kIng who makes himself inaccessible to his people (*durdarśa*) and entrusts his work to his officers in attendance will cause confusion in business and even public disaffection. It may be noted that the term *Upasthāna* signifies the *sthāna* or place where people wait to have a *sight* of king (*Upatishṭhante sandarśanārthino rājānāmatra iti Upasthānagriham* [Commentator on X I].

Among the items of business that the king should personally attend to is mentioned the business concerning the gods, hermits, heretics, learned brahmins (*Śrotriya*), cattle, sacred places, minors, persons disabled by age, disease or misfortune, orphans and women. These he should attend to in the order of this enumeration, or in accordance with their urgency or gravity. In fact, the king is asked to respond to all urgent calls of business which he must dispose of at once without putting it off.

It is further laid down that while he is seated in the hall of worship (*Agnyāgāra*), he should attend to the business of physicians and ascetics in the company of his chief priest and preceptor.

For purposes of the king's safety at these public interviews, Kauṭilya makes the provision [I. 21] that the king must not give interviews to strangers, saints, and ascetics unless he is duly protected by his trustworthy bodyguard (*āptaṣastragrāhādhishṭhita*). He is also to interview the ambassadors from foreign kings with his whole Council of Ministers in attendance (*Mantriparishadā Sāmantadūtam*).

Maxims for Royalty. Lastly, the *Arthaśāstra* contains the following eloquent exhortation to the king: "For a king, his *vrata* (religious vow) is constant activity in the cause of his people (*Utthānam*); his best religious ceremony is the work of administration (*Kāryānuśāsanam*); his highest charity (*Dakshinā*) is equality of treatment meted out to all."

"In the happiness of his subjects lies the happiness of the king; in their good is his own good, and not in what is pleasing to him. He must find his pleasure in the pleasure of his subjects."

Thus exertion is emphasised as "the root of success in administration (*Arthasya mūlaṁ utthānam*)" [I. 19]. In another place [VI. I], Kauṭilya points out the king's virtues to be "abundance of enthusiasm and freedom from procrastination (*mahotsāho adīrghasūtraḥ*). And again [XII. 11]: "the king who is a fatalist (*daivapramāṇaḥ*), devoid of energy (*mānushahīnaḥ*), or of initiative (*nirārambhaḥ*), will come to grief."

These admonitions of Kauṭilya are echoed by Asoka in his Rock Edict VI: "For there is no satisfaction of mine in exertion (*Usṭānam*) or despatch of business (*Arthasamtīraṇa*). My highest duty is, indeed, the promotion of the good of all (*Sarva-loka-hitam*). Of that, again, the root is this: exertion (*Utthānaṁ*) and despatch of business. There is no higher work than the promotion of the common weal."

Asoka's Time-Table. It is interesting to note that Asoka's own Time-table follows that of Kauṭilya. In his Rock Edict VI, Asoka states that he holds himself ready for public work, whether despatch of business (*artha-karma*) or receipt of reports (*prativedanam*), at all hours and places, "when he is dining, or in his harem (*orodhanamhi*), or in the inner apartments (*gabhāgāraṁhi*) or in the ranches (*vachaṁhi*), or in the place of religious instruction (*vinītaṁhi*), or in the parks (*uyānesu*)."

Testimony of Megasthenes. That all this programme of the king's daily duties was not meant as a mere counsel of perfection is indicated by what Magasthenes reports on the subject. Megasthenes saw with his own eyes how busy the king, Chandragupta, was, and how he was found always engaged in public work. He states: "The king may not sleep during the day time. He leaves his palace not only in time of war but also for the purpose of judging causes. He then remains in court for the whole day without allowing the business to be interrupted, even though the hour arrives when he must needs attend to his person" [McCrindle, *Ancient India*, p. 58]. Curtius [VIII. 9] also adds: "The palace is open to all comers, even when the king is having his hair combed and dressed. It is then that he gives audience to ambassadors, and administers justice to his subjects." [*Ib.*].

We see here how closely Kauṭilya is confirmed by the evidence of the Greek eye-witness. Both point out how the king was always accessible to the public and how the greater part of his work concerned disposal of suits. What Megasthenes calls "court" Kauṭilya calls *Upasthāna* and *Agnyāgāra*. Where Megasthenes mentions the administration of justice by the king or "his judging causes", Kauṭilya describes the king's administrative work in more general terms including disposal of petitions from the public. It is also apparent from Kauṭilya's time-table that the "judging of causes" might easily encroach upon the time fixed for the king's bath and meals, as the Greek writers state. For it will be seen that the king disposes of public business at the *Upasthāna* from 6 to 9 A.M., after which comes the time fixed for his bath. It is also to be noted that the king in Kauṭilya's scheme has another spell of adminstrative work for three hours after meals from 12 noon and after an interval of rest he has further hard work to go through with the Military and Intelligence Departments from 3 to 7-30 P. M. Thus Greek evidence fully corroborates that of Kauṭilya on the king's strenuous daily work.

A high purpose informed this exacting programme of work and gave it shape. It has been thus summed up by Kauṭilya [I. 7]: "The king is to grow in wisdom and statesmanship (*prajñā*) by contact with the elders in wisdom; to develop insight (*chakshu*) into the affairs of the people through the instrumentality of his Intelligence Officers (*chāreṇa*); to achieve the welfare and happiness of his people by his constant labours (*utthānena*); uphold the social order (*svadharmasthāpanaṁ*) by the exercise of his administrative authority (*kāryānuśāsanena*); to attain discipline by following the injunctions of his teachers; to achieve popularity through proper administrative measures securing the employment of the people (*arthasaṁyogena*); and to regulate his life (*vṛittim*) by the standard of promoting public good (*hitena*)."

All this burden placed upon royalty was a consequence of the very conception of royalty in Hindu Polity. It is thus stated by Kauṭilya [I. 13] : "The people overwhelmed by the evils of anarchy, wherein the strong prey upon the weak as among fishes, chose the king and assigned to him a sixth of agricultural produce and a tenth of sales of merchandise as revenue, in return for which the king was to protect the people, promote their welfare, by levy of punishment and taxes, and was answerable for their sins, if he did not punish them. Even hermits pay a sixth of the grain they glean to the king as their protector (*yosmān gopayatīti*). The king is thus the fountain of favours and justice like Indra and Yama, and is entitled to the loyalty of his subjects." This points out the origin of kingship in contract and election and the binding of the king to his people in ties of service. Thus Hindu political theory insists on the democratic foundations of kingship and imposes heavy obligations upon the king as 'the father' of the people. Kauṭilya is fond of the expression : "the king must treat his subjects as his sons" (*tān piteva anugṛihṇīyāt*) [II, 1 ; IV. 3.].

The *Mahābhārata* [Śānti P. 56, 45] describes the king as mother who sacrifices all that she holds dear for the good of her child (*yathā hi garbhiṇī hitva syaṁ priyaṁ garbhasya hitamādhatte.*) Asoka also repeats the same doctrine for himself : " All people are my children for whom, like their father, he wishes all happiness both in this world and in the next' (*sava-munisā me pajā* in Jaugada R. E. II, also Dhauli R. E. I).

Lastly, it may be noted that the same spirit of idealism informed the king's foreign policy. If he is bent on conquest, it should not be for mere power, pelf and greed, lust for dominion. Kauṭilya [XII. 1] mentions three classes of conquerors in the order of merit : (1) *Dharma-vijayī* (2) *Lobha-vijayī* and (3) *Asura-vijayī*. Thus Asoka follows this ideal by declaring that 'the best of all conquests is *Dharma-vijaya*' [R. E. XIII).

Other Features of Royalty: Bodyguard of armed women. We shall now turn to the other habits and paraphernalia of the king, as these were witnessed by the Greek ambassador, Megasthenes.

Greek Evidence. Strabo states : "The care of the king's person is entrusted to women. . . When he goes to hunt, it is in a kind of Bacchic procession, surrounded by women who form a circle. . . Some of the women are in chariots, some on horseback, some on elephants, fully armed as in war [XV. I, 55].

Evidence of Kautilya. The Greek evidence is confimed by Kautilya [I. 21]. He states that the king on rising from bed shall be received first by troops of women armed with bows (*strīgaṇairdhanvibhiḥ*), who must have formed his immediate body-guard, and that female-slaves should bathe and massage the king, make his bed, wash his clothes, and adorn him with garlands [*Snāpakasaṁvāha-kāstaraka-rajaka-mālākārakarma dāsyaḥ kuryuḥ.*]. The king, according to Kauṭilya, had a regular staff of public women (*gaṇikā*) in his household in three grades of service for his personal attendance. Of these, the lowest grade of *gaṇikās* was employed to hold the royal umbrella over him and the golden pitcher (*chhatra-bhṛiṅgāra*); the next grade carried the fan and attended on him seated in the royal pavilion (*vyajana-śibikā*); and the superior grade served him seated on the throne or in the chariot (*pīṭhikā-ratheshu*). The aging ones would be transferred to work in the royal store-house (*koshṭhā-gāra*) or in the royal kitchen (*mahānase*) [II. 27]. A *gaṇikā* could also obtain her liberty to lead a different life by payment of a ransom (*nishkraya*) of 24,000 *paṇas* (*Ib*). Girls above eight were employed to act and sing before the king (*ashṭavarshāt prabhṛiti rājñaḥ kuśīlava-karma kuryāt.*) [*Ib*]. We may note in this connection the statement of Megasthenes [Frag. XXVII] that "the women who take care of the King's person are bought from their parents."

It is interesting to note that there is a representation of a procession in a Bharhut Sculpture (*c.* 2nd century B. C.) of the figure of a woman riding a horse fully caparisoned and carrying a standard, the *garuḍadhvaja* [*A guide to Sculptures in the Indian Museum*, I. 24).

Hunting. According to the Greek writers, the king leaves the palace and goes about among the public on three occasions. "One is for the purpose of hearing cases which occupy him throughout the day," as we have already seen. The second occasion is when he goes to hunt, surrounded by his women-hunters, as already stated. "A rope is stretched to mark the road, and it is death for any one to go past it among the women. Drummers and bell-ringers lead the way. In his hunting enclosures, the king shoots with a bow from an elevated place, two or three armed women standing beside him. When hunting in a place not enclosed, he shoots from an elephant."

It may be noted that Kauṭilya (II. 2) provides for a reserved forest for purposes of the king's *vihāra* or sport. Asoka in his Rock Edict VIII speaks of the king's *vihārayātrās*. According to Kauṭilya, this reserved forest was to be protected by a ditch (*khātaguptam*), to have only one entrance, and to be stocked with tigers, beasts of prey, and bisons (*kalabha*) with their claws and teeth cut off, so that the king could have his sport without any risk to his life. Kauṭilya further provides that the king should go out a-hunting into such forests as are previously cleared of all sources of danger, robbers, tigers and the like, by his foresters (*lubdhaka*), with the hounds of the king's kennels. Under these conditions, the king was to learn the difficult art of shooting at a moving mark, such as running deer (*chalalaksha*) [I. 21]. The *Mudrārākshasa* tells of a park (*udyāna*) where the Nanda king used to shoot at moving objects.

It may be noted that Hunting was a standing pastime of kings. Kauṭilya (VIII. 3) fully discusses the virtues of hunting for the king. While Piśuna condemns it as a *vyasana*, or indulgence, chiefly for its physical dangers from robbers, enemies, wild animals, forest fires, accidents, hunger, thirst, and even its chance of mistake about direction and destination, Kauṭilya approves of it as a *Vyāyāma* or healthy physical exercise, destroying the excess of phlegm, bile, fat and perspiration, and improving one's marksmanship and knowledge of the tempers of wild beasts.

Megasthenes (Fragm. XII), along with Aelian and Strabo, speaks of hunting lions with dogs. Kauṭilya also refers to hunters going about the forests with their packs of hounds (*Śvagaṇinaḥ*) and also to the hunting of tigers with dogs (IV. 3). In I. 14, Kauṭilya refers to keepers of dogs fed by the milk of their cows (*Svagaṇinām dhenuḥ*).

It was, however, left to Chandragupta's grandson, Asoka, to abolish *Mṛigayā* or hunting and other such sports of pleasure (*Abhiramani*) by royal decree [R. E. VIII.] It may be noted that, according to *Mahāvaṁsa* [V. 154], Asoka's own brother, Tissa, had indulged in hunting as his *Uparāja*, so that hunting was permitted by him as a royal pastime down to at least 266 B.C., when Tissa left the world and became a monk.

Races. Next to Hunting were the Races in which the kings indulged in those days. In Chandragupta's time, there was a special trotter breed of oxen "which equalled horses in speed". A carriage was harnessed to a mixed team of two such oxen with a horse between. The course was about a mile and three quarters in length, and the king and his nobles betted keenly in gold and silver on the result. Kauṭilya also knows of oxen which equalled horses in speed (*Balīvardānāṁ nasyāśvabhadragativāhināṁ*) [II. 29].

Animal Fights. Among other pastimes of the king, Aelian mentions the prevalence of even gladiatorial contests. But more usual were contests arranged between "brute animals that are horned and butt each other, such as wild bulls, tame rams and rhinos. There were also arranged fights between elephant tuskers." The *Dīgha-Nikāya* calls such sport as *Samāja* which it condemns and describes as fights arranged between animals such as "elephants, horses, buffaloes, bulls, goats, and rams," and even between "birds like cocks and quails."

Royal Processions. The third occasion on which the king came before the public was the occasion of a religious festival or the performance of a religious sacrifice. As Strabo states [XV. I. 69]: " In the processions at their festivals, many elephants adorned with gold and silver are in the train, as well as four-horsed chariots and yokes of oxen. Then comes a great host of attendants in their holiday attire, with vessels of gold, such as large basins and goblets six feet in breadth, tables, chairs of state, drinking-cups and lavers all made of Indian copper, and set many of them with precious stones—emeralds, beryls, and Indian garnets—garments embroidered and interwoven with gold, wild beasts—such as buffaloes, leopards, tame lions—and multitude of birds of variegated plumage and fine song." Kleitarchos mentions "four-wheeled carriages carrying trees of the large-leaved sort, from which were suspended in cages different kinds of tame birds, among which he speaks of the *orion* as that which had the swestest note, and of another called the *katreus*, which was the most beautiful in appearance and had the most variegated plumage."

Courtly Pomp. Curtius also gives the following account of the magnificence of the Indian court under Chandragupta Maurya : "When the king condescends to show himself in public, his attendants carry in their hands silver censors and perfume with incense all the road by which it is his pleasure to be conveyed. He lolls in a golden palanquin, garnished with pearls which dangle all around it, and he is robed in fine muslin embroidered with purple and gold. Behind his palanquin follow men-at-arms and his body guards, of whom some carry boughs of trees on which birds are perched, trained to interrupt business with their cries."

Washing of Hair. According to Strabo, a great occasion at the court was the ceremonial washing of his hair by the king on his birthday, when people sent him "great presents, each person seeking to outrival his neighbour in displaying his wealth [XV. I, 69]." A form of presents favoured by the king was the "present of animals, even wild ones, like deer, antelopes, or rhinos, also birds like cranes, geese, ducks and pigeons. The Indians bring to their king tigers made tame, domesticated panthers, oxen fleet of foot, or the yaks, pigeons of yellow plumage, hunting hounds and apes" [Aelian. p. 144, McCrindle's *Ancient India*].

Elephant Guard. We are also told that the king had a guard of twenty four elephants, and when he went out to administer justice, the first elephant was trained to do him obeisance. As the king passed, the elephant gave him a sort of a military salute on a hint from the driver and a stroke of his goad [Megasthenes, *Frag.* 25].

Journeys. As regards the king's journeys, "he rides on horseback when making short journeys, but when bound on a distant expedition, he rides in a chariot mounted on elephants, and, huge as these animals are, their bodies are covered completely over with trappings of gold" [*Ib.*].

We are also told that while on such tours the king has his food prepared by women [Strabo, VIII. 9].

According to Kauṭilya [I. 21], the king mounted a horse, a chariot, or an elephant in full military attire when he goes out to inspect his army to be paraded before him in its full military equipment.

In his progresses, whether excursions or incursions (*niryāṇo abhiyāne cha*), the road will be lined on both sides (*ubhayataḥ*) by police bearing *lāthīs* (*Daṇḍibhiḥ*) who will clear it of all armed persons (*apāstaśastrahasta*), ascetics, and cripples. The king must not enter a crowd (*Na purushasambādhamavagāheta* [*Ib.*].

Kauṭilya speaks of the king's journeys to witness festive processions (*yātrā*), popular gatherings (*samāja*), seasonal celebrations (*utsava* 'such as Vasantotsava') and picnic parties at parks (*pravahanaṁ udyāna-bhojanādi*), provided they are policed by companies of soldiers (*daśavargika*) [*Ib.*].

Measures of Safety. Kauṭilya is prone to provide for the king's personal safety on occasions of his journeys in all possible manner. The king must not mount a chariot or a horse or an elephant (*yānavāhanam*) unless it is certified to be reliable by his trusted officers concerned. He shall also board a ship (*nāvam*) only when it is piloted by a trustworthy sailor and is also attached to a second boat. He must not, however, sail in any ship which is not found to be seaworthy from the damage done to it by winds (*vātavegavaśām*) [*Ib.*].

Palace. We shall now describe the splendours of the royal palace at the imperial capital at Pāṭaliputra. According to Aelian, "neither Memnonian Susa with all its costly splendour, nor Ekbatana with all its magnificence" can vie with it.

"The palace is adorned with gilded pillars clasped round with a vine embossed in gold, while silver images of those birds which most charm the eye diversify the workmanship."

The palace stood in an extensive park. It was full of "tame peacocks and pheasants, shady groves and trees set in clumps with branches woven together by some special cunning of horticulture, trees that are always green, that never grow old and never shed their leaves. Some of them are native, and some are brought from other lands with great care, and these adorn the palace and give it glory. Birds are there, free and unconfined. They come of their own accord and have their nests and roosting places in the branches, birds of various kinds. But parrots are specially kept there, and these flock in bevies about the king. In this royal pleasance, there are lovely tanks made by hand of men, in which they kept fish of enormous size, but quite tame. No one has permission to fish for these except the king's sons while yet in their boyhood. These youngsters amuse themselves without the least risk of being drowned, while fishing in the unruffled sheet of water and learning how to sail their boats."

Its Apartments. While the exterior and the grounds of the palace are thus described by the Greek writers, more light is thrown on its interior and its design by Kauṭilya [I. 20-21]. The palace was to be protected by an outer wall and a moat (*saprākāra-parikhā*). In its rear were the women's apartments with stores of medicine useful in midwifery. Outside these apartments were residences of the princes and princesses. In front of these came the toilet chamber (*Alaṁkārabhūmi*), the Council-house (*Mantrabhūmi*), the Hall of Audience (*Upasthāna*), and, lastly, the administrative offices of the heir-apparent (*Kumāra*) and of the Heads of Departments (*Adhyakshasthānaṁ*). In the intervening places between these apartments, the troops in charge of the harem (*antarvaṁśika-sainyaṁ*) shall be stationed. A special household guard (*Abhyāgārika*) comprising 80 men and 50 women (or old men of 80 and women of 50) was to look after the morals of the harem [*Ib.*].

The king had his own suite of rooms. On rising from bed the king was to be received by his Amazonian bodyguard, women archers (*strīgaṇairdhanvibhiḥ*). In the second apartment, he will be received by his personal servants to give him coat and head-dress, and other aged attendants and attendant eunuchs. In the third apartment was stationed a sham bodyguard of dwarfs, hunchbacks and *kirātas*, or mountaineers, of foreign origin, *Mlechchhas*. The outermost of the king's apartments which communicated with the exterior was to be in charge of an armed retinue (*prāsapāṇibhiḥ*), door-keepers (*dauvārikaiḥ*), as well as the king's ministers and kinsmen.

Menial Staff. Thus the king's menial staff comprised (1) *Kañchuka* (2) *Ushnīshi* (3) *Kalpaka* (4) *Prasādhaka* (5) *Snāpaka* (6)

Saṁvāhaka (7) *Āstaraka* (8) *Rajaka* (9) *Mālākāra* and (10) *Māhānasika*. As to (6) *Saṁvāhaka*, Strabo says that the king's "favourite mode of exercising the body is by friction in various ways, but especially by passing smooth ebony rollers over the surface of the body" [XV. i. 41].

To these menials are also added [I. 12] *Sūda* and *Ārālika*, cooks for preparing varieties of food and beverage, *Udaka-parichāraka* for supplying water, while the king also had personal attendants of various types such as (1) *Kubja* (hunchback) (2) *Vāmana* (dwarf) (3) *Kirāta* (of small body, *alpatanu*) (4) *Mūka* (dumb) (5) *Badhira* (deaf) (6) *Jaḍa* (idiot) (7) *Andha* (blind). Even deformities were utilized in the service of the king!

There were also several other servants in charge of the king's bodily requisites such as Umbrella (*chhatra*), Goblet (*bhṛiṅgāra*), Fan (*vyajana*), Shoes (*pādukā*), Seat (*āsana*), Carriage (*yāna*) and Horse (*vāhana*). Some of these were women, as already shown.

Lastly, the king had a special staff to cater for his amusements, as indicated in the series *Naṭa-Nartaka-Gāyana-Vādaka-Vāgjīvana-Kuśīlava* [I. 12].

According to Kauṭilya [I. 21], the personal attendants of the king [*Āsanna* staff] should be natives and not foreigners and should be recruited from approved families who are related to the king by hereditary service and known for their loyalty and accomplishments. They should also be proof against fear and incapable of being coerced into disloyalty [I. 10].

Elaborate Provisions for the King's Safety. The design of the palace is determined by suspicion and precaution for the king's safety. Its structure includes any number of mazes, secret and subterranean passages, hollow pillars, hidden staircases, collapsible floors. There is also diverse provision against fire, poisonous animals and poisons. There are introduced trees which are avoided by snakes. There are parrots because they cry at the sight of a serpent and give the alarm signal. There were other birds also which were differently affected by the sight of poison [I. 20].

Precaution against Poisoning. The kitchen is carefully guarded and is constructed in a secret place. The food for the king is tested by a multitude of tasters. Examination is made of any traces of poison found in the viands and in the demeanour of the tasters. Medicaments for the king must pass similar tests. Servants in charge of the king's dresses and toilets must appear bathed, and in washed clothing, to receive the toilet requisites, duly sealed, from the bodyguard in charge of same before applying them on the king. Articles of ornament and apparel are inspected by the king's maid servants. Cosmetics etc. are first tried on those who apply them. Those who perform physical feats before the king must use appliances which cannot do any harm from fire, poison or any weapon. Musicians will perform before the king on instruments kept in the palace and thus free from any taint of poison. Similarly, even the equipment for horses, chariots and elephants to be used by the king is to be supplied from the palace The king should have always in attendance physicians and experts in the science of poisons (*Jāṅgalīvids*) [I. 21].

Treatment of Princes. In connection with the king's personal safety about which the *Arthaśāstra* is so particular, it deals with the problem of the grown-up sons of the king, a "problem of polygamous sovereignty," as F. W. Thomas pithily puts it. It is plainly recognized that 'princes like crabs devour their parents' (*karkaṭasadharmāṇo hi janakabhakshāḥ rājaputrāḥ*) [I. 16.] The question is, should they live with the king or at a distance ? If the latter, should they be in a detention camp (*ekasthānāvarodhaḥ*), or in a frontier fort (*antapāladurge*), or in the fort of a foreign king (*sāmantadurge*)? But the last measure will make the foreign king milk him. through the calf of his son so as to exploit the situation against him (*vatseneva hi dhenuṁ pitaramasya sāmanto duhyāt*). The last alternative is to place these princes in rustic seclusion with their maternal relations. In any case, they are to be kept under surveillance with spies set on them, to betray them, if necessary. Where a king has many sons, he may send some of them away to frontier or foreign States (*pratyantaṁ anyavishayaṁ vā preshayet*), where there is not, nor is to be, an heir-apparent (so that they may have a chance of being adopted and chosen for the throne). The worthy son is to be made Commander-in chief or the Crown-Prince.

Succession. The eldest son is to be preferred for the throne as a general rule (*aiśvaryaṁ jyesṭhabhāgī*). But Kauṭilya is emphatic that even the only son of the king should not be placed on the throne if he is devoid of education, discipline, and character (*na chaikaputramavinītaṁ rājye sthāpayet*). It is also stated that the king is justified in deporting the wicked son among his many sons. It is also pointed out that normally the father is the well-wisher of his sons. To solve the problem of succession among many sons, Kauṭilya contemplates the device of a joint-family sovereignty, on the ground that such a collective sovereignty will be of invincible strength, while free from the evils caused by the defects of a single sovereign. Such a sovereignty will be permanent (*Kulasya vā bhaved* *rājyaṁ kulasaṁgho hi durjayaḥ| Arājavyasanābādhaḥ śaśvadāvasati kshitīm ||*)

Some scholars take the sovereignty of the Nandas as a joint sovereignty held by their family. According to *Chāṇakya-kathā* (ed. N. Law, v. 7), Mahapadma was succeeded by his sons who ruled conjointly, and one of them was selected by lot annually to act as king, while the sovereign authority was vested in all.

It may be noted that Kauṭilya who, according to tradition, forced upon the throne of Magadha a king of his choice, believed more in merit than in hereditary right as the title to kingship. He has, however, no faith in mere usurpers as such [VIII. 2]. Some believe in a new king as being more acceptable for his readiness to please the people by means of 'favours, concessions and gifts and honours' (*Navastu Rājā sva-dharmānugraha-parihāra-dāna-māna-karmabhiḥ prakṛitirañjanopakāraiścharati iti*), but Kauṭilya thinks it is not so, because ultimately a new king's rule will be a rule of might, since he will feel that he has conquered the country by his own might (*Balāvarjitaṁ mamedaṁ rājyaṁ iti*). Even where a king dies without leaving a competent heir to succeed him, Kauṭilya would prefer him to be placed on the throne and announced as king before the public, with the co-operation of the other princes and chiefs (*Mukhya Rāshṭramukhya*). 'Or the minister having gradually placed the burden of administration on the shoulders of the heir-apparent may announce finally to the public the death of the king.' Ordinarily, "that son of the king who is possessed of self-control should succeed him on the throne. Failing such a qualified prince, the Chief Minister will place on the throne even the unworthy prince (*Kumāra*), or princess, or even the pregnant queen (*Devī*), and, calling a meeting of the ministers and magnates (*Mahāmātrān sannipātya*), should say: 'the kingdom is your trust (*nikshepa*): think of their father and of your own power and pedigree: this successor of the king is a mere symbol of sovereignty (*Dhvajāmātroyam*): you are the real sovereign.' Thus saying, he will anoint to sovereignty the prince or the princess or the pregnant queen (*Tatheti Amātyaḥ Kumāraṁ Rāja-kanyāṁ garbhiṇīṁ Devīṁ vā adhikurvīta ..abhishiñchet*). He will then undertake the education of the prince as king (*Vinayakarmaṇi cha Kumārasya prayateta*). If it is the princess on the throne, then her son, born of the father of the same caste (*samānajāti*), will ultimately succeed her. The minister must make ample provision for the paraphernalia due to royalty in respect of conveyances, chariots, horses, elephants, (*yāna-vāhana*), jewellery (*ābharaṇa*), robes, harem, residence and its fittings (*vastra-striveśma-parivāpān*)" [V. 6]. Thus Kauṭilya contemplates a

Regency administration to meet such an emergency, and prevent a possible revolution following the advent of a new king supplanting the dynasty of hereditary kings.

Capital at Pataliputra. According to Megasthenes who lived at the city, Pāṭaliputra was built at the confluence of the two rivers, Ganges and Son, at *nadī-saṅgama*, as it is called by Kauṭilya [II. 3]. In shape it was an oblong, with a length of 80 *stades* (=9 1/5 miles) and a breadth of 15 *stades* (=1 mile 1270 yards). The city was protected by a moat which had a depth of 30 cubits (=about 60 feet) and a width of 6 plethra (=200 yards). The moat was thus navigable. It was filled from the waters of the Son. It received the sewage of the city. The city was further protected by a massive timber palisade surrouding it along the moat. The palisade was pierced by loopholes through which archers were to shoot. It had also 64 gates and 570 towers. (Megasthenes, Frag. 25=Strabo, XV. c. 702).

Rhys Davids [*Buddhist India*, p. 262] calculates that "the number of *towers* allows one to every 75 yards, so that archers, in the towers, could cover the space intervening between any two. The number of *gates* would allow one to each 660 yards, which is quite a probable and convenient distance. The extent of the fortifications is, indeed, prodigious. . . But the native records confirm the impression that then, as now, an Indian town tended to cover a vast extent. And we may accept the estimate made by Megasthenes of the size of the city wherein he dwelt."

According to Megasthenese wood was the material mainly used in the construction of Pāṭaliputra, because it was a city built on the banks of rivers and had to be protected against floods by wood [1. 6]. It may be noted that excavations at the site of Pāṭaliputra have brought to light portions of wooden palisade at depth of ten to fifteen feet below the surface. These must have formed portions of the ancient wooden wall of the Maurya city.

The construction of the city corresponds closely to what Kauṭilya prescribes on the subject. Kauṭilya builds up the capital as a fort (*durga*) to protect the country (*janapadārakshasthānam*). In that view, it should be on a river or a hill. Or it may be built at the centre of the kingdom (*Janapadamadhye*) in a suitable locality approved by engineers (*Vāstuka-praśaste Vāstuvidyābhijñanirdishṭe deśe*) at the confluence of rivers (*nadīsaṅgame*), or on a lake (*hrada*), or tank (*taṭāka*) for unfailing supply of water. It should be surrounded by a canal (*pradakshiṇodakam*) and accessible by both land and water routes. It should be further protected by a ring of three moats (*parikhā*) with an interval of one *daṇḍa* (=6 ft.) between each. The three moats are to be of the width of 14, 12 and 10 *daṇḍas* (=84′, 72′ and 60′) each, and with sides made of stone or brick. The depth is to be one-fourth or half of width (so as to lend itself to boating). The moats should be running streams connected with natural sources of water, with rivers, into which they can flow, and bearing lotuses and crocodiles (*toyāntikīḥ āgantutoyapūrṅā vā saparivāhāḥ padmagrāhavatīḥ*).

At a distance of 4 *daṇḍas* from the innermost ditch was to be constructed a rampart (*vapra*) of pressed mud, 6 *daṇḍas* in height and 12 in width, solidified by the tramp of elephants and cattle, and further consolidated by the planting on it of thorny bushes and poisonous creepers. The rampart was to be surrounded by parapets (*prākāra*) of bricks and square towers (*aṭṭālaka*). Between each tower was to be a cloister (*pratolī*). Between the tower and the cloister was to be a stand (*indrakośa*) to accommodate three archers (*tridhānushkādhishṭhānam*). There were secret passages between the parapets and ramparts (*devapatha* and *chārya* and *chhannapatha*). These were also provided with openings (*dvāra*) and gates (*gopuram*). On the rampart were to be constructed at intervals hollows (*kulyā*) for the storage of weapons of all kinds, such as spades (*kuddāla*) of stone, axes (*kuṭhārī*), arrows (*kāṇḍa*), goads for elephants (*kalpanā*), clubs (*musṛiṇṭhi*), bayonets (*mudgara*), missiles (*daṇḍa*), discus (*chakra*), machines (*yantra*), weapons fitted with spikes of iron (*śataghni*), weapons of steel (*kārmārikāḥ*), tridents (*śūla*), bamboos fitted with iron points, explosives (*agnisaṁyogāḥ*) and the like.

The city should be provided with 12 gates out of which roads will lead to different stations in the country and to forests.

In its strongest part (*pravīre vāstuni*) is to be built the royal residence (*rājaniveśa*) covering a ninth of its area (*navabhāga*).

Adjoining the palace are to be the buildings for the king's preceptor, priest, sacrificial ceremonies (*ijyā*) and reservoir of water (*toyasthānam*), as also the residences of the Ministers.

Adjoining these will be the royal kitchen, the Assemby Hall (*Hastiśālā hastipṛishṭhākāraṁ sabhāgṛiham*) and the store house.

Outside the palace (*tataḥ paraṁ rājabhavanāt vahiḥ*, will be the dwellings of dealers in perfumes, garlands, grains, and drinks, dwellings of principal artisans, and of Kshatriyas.

Next will come the Treasury building, Accounts office, and the shops of goldsmiths and silversmiths (*Karmanishadyāḥ svarṇarajataśilpasthānāni*).

Then will come the shops of workers in other metals (*Kupyagṛihaṁ svarṇarajatetarasthānam*) and the arsenal.

These will be followed by the offices of the Municipal Corporation (*Nagara-vyāvahārika*), the Controller of Grain Market (*Dhānya-vyāvahārika*), the Superintendent of Mines and the Commander of the Army.

Next will follow the hotels and restaurants supplying cooked foods, meats, and wines, and dwellings of prostitutes, and actors (*tālāvachārā naṭāh*), as well as of the Vaiśyas.

Next will be the stables for asses, camels, the workshop, and the garages for vehicles and conveyances.

After these will come the quarters of different craftsmen, workers in wood, cotton, hemp, leather and of the Śūdras.

These will be followed by shops of medical stores (*bhaishajya-griham*).

Next will come the granary and the cattle shed and stable for horses.

After these will be located the temples of the royal dynastic deities and of the gods worshipped by the citizens at large: then the shops of the blacksmiths, and jewellers and then the dwellings of the Brāhmaṇas.

In the available space of the city will be located the craft guilds and companies of foreign merchants (*pravahaṇika-nikāyāḥ pravahaṇikāḥ videśāgatā vaṇijaḥ teshāṁ samūhāḥ*).

Within the city will also be located the temples of Durgā (*Aparājitā*), Vishṇu (*Apratihata*), Subrahmaṇya (*Jayanta*), Indra (*Vaijayanta*), Śiva, Vaiśravaṇa, Aśvins, Lakshmī and Madirā.

Heretics like *Kāpālikas* and Chaṇḍālas will live beyond the cremation grounds.

The store house of the capital must contain sufficient quantities of the necessaries of life to last for many years (against a prolonged siege of the city), necessary articles of food, medicines, and defence.

No quarters are to be given to the *Bahirikas*, such as acrobats, actors, and dancers, who are dangerous to the well-being of both urban and rural people.

Pataliputra in Indian Literature: Buddhist Texts. Pāṭaliputra has figured for a long time in Indian literature both before and after Chandragupta. Its foundation is traced in the Pali texts to the famous emperor of Magadha, Ajātaśatru, c. 551-519 B. C. who selected for the city a convenient site on the Ganges and had it constructed under the supervision of his chief ministers named Sunīdha and Vassakāra. The Buddha visited the city on the occasion of its foundation and made the following prophecy about its future greatness: "And among famous places of residence and haunts of busy men, this will become the chief, the city of Pāṭaliputra, a centre for interchange of all kinds of ware" [*Mahāprinibbāna Suttanta*, p. 18, tr. SBE.] The same prophecy is repeated in the *Mahāvagga*, VI. 28, 8: "(At the right place), Ānanda, the Magadha ministers, Sunīdha and Vassakāra, build this town at Pāṭaligrāma in order to repel the Vajjis. As far, Ānanda, as Aryan people dwell, as far as merchants travel, this will become the chief town, the city of Pāṭaliputta. ."

Patanjali. Patañjali (c. 2nd century B. C.) describes Pāṭaliputra as '*anuśoṇam Pāṭaliputraṁ*' in his *Mahabhāshya* [II, 1, 2] which means that Patañjali knew Pāṭaliputra as situated on the banks of the Śoṇa. The lofty buildings and the parapets for which the city was known impressed Patañjali so much that he refers to them as grammatical examples. Thus in IV, 3.2 he says: *Pāṭaliputrakāḥ prāsādāḥ Pāṭaliputrakāḥ prākārāḥ iti.*"

Mudrā-Rākshasa. In the later drama of *Mudrā-Rākshasa*, there is an interesting description of Pāṭaliputra. It indicates that Pāṭaliputra was situated at the confluence of the two rivers, Gangā and Śoṇa. In the drama, Chandragupta after taking possession of the Nanda king's palace called Sugāṅga-prāsāda sees from the palace the beauty of the river Gaṅgā being led fast, as a declining stream, after the rains, by the season of autumn towards her lord, the sea [III, 9]. This shows that the city was directly on the river Ganges. At the same time, the drama tells us that Malayaketu had to cross the river Śoṇa to be able to reach Pāṭaliputra. He says: "My elephants in their hundreds will drink up the waters of the river Śoṇa in their march towards the city" [IV, 16].

It is also stated in the drama that the city was surrounded by a rampart (*prākāra*) on which archers (*śarāsandharāḥ*) could be posted in its defence. The city is also described to be of many gates at which were stationed elephants strong enough to break through the array of the enemy's elephants [II, 13]. We are further told that one of the gates was fitted with a mechanical gate (*Yantra-toraṇa*) which could be let down by manipulating an iron bolt (*loha-kīlakam*) [II, 15].

It may be noted that the Greeks use the term Erannobaos which corresponds to Sanskrit *Hiraṇya-vāha*, a name of the Śoṇa river (Bāṇa's *Harsha-charita*, p. 19, ed. Parab).

Fa-hien. We may further note that the Chinese traveller Fa-hien who travelled in India between the years 319-414 A.D. saw the Mauryan palace in a good condition and describes it as follows: "The king's (Asoka's) palace in the city, with its various halls, all built by spirits who piled up stones, constructed walls and gates, carved designs, engraved and inlaid, after no human fashion, is still in existence."

Royal Decrees. The king had to perform his administrative work by means of his decrees which Kauṭilya calls *Śāsanas* [II, 10]. The king was to appoint a qualified writer called *Lekhaka* who will listen to the king's order, and comprehending it fully, will reduce it to writing. The king's writs are issued to his Viceroys (*Īśvaras*) or to other officials. Therefore, the writer must be one of high qualifications such as those of an *Amātya* or Minister, with a knowledge of different customs, good hand-writing, quick at composition, and able to decipher writing.

The qualities of a good composition (*lekha-sampat*) consist of a logical arrangement of matter (*arthakrama*), relevancy (*sambandha*), fulness of expression (*paripūrṇatā*), agreeable expression (*mādhuryaṁ*), dignity of language (*audāryaṁ*) and clearness of expression (*spashṭatvaṁ*).

Dr. F. W. Thomas suggests [*Cambridge History of India* I. 488] that these *Lekhakas* belonged to the office of the Minister of Correspondence called *Praśāstā* in charge of the issue of the king's *śāsanas*.

The royal writs may be those of notice (*prajñāpana*), command (*ājñā*), gift (*paridāna*), remission (*parīhāra*), authorisation (*nisṛishṭi*), intelligence (*prāvṛittika*), reply (*pratilekha*), and of general proclamation (*sarvatraga*). "Having studied all the Śāstras and having also considered the applications of their injunctions, Kauṭilya has thus laid down the procedure for royal ordinances in the interests of Narendra" (which is supposed to be the name of Chandragupta according to some tradition).

CHAPTER V

MINISTERS : RULES OF SERVICE

Constituents of the State. The machinery of administration has been modelled by Kauṭilya with reference to the seven constituent elements of the State in the theory of Hindu polity. These consist of (1) the sovereign (*svāmī*) (2) the ministers (*amātya*), (3) the territory (*janapada*), (4) fortifications (*durga*), (5) financial strength (*kośa*), (6) military strength (*daṇḍa* or the army made up of its four limbs, infantry, cavalry, elephants and chariots) and (7) alliances (*mitrāṇi*).

Territory. Of these, Kauṭilya duly emphasises the importance of the territorial basis of the State upon which its progress and future so much depend. First of all, Kauṭilya [IX. 1] gives utterance to his innate sense of patriotism and love of country by stating that "of the whole world, the northern part of the country which stretches from the Himalayas up to the seas (*Himavatsamudrāntaramudīchīnaṁ*) is marked out as the natural sphere of imperialism" (*Chakravarti-kshetram*). Here Kauṭilya is evidently thinking of the empire already established by Chandragupta in northern India by his overthrow of Greek rule in the Punjab, of Nanda empire of Magadha, and his rule over Surāshṭra in western India. This country is rich in its economic resources and potentialities, in its abundance of all varieties of land, cultivated (*grāmya*), uncultivated forests (*āraṇya*), highlands (*pārvata*), well-watered lands (*audaka*), dry land (*bhauma*), stretches of even land (*sama*), and undulating land (*vishama*), so as to give scope to the growth of every kind of agricultural produce, both wet crops and dry crops. India to this day remains pre-eminently the land of agriculture, with its capacity for economic self-sufficiency depending upon its variety of climates so as to make India an 'epitome of the world.' In another passage [VII. 1], Kauṭilya approves the country of warriors (*āyudhīyaprāya*), agriculturists, and craftsmen (*śreṇīprāyo*), and protected by forts on hill, or river, or by forest-fastnesses. Kauṭilya, as a man of the Frontier Province, was impressed by its many hill-forts. He also mentions the following essentials of a flourishing country : (1) Fort (2) Agriculture (*Setu*) (3) Roads (4) Mines as source of weapons of war (*saṁgrāmopakaraṇānām yoniḥ*) (5) Timber forests supplying materials for constructing forts, carts, and chariots (*durgakarmaṇāṁ yānarathayośca*) (6) Forests of Elephants and (7) Pastures for cattle (*vraja*) including Cow, Horse, Ass, and Camel (pointing to the Frontier Province) [VII. 14]. Among other valuable virtues which a country should possess (*jaanapadasampat*), Kauṭilya mentions them as follows [VI 1] : It should be fortified in all its parts. It should be capable of supporting not merely the indigenous population but also the immigrants from foreign countries (*ātmadhāraṇaḥ paradhāraṇaśca*). It should be possessed of means of defence, natural, and artificial, such as mountains, forests, rivers and forts (*svārakshaḥ*). It should be economically self-contained (*svājīvaḥ*). It should have a loyal people who would resent foreign invasion (*śatrudveshī*). It should have weak neighbours (*śakya-sāmantaḥ durbala-sāmantaḥ*). It should have abundance of agricultural land, being not too marshy, or rocky, or dry, or undulating, or jungly, nor should it be exposed to the depredations of wild tribes (*kaṇṭaka-śreṇī*). It should be *kānta*, i.e. 'endowed with all works and facilities of public utility and convenience such as provision of shade-giving and fruit-growing trees, gardens of medicinal plants, rivers, lakes, tanks, and resthouses' (for which Asoka was so famous). It should be further possessed of abundance of fertile lands (*sītā*), mines yielding gold and precious stones (*khanirvajrādimaṇi-suvarṇādyākaraḥ*) ; vegetable gardens and timber forests and also forests of elephants, grazing grounds for cattle (*gāvyaḥ*), lands for settlements (*paurusheya*), reserves for hunters and forests (*guptagocharo lubdhakādirakshitabhūmiḥ*) and abundance of livestock (*paśumān*). It should be independent of rainfall in its own supply of waters from its rivers (*adevamātṛikaḥ*). It should be possessed of roads of traffic by water and land. It should be rich in valuable merchandise and manufactures of various kinds (*sāra-chitra-bahu-paṇya*). Its people should be capable of bearing the burden of an adequate army and taxation (*daṇḍakara-sahaḥ*). It should have an industrious agricultural population (*karmaśīla-karshaka* , a body of able administrators. It should have a vast population belonging to the lower castes or the aboriginal tribes who may aid in the development of its arts and crafts (*avaravarṇa-prāyaḥ adhama-varṇa-bahulaḥ*). It may be noted that Manu welcomes this kind of population in a country to form the artisan classes "whose hand was always pure (*nityaṁ śuddhaḥ kāruka-hastaḥ*) [V. 129]." Lastly, the prosperity and future of a country ultimately must depend upon the quality of its people, its loyalty and character (*bhaktaśuchi-manushya*). No better picture can be given of India than the one given here by Kauṭilya.

Megasthenes on India as a Country. It is interesting to note that Megasthenes has left a description of India and its natural and economic resources, which corresponds closely to that of Kautilya. He has observed : "India has many huge mountains which abound in fruit trees of every kind and many vast plains of great fertility, intersected by a multitude of rivers. The greater part of the soil is under irrigation and bears two crops in a year. The country teems at the same time with animals of all sorts, beasts of the field and fowls of the air, of all different degrees of strength and size. It is prolific besides in elephants. The Indians are well skilled in arts. They inhale a pure air and drink the very finest water.

"And while the soil bears on its surface all kinds of fruits which are known to cultivation, it has also underground numerous veins of all sorts of metals, for it contains much gold and silver, and copper and iron in no small quantity which are employed in making articles of use and ornaments, as well as the implements and accoutrements of war.

"In addition to cereals, there grow throughout India much millet which is kept well watered by the profusion of river streams, and much pulse of different sorts, and rice also, as well as many other plants useful for food. It is accordingly affirmed that famine has never visited India, and that there has never been a general scarcity in the supply of nourishing food.

"The fruits, moreover, of spontaneous growth, and the succulent roots which grow in marshy places and are of varied sweetness, afford abundant sustenance for man. The fact is that almost all the plains in the country have a moisture which is alike genial, whether it is derived from the rivers, or from the rains of the summer season, which are wont to fall every year at a stated period with surprising regularity."

Treasury. The next vital factor of the State is the strength of its Treasury (*kośasampat*) built upon the basis of a sound and just system of taxation (*dharmādhigataḥ*), abundance of gold and silver, precious stones and gold coins (*hiraṇya*), so as to be able to sustain the country against calamities of long duration such as famines and the like (*dīrghāmapyāpadamanāyatiṁ saheteti kośasampat*) [VI. I].

Army. As regards the army, Kauṭilya prefers it to be hereditary (*pitṛipaitāmaho*), well paid, and contented, recruited from householders (*bhṛitapūtradāraḥ*), experienced in many battles (*bahuyuddhaḥ*), proficient in all the arts of war, completely identified with the king, and mainly composed of Kshatriyas [*Ib.*].

Kauṭilya concludes with the following wise saying: "Even if the king is possessed of a small territory (*alpadeśopi*), if he is possessed of the other elements of sovereignty, he will make himself invincible and will be able to conquer the whole earth [*Ib.*]." This is an incentive to the conquests which Kauṭilya had in view for his protege, Chandragupta.

Powers reserved to the King. It may be noted that of the several elements making up the State, the king was to retain in his own hands his ultimate control over two elements viz, *Kośa* and *Daṇḍaśakti*, the power of purse and the military, by which he will be able to prevail over *Amātyas* or Ministers, in case they are disloyal to him. The disloyalty of Ministers is described as an internal trouble which is far more dangerous to the State than any of its troubles from an external source and is described as a snake (*Ahi-bhayāt abhyantaraḥ kopo bāhyakopāt pāpīyān | Antarāmātya-kopaśchāntaḥ kopāt | Tasmāt kośadaṇḍa-śaktimātmasaṁsthāṁ kurvīta*) [VIII. 2].

Famine Code. The king also exercised his extraordinary powers for the welfare of his people against emergencies like famines (*durbhiksha*). First, he is to help the people with a supply of seeds and provisions (*bhakta*). Secondly, he may provide for employment of the people by undertaking construction of public works such as buildings (*durgakarma*) or bridges (*setu*). Failing this, he is to supply the people with food (*bhakta-saṁvibhāgam*). Or he may remove the famine-stricken to another country for the time being (*deśanikshepaṁ vā*) or he may seek the help of a friendly State. Or he may contract (*karśana*) his population by emigrating its unemployed portion to a foreign country (*nirupayogajanānāṁ tatkāle deśāntarapreshaṇena alpatva-karaṇam*). Or he may arrange a wholesale emigration of his people to another flourishing country; or take recourse to the sea-coast or a country with lakes and tanks as sources of fish, tortoise or birds upon which to live. Or he may extend agriculture. Or he may employ his people on hunting and fishing [IV, 3].

Patañjali mentions an interesting tradition about the Mauryas that they, in need, took to the manufacture of images of deities, and to trading in them as a source of profit (*Mauryaiḥ hiraṇyārthibhiḥ archāh prakalpitāḥ*). The images thus fashioned and sold as articles of trade were named differently from the images that were worshipped: e.g., *Śivaka* instead of *Śiva* [Patañjali on Pāṇini, V. 3, 92].

It may be recalled against these extraordinary measures for raising revenue that the Maurya empire had to face a twelve year's famine, as already described.

Hierarchy of Officers. It will appear from the above conception and description of the various needs of a country and the factors upon which its economic and political progress depends that there should be devised an elaborate system of administration, and a complex machinery to cope with the problems of government. Kauṭilya has well said [I, 7] : " Administration cannot be the work of one man, just as one wheel cannot drive a car" (*Sahāyasādhyaṁ rājatvaṁ chakramekaṁ na vartate*). Therefore, the king must carry on the administration with the help of a hierarchy of agents of different grades and jurisdictions extending and descending up to the village.

Normal Administrative Machinery. We have already referred to the many Viceroys and Governors whom the Mauryan emperor placed in charge of the different provinces and local governments among which the burden of Imperial Administration from headquarters was conveniently distributed. But it is to be noted that each such Viceroyalty or Governorship was functioning like a State by itself after the pattern and standard laid down for it in the time-honoured science and theory of Hindu polity. Every State in the Hindu scheme of polity thus adopted a prescribed system of government and corresponded to the type and structure of administrative machinery laid down as the standard.

The normal administrative machinery prescribed for the government of a State was made up of the following elements, viz., (1) the Sovereign, (2) the Viceroys and Governors functioning as deputy kings as the sovereign's representatives, (3) the Ministers, (4) the Heads of Departments, (5) the subordinate Civil Service, and (6) Officers in charge of rural administration, of the villages. In addition to these, there was, of course, the branch of administration dealing with the Military in all its Departments. The administrative system of Chandragupta will, therefore, be described with reference to the aforesaid elements in the order in which they are mentioned.

Counsellers (*Mantrīs*). The policy and plan of administration count more than its details. The first duty that awaits the king as he arises from sleep is, as we have seen, his contemplation of the policy which must inform his government (*mantraṁ adhyāsīta*). As Kauṭilya points out [1. 15], all administrative work is preceded by the determination of policy (*mantrapūrvāḥ sarvārambhāḥ*). At the same time, it is recognized that the policy must be hatched in secret, while it cannot be determined by the king himself. Thus the question is, How many should the king take into confidence and consult as his counsellors or advisers ? Therefore, Bhāradvāja thought that secrecy of policy would be impossible except with one counsellor. Viśālaksha answers him by saying that it might be *mantragupti* but not *mantrasiddhi.* Success of policy is more important than its secrecy. "Therefore," says he, "the king should take counsel with a number of wise men." According to the School of Parāśara, however, this is only *mantrajñāna* but not *mantrasaṁrakshaṇam,* that is, 'Knowing Policy, but not keeping its secrecy.' They rather advise consulting a Minister on a hypothetical case. According to Piśuna, such a Minister will not take the matter seriously but will give his advice half-heartedly. Advice is responsible only on business that is pending. By this is secured both good counsel (*mantrabuddhi*) as well as its secrecy (*gupti*). Kauṭilya objects to this method as being uncertain (*anavasthā*). He recommends the appointment of permanent Advisors of the king, either three ot four in number. He does not recommend two for fear of their combination against the king. It should of course be open to the king to take counsel with only one or two of them according to need (*deśakāla-kāryavaśena*).

Objectives of Mantra or Policy. Mantra is described to be *panchāṅga*. The policy of government is bound up with the consideration of the following five subjects. The first will be Ways and Means of ensuring the defence of the country and proper foreign relations (*karmaṇāmārambhopāyaḥ*). The second is the resources of the State in men and material (*purushadravya-sampat*). The third is the determination of time and place for action (*deśakālavibhāgaḥ*). The fourth subject is provision against unforeseen calamities (*vinipāta-pratīkāraḥ*). The fifth is successful prosecution of administrative measures (*kāryasiddhiḥ*).

Council of Ministers (*Mantriparishad*). Besides this small body of Counsellors or Advisers (*Mantriṇaḥ*), the king must have a regular Council of Ministers (*Mantriparishad*). The Mānavas fix its number at 12, the Bārhaspatyas at 16, the Auśanasas at 20 but, according to Kauṭilya, it should be as required. Kauṭilya is evidently for a large Council. He cites with approval Indra's Council of 1000 Ṛishis. Though of only two eyes, He is known as one of thousand eyes, for these Rishis are his eyes, (*tasmād imaṁ dvyaksham sahasrākshamāhuḥ*) [I.15]. Kauṭilya mentions as one of the strong points of kingship the strength of his Council or *Parishad*. In his opinion, a king who is an *akshudraparishatka* lacks an important source of his power [VI. 1]. We may note that much earlier than the time of Chandragupta, Pāṇini, who did not live later than 500 B. C., refers to the *Parishad* as an accompaniment of kingship. He states [IV. 4, 44] that the members of a *Parishad* should be called *Pārishadyas,* while the king whose position was strengthened by his *Parishad* was called *Parishadvalaḥ* [V. 2, 112].

Procedure of Business in Council. The procedure of the king's business in the Council is also indicated by Kauṭilya. As has been already stated, the king had to transact some classes of administrative business with his whole Council of Ministers in attendance. For instance, the king was not to give interviews to the ambassadors from foreign kings without being attended by his Council of Ministers. Generally, he was to transact all administrative business along with the Ministers in attendance (*Āsannaissaha kāryāṇi paśyeta*). In the case of Ministers who were not present, he sought their advice by despatch of letters (*anāsannaissaha patrasampreshaṇena mantrayeta*). In the case of any urgent business cropping up, the king summoned to his presence both his Advisers (*Mantriṇo*) and his Council of Ministers (*Mantriparishadaṁ*) to whom he would explain it (*brūyāt*). He would generally act on the opinion of the majority in that joint meeting of his Counsellors and Ministers (*tatra yadbhūyishṭhāḥ brūyustat kuryāt*), or whatever was considered to be contributory to success (*kāryasiddhikaram*).

Asoka's Council. The inscriptions of Asoka mention his *Parisad* [R.E. III and VI]. Asoka speaks of his reference of urgent matters (*āchāyike* or *atiyāyike*=*ātyayika* of Kauṭilya) to his Council (*Parisā*) of Ministers (*Mahāmātras*), and of their debate or deliberation (*vivado nijhati*) thereon (*tāya aṭhāya*).

It may also be noted that, according to *Divyāvadāna* (p. 372, Cowell's ed.), Bindusāra (Chandragupta's son) had as many as 500 *Amātyas*.

Patañjali, in his *Mahābhāshya*, mentions *Chandragupta-Sabhā* [Gloss on I. 1, 68].

Secretary to Council. The Council or *Mantri-Parishad* had its Secretary in charge of its office. He is called by Kauṭilya *Mantri-Parishadadhyaksha* [I. 12].

Greek Accounts. We may now consider the Greek evidence on the subject of the king's Council.

Diodorus Diodorus, in his epitome of Megasthenes, mentions "the Councillors and Assessors who deliberate on public affairs. It is the smallest class, looking to number, but the most respected, on account of the high character and the wisdom of its members; for from their rank the Advisers of the king are taken, and the treasurers of the State, and the arbiters, who settle disputes. The generals of the army also, and the Chief Magistrates usually belong to this class."

Strabo. Strabo [XV, I, 46-9] referring to the "Councillors and Assessors" of the king states that "to them belong the highest posts of government, the tribunals of justice, and the general administration of public affairs."

Arrian. Arrian [*Indika*, XI, 12] says: "There are the Councillors of the State who advise the king or the magistrate of the self-governed cities, in the management of public affairs. In point of numbers, this is a small class, but it is distinguished by superior wisdom and justice, and hence enjoy the prerogative of choosing governors, chiefs of provinces, deputy governors, superintendents of the treasury, generals of the army, admirals of the navy, controllers, and commissioners, who superintend agriculture."

Council in Republics. It is to be noted that, according to Arrian, the Council of Ministers was a part both of monarchical and republican constitutions. We have already seen how many were the republican peoples who had taken a prominent part in the politics of Mauryan India.

Correspondence to 'Amatyas'. We have also to observe that the Greek descriptions of the Councillors and Assessors probably correspond to what Kauṭilya says about the class of officers called by the general name of *Amātyas*. It is out of these *Amātyas* that the Ministers themselves are recruited, as also the Heads of Departments, on the basis of certain tests and qualifications. Thus the body of *Amātyas* made up the Civil Service of the country, to which were recruited persons possessing the highest qualifications.

Mantri proper or Prime Minister. The full scheme of Kauṭilya's administrative arrangements may be thus stated. Firstly, the king depends most upon what is called his *Mantrī*, the Chief Minister, or the Prime Minister, as well as his preceptor or *Purohita*. They were of the first rank in administration. Next to them come the king's Counsellors or Advisers who are called *Mantrīs* or Ministers, and the other class of Mantrīs who form the *Mantriparishad*. All these come under the general class of officers called *Amātyas*.

His Rank. It would appear that the rank of the Chief Minister as the Mantrī proper is indicated by the payment of the highest salary to him, a salary of 48,000 *paṇas*. The salary attached to a Mantrī, who was a member of the *Mantriparishad*, was only 12,000 *paṇas*.

Qualifications. As regards the qualifications of the Chief Minister, it is laid down that he must be a native of the country (*Jānapada*). He should be senior in age (*pragalbha*), possessed of eloquence (*vāgmī*), resourceful (*pratipattimān*), of unimpeachable honesty, of good physique.

Agramatya. It is interesting to note that, according to *Divyāvadāna*, Bindusāra, Chandragupta's son, had Khallāṭaka as his Prime Minister called *Agrāmātya*, and that the *Agrāmātya* of Asoka was Rādhagupta.

Purohita as Minister of first rank. As regards the *Purohita*, he should be proficient in the Vedas and the six Aṅgas, in Jyotisha (*Daiva*), in the science of Omens (*Nimitta*), and also in the science of Polity (*Daṇḍanīti*), and the practices of Atharvaveda. "Him the king should follow as a pupil his preceptor, a son his father, and a servant his master. Thus brought up by Brāhmanas and trained in statecraft by a qualified Minister, and disciplined by the precepts of the Śāstras, the king will conquer the invincible [I. 9]."

Public Service Commission. There is a constitutional importance attaching to the offices of the Prime Minister and the Purohita. It appears that the king appointed by himself the *Amātyas* who should serve him as Ministers or *Mantrīs* either as (a) the Prime Minister (*Mantrī* proper) and Chief Purohita or as (b) the group of three or four Mantrīs who should be always ready to hand (*Āsanna*) as the king's Counsellors or Advisors, or as (c) Ministers who would constitute the *Mantriparishad* or Council of Ministers. All appointments other than those of the Ministers of these three classes were made by the king acting with his two Ministers, the Prime Minister, and the High Priest (*Mantripurohitasakhaḥ*) [I. 10]. Thus these two Ministers and the king formed an inner Council functioning as a sort of a Public Service Commission for making the higher administrative appointments, such as the Heads of Departments. These appointments were made upon the basis of both mental and moral qualifications out of candidates who were considered eligible for appointment as *Amātyas* [I. 8]. They were tested by temptations pertaining to *Dharma* (Duty), *Artha* (Wealth), *Kāma* (Moral Character) and *Bhaya* (Fear) [I. 10].

It is interesting to note that Megasthenes also mentions that it was the Council which appointed all higher officers of the State including provincial Governors.

Tests for Appointments. In the first, a priest is dismissed and is set upon *Amātyas* whom he incites to rebel against the king on the ground that he is unrighteous (*Adhārmikaḥ*). In the second, a general is dismissed for supposed embezzlement to tempt *Amātyas* by money for conspiring to murder the king. For the third test, a woman spy in the guise of an ascetic (*parivrājikā*) is employed to corrupt the *Mahāmātras*, telling each in turn that the Queen is in love with him. For the fourth test, Ministers are tempted to enter into a plot against the king's life. [*Ib*].

Principle of Selection: Appointments to Courts of Justice. The rule of appointment is that those Ministers who have stood the religious test should be appointed as judges, both civil (*Dharmasthīya*), and criminal (*Kaṇṭakaśodhana*) [*Ib.*].

Revenue and Stores. *Amātyas* who proved themselves above bribery should be appointed as Heads of Departments dealing with Revenue and Stores (*Samāhartṛi-Sannidhātṛinichay-akarmasu*) [*Ib.*].

Harem. *Amātyas* who have shown themselves as proofs against temptations of flesh would be the best officers to take charge of Departments concerning women. They are to be placed in charge of the king's harems both in capital, and also in the outlying parts (*Bāhyābhyantara-vihārarakshāsu*) [*Ib.*]. The king's harems outside the capital were meant for the king's female companions (*Bhoginyaḥ*) The harem of the Palace accommodated the Queens known as *Devīs* [Commentator].

Asoka's Harems. It is interesting to note in this connection that Asoka in one of his inscriptions [R.E. V] speaks of his harems (*orodhana*) and those of his brothers, and also the residences of his sisters, situated both in the capital at Pāṭaliputra (*hida Pāṭālipute cha*) and also in the outlying towns (*bahiresu cha nagaresu*). Asoka also refers to his second Queen (*Dutīyāye devīye*) named Kāruvākī, mother of Prince Tīvara, and to her residence at the *bāhira nagara* of Kauśāmbī. In his Pillar Edict VIII, Asoka makes another mention of his Queens and harems both at Pāṭaliputra and in the provinces (*diśāsu*) and also refers to his sons, whether the sons of his Queens (*Devikumāras*) or of his other wives (*Dārakas*). Asoka also, following Kauṭilya's injunctions, places special officers called *Dharmamahāmātras* in charge of these harems. One is tempted to suggest that the very title of these officers called *Dharmamahāmātras* is due to the fact that these must have been tested by the *Dharma-upadhā* or *Kāma-upadhā* of Kauṭilya (*Kāma* being taken to be included in the *Dharma* test). In his Rock Edict XII also, Asoka creates special officers to take charge of the interests of the women-folk and designates them as *Strī-Adhyaksha-Mahāmātras*. Apart from these Inscriptions referring to the many harems of Asoka, we know from *Mahāvaṁsa* of Asoka marrying the lady called Vedisa-Mahādevi-Śākyakumāri when he was serving as Viceroy at Ujjain. She did not follow Asoka as king to Pāṭaliputra where he lived with his chief Queen (*Agramahishī*), Asandhimitrā, but she lived on at Vedisa which was thus another outlying town where Asoka had a harem [V. 85 and XX).

Appointment of King's Bodyguard. Lastly, there were the officers who would prove themselves to be proof against fear, and would not by any means be coerced into disloyalty to the king. These ardent loyalists, dare-devils, and desperados would be chosen to constitute the king's bodyguard (*Āsanna-kāryeshu*).

Out of the way Posts. Officers who fail in one or the other of the above tests were to be employed at a distance as Superintendents of Mines, Timber or Elephant forests, or Manufactories (*Karmānta*).

Mantris. *Amātyas* who successfully stood all the above four tests were eligible for appointment to the exalted office of Mantri or Ministers of aforesaid three grades.

Ordinary Employees. It is also laid down that persons qualified to be *Amātyas* but not tested and tried will be employed in the general departments (*sāmānya-adhikarṇa*).

Ambassadors, Secretaries and Heads of Departments. *Amātyas* were also eligible for appointment as Ministers Plenipotentiary (*nisṛishṭārthaḥ*). An *Amātya* not fully qualified to be Ambassador was employed on special missions (*parimitārthaḥ*) or as bearer of royal writs (*śāsanaharaḥ*) [I. 16]. *Amātyas* were also appointed as *Lekhakas* or the king's Secretaries in charge of correspondence [II. 10,] and also *Adhyakshas* or Heads of Departments [II. 9].

Intelligence Department. Kauṭilya further prescribes [I. 11] that the king, acting with his ministers, will make appointments to the Intelligence Department of administration. The appointing authority for this rather difficult Department is specified as *Amātyavarga* of proved qualifications (*upādhibhiśśuddha*). This should mean the group of Ministers including the Prime Minister or *Mantrī*, th ePurohita, and the king's Advisors aforesaid. For it is laid down [I. 10] that those *Amātyas* who were found competent by all possible tests were appointed as Mantris (*Sarvopadhāśuddhān Mantriṇah kuryāt*).

The King's extraordinary powers. It may be noted that the king, besides reserving to himself the power of making the higher appointments of Ministers, Informers, and Heads of Departments, had to reserve to himself certain extraordinary powers against emergencies arising out of internal (*abhyantara*) or external (*bāhya*) troubles (*kopa*). The internal trouble is more serious for the State, and has to be put down by drastic measures. It is stated that such a trouble arises out of disloyalty or disaffection of the king's highest officers, namely, (1) *Mantrī* (Prime Minister) (2) *Purohita* (3) *Senāpati* and (4) *Yuvarāja*. If the king is at fault, he must acknowledge and abandon it (*Ātma-dosha-tyāgena*). Otherwise, his only remedy is to imprison (*saṁrodhana*) or to banish (*avasrāvaṇa*) them. In the case of the rebellious

Crown Prince, it may even extend to extreme punishment (*Nigraha*). The disaffection of other officers (*Amātyas*) is to be dealt with by suitable means (*yathārhamupāyān prāyuñjīta*).

The sources of external trouble are stated to arise out of disaffection of officers named (1) *Rāshṭramukhya* (2) *Antapāla* (3) *Āṭavika* (4) and the subdued king (*daṇḍopanata*). The remedy is stated to be that one may be set against the other (*tamanyonyenāvagrāhayeta*) [IX. 3].

Rules of Administration and Service. The rules by which the Heads of Departments are to administer them are indicated by Kauṭilya [II. 9]. The fundamental duty of each departmental Head is to see that he can balance the budget of his Department so as to be able to realise the receipts of revenue estimated. Heads of Departments are called *Adhyakshas* by Kauṭilya and also under the general name of *Upayuktas* or superior officers (*yuktānāṁ upari niyuktāḥ*). The Head of a Department is to be appointed by his fitness (*śaktitaḥ*) for it. He should work according to instructions (*yathāsandeśam*) and should not commence any costly schemes without previous sanction except to meet emergencies 'due to fire or flood.' Strict discharge of duty or work done better than instruction is to be rewarded with promotion and honours (*sthānamānau*). One should not realise more than estimated revenue. For this will be "eating up the country" (*janapadaṁ bhakshayati*). The main business of the Head of a Department is to check the accounts of income and expenditure both by general and detailed examination.

It will be seen that most of the Heads of Departments are to work at mofussil centres and in the interior of the country. There the Head of a Department is to keep eye on people who are drifting towards bankruptcy by wrongly spending away all their ancestral assets (*mūlaharaḥ*), or those who are spendthrifts and do not save but live from hand to mouth (*tādātvika*), or those who are contemptible misers (*kadarya*) and hoard wealth by famishing themselves and their dependents (*yobhṛityātmapīḍābhyāmupachinotyartham*). He should particularly keep a watch on the monetary transactions of the miserly and rich capitalists and see how they hide their wealth by hoarding it in their homes in secret places underground or in holes in pillars (*svaveśmani bhūgartastambhakoṭarādishu*); or by depositing it with others, urban or rural people (*avanidhatte paurajānapadeshu*); or by spiriting it away to foreign countries (*avasrāvayati paravishaye*). Such people are potential dangers to the State to whose prosperity they do not make their due contributions by evading and avoiding taxation.

Since the chief concern of the Head of a Department is thus finance and solvency, he is to be associated with a number of appropriate officers to assist him in his work. These are mentioned as Accountant (*Saṅkhyāyaka*), Scribe (*Lekhaka*), Examiner of coins (*Rūpadarśaka*), Treasurer (*Nīvīgrāhaka*), and their superior officer (*Uttarādhyaksha=auparika*). These superior officers are to be recruited from retired military officers (*Vṛiddhabhāvādinā yuddhākshamatvaṁ*).

It is also provided that each Department should have a number of sectional Heads (*bahumukhyaṁ*), but they should be appointed on a temporary and not a permanent basis (*anityaṁ*). 'Permanent service by its security is liable to make its incumbent independent and mischievous, while the country people (*Jānapadāḥ*) have no interest in reporting his defects.'

The authorities are asked to guard against embezzlement to which government servants dealing with large amounts of receipts are liable. It is difficult to detect embezzlement, just as it is difficult to detect fishes drinking in water as they swim in it. Officers found guilty of corruption or embezzlement are to be proceeded against and made to refund the public money embezzled (*Āsrāvayechchopachitān*). They will be further punished by being degraded to lower posts (*viparyasyechcha karmasu, "karmasu viparyasyat vyatyayena niveśayet uchchakarmasthānebhyo-varopya nīchakarmasthaneshu niyuñjīta"*). The two punishments for embezzlement are thus (1) *Āsrāvaṇa* (refunding) and (2) *Viparyasana* (degrading). On the other hand, those officers who distinguish themselves by not merely abstaining from embezzlement of public revenue but even by increasing it in accordance with law (*nyāyataḥ*) will be made permanent in their service (*nityādhikārāḥ*).

The rules of Service show that there was a period of probation for every government servant, which was followed by his confirmation on approved work.

Grades of Pay and Service. The entire Civil Service was of different grades and scales of salary attaching to each grade. Kauṭilya gives an account of these grades [V. 3] which very well show the vastness and complexity of the administrative machinery that was created to look after the manifold interests and requirements of the country. Kauṭilya, however, lays down the rule of administration that its establishment charges should not exceed a fourth of total provincial revenue (*Durga-janapadaśaktyā bhṛityakarma samudayapādena sthāpayet*) [V. 3]. His account of the grades of officers in terms of salary may be thus presented :

Grade of salary 48,000 *paṇas*

1. Prime Minister (*Mantri*).
2. Chief Priest (*Purohita*).
3. Commander-in-Chief of the army (*Senāpati*).
4. Crown-prince (*Yuvarāja*).

The following members of the royal family and household also received the same allowance: the king's Preceptor (*Āchārya*), sacrificial priest (*Ritvik*), Queen (*Rāja-Mahishī*), and the Dowager Queen (*Rāja-mātā*).

Grade 24,000 *paṇas*

1. The Warden of the Palace (*Dauvārika*).
2. The Overseer of the Harem (*Antarvaṁśika*).
3. The Officer in-charge of Munitions (*Praśāstṛi*).
4. The Collector-General (*Samāhartṛi*).
5. The Treasurer-General (*Sannidhātṛi*).

Grade 12,000 *paṇas*

1. The Prefect of the city (*Paura-vyāvahārika*).
2. Superintendent of Agriculture and Forests (*Kārmāntika*).
3. The Members of the Council (*Mantri-parishat*).
4. Provincial Governor (*Rāshṭra-pāla*).
5. The Warden of the Marches or Frontiers (*Antapāla*).
6. The Commandant of the Cavalry (*Kumāra=Aśvānucharaḥ*).
7. Commander of a Company of Eighty (*Kumāra-mātā=aśītijananetā*).
8. Commandant of the Infantry (*Nāyaka=Padātinetā*).

Grade 8,000 *paṇas*

1. Presidents of Guilds (*Śreṇī-mukhyāḥ*).
2. Officers in charge of elephants, chariots and cavalry (*Hastyaśva-rathamukhyāḥ*).
3. The Judge (*Pradeshṭā*).

Grade 4,000 *paṇas*

1. The Superintendents of Infantry, Horses, Chariots and Elephants (*Pattyaśva-ratha-hastyadhyakshāḥ*).
2. The Superintendents of (a) Timber-forests (b) Elephant-forests (*Dravya-hasti-vanapālāḥ*).

Grade 2,000 *paṇas*

1. The teacher of Charioteering (*Rathika*).
2. The physician and surgeon (*Chikitsaka*).
3. The trainer of horses for the army (*Aśvadamaka*).
4. The carpenter or mechanic for the army (*Vardhakiḥ*).
5. The rearers of animals (*Yoniposhakāḥ*).
6. The trainer of elephants (*Anīkasthaḥ*).

Grade 1,000 *paṇas*

1. The Foreteller (*Kārtāntika*).
2. The Diviner (*Naimittika*).
3. The Astrologer (*Mauhūrtika*).
4. The Expounder of Purāṇas (*Paurāṇika*).
5. The Charioteer (*Sūta*).
6. The Bard or Ministrel (*Māgadha*).
7. The Priestly Staff (*Purohita-purushāḥ*).
8. All Departmental Superintendents (*Sarvādhyakshāḥ*).

Grade 1000-500 *paṇas*

1. Chief (*Ārya*) of a class.
2. Skilled trainer of untamed horses and elephants (*Yuktārohaka*).
3. Experienced Detective (*Māṇavaka*). (recruited from criminal classes).
4. Builder in stone (*Śailakhanaka*) or State Sculptor.
5. Teachers of Music, preceptors, and specialists in *Dharma-* and *Artha-śāstras* to receive above as honorarium, as their services are available for the public (*Sarvopasthāyina āchāryā vidyāvantaścha pūjāvetanāni*).

Grade 500 *paṇas*

1. Foot-soldiers (*Pādāta*).
2. Accountants (*Saṅkhyāyaka*).
3. Clerical staff (*Lekhaka*).
4. Artists (*Śilpavantaḥ*).
5. Directors of Music (*Tūrya-karāḥ*).

Grade 250 *paṇas*

Musicians (*Kuśīlavāḥ*).

Grade 120 *paṇas*

Skilled artisans (*Kāru-śilpī*).

Grade 60 *paṇas*

1. Menial staffs (*Parichāraka*) in charge of animals and birds and their chiefs (*Pārikarmika*).
2. The king's personal attendants (*Aupasthāyikaśarīra-parichāraka*):
3. Cowherds (*Gopālakas*).
4. Labourers (*Vishṭi*).
5. Trappers (*Bandhaka*).

Couriers (*Dūtas*) are to be paid ten *paṇas* for carrying messages up to ten yojanas ; twenty *paṇas* for a distance up to hundred yojanas.

Special pay is to be given on occasions of *Rājasūya* to Mantrī and Purohita which may be three times their usual salary. The king's charioteer is to be paid 1,000 on that occasion.

Spies of different classes are to get 1,000 *paṇas*.

The village staff (such as washermen and spies) are to get 500.

Attendants of spies are to get 250 *paṇas* or more in proportion to work (*prayāsa-vṛiddhavetanā vā*).

Government servants of grades (*varga*) from 100 to 1,000 are to be placed under *Adhyakshas* who will determine their subsistence, wages, rewards, instructions (*ādeśa*), and assignment of work (*vikshepa*).

When there is no work (*avikshepa*), they will be transferred to take charge of looking after Government buildings (*rājaparigraha*), fortifications (*durga*), and the defences of the realm (*rāshṭrarakshā*).

Pensions. There were some very generous and humane regulations which added to the attractions of the public service. When an officer died in the discharge of his duties, his sons and wives were entitled to a subsistence allowance (*bhakta-vetana*) from the State. Consideration was also shown to such dependents of the deceased officer as were incapacitated from earning their livelihood, e.g. infants, aged and afflicted persons.

Payments in Cash or Kind. Payments of salaries might be made both in cash and kind. When short of money, the king paid the salary in forest produce, cattle, or land for cultivation, together with some cash. But payment in cash was the rule when new colonies or settlements were projected [V. 3].

It is to be noted that grants of land were also made without the right of alienation (*vikrayādhānavarjam*) to officers like (1) *Adhyaksha* (2) *Saṁkhyāyaka* (Accountant) (3) *Gopa* (4) *Sthānika* (5) *Anīkastha* (elephant-trainer) (6) *Chikitsaka* (physician) (7) *Aśvadamaka* (trainer of horses) and (8) *Jaṁghārika* (*Jāṁghika*, courier) [II. 1].

Special scales of pay were granted in accordance with qualifications and administrative efficiency shown (*vidyākarmabhyām bhakta-vetanaviśeshaṁ cha kuryāt*).

These were the Civil Service regulations which determined and governed the appointments, pay, prospects, and grades of the men who carried on the complex and difficult work of administration from day to day.

CHAPTER VI

ADMINISTRATIVE DEPARTMENTS AND OFFICERS

Departments and Officers : Greek Accounts. An interesting and valuable account of these is given by Megasthenes from what he had himself seen of the working of the Indian Administration under Chandragupta Maurya. E. R. Bevan, who has critically examined the Greek evidence in the original, states [*Cambridge History of India*, Vol. I, ch. XVI] : "The account which Megasthenes gave of the various officials points to a highly organised bureaucracy. They were, he said, of three kinds : (1) *Agronomoi* 'District Officials' ; (2) *Astynomoi*, 'Town officials' ; and (3) Members of the War office.

District Officials (*Agronomoi*). "The duties of the first kind were to supervise (1) Irrigation and Land Measurement, (2) Hunting, (3) the various Industries connected with Agriculture, Forestry, work in Timber, Metal Foundries, and Mines, and they had (4) to maintain the Roads and see that at every ten *stadia*[1] ($1\frac{1}{3}$ miles) there was a mile-stone indicating the distance (this is the passage which proves that Megasthenes did not mean to assert a general ignorance of the art of writing in India.")

The Town Officials (*Astynomoi*): "The second kind, the Town Officials, were divided into six Boards of five. Their respective functions were (1) Supervision of Factories (2) Care of strangers, including control of the Inns, provision of Assistants, taking charge of sick persons, burying the dead (3) the Registration of Births and Deaths (4) the Control of the Market (5) Inspection of Weights and Measures, the inspection of manufactured goods, provision for their sale with accurate distinction of new and second-hand articles (6) Collection of the Tax of 10 per cent charged on sales.

" The six Boards acting together exercised a general superintendence over public works, prices, harbours and temples."

To these officers we may add the following in the words of Megasthenes.

Priests. " The philosophers who are engaged by private persons to offer the sacrifices due in life-time and to celebrate the

1. 1 *Yojana*=8 miles ; 10 *Stadia*=$2022\frac{1}{2}$ yards=$\frac{1}{8}$ of a *Yojanā*=$1\frac{1}{3}$ of a mile [Rhys Davids, *Buddhist India*, p. 265 ; *Cambridge History*, I. 185]. McCrindle takes a unit of 10 *Stadia* to stand for an Indian *Krośā* or *Kosa*.

obsequies of the dead. In requital of such services they receive valuable gifts and privileges." This really points to the Ecclesiastical Officers or priests who ministered to the religious interests of the people.

Espionage. " The *Overseers* whose province it is to enquire into and superintend all that goes on in India, and make report to the king, or, where there is not a king, (i.e , in the case of the Republics which were seen to be as prevalent as the monarchies in his time by Megasthenes) to the Magistrates" (i.e. the Chief Officers of the Republics). Strabo adds [XV. 1, 46-9]: " Some are entrusted with inspection of the City, and others with that of the Army. The former employ as their co-adjutors the courtesans of the city, and the latter the courtesans of the camp. The ablest and most trustworthy men are appointed to fill these offices." To this Arrian adds : " It is against use and wont for them to give in a false report, but, indeed, no Indian is accused of lying."

Councillors. " The Advisers of the King, the Treasurers of the State, the Arbiters who settle disputes (i.e., the judges both civil and criminal) ; the Generals of the Army and the Chief Magistrates (i.e. the Heads of Departments who are called *Adhyakshas* by Kauṭilya)."

Megasthenes further states that these high Officers of the State were recruited from the class of Officers described by him under the general name of Councillors and Assessors. It is interesting to note that these correspond to the general body of Officers called *Amātyas* by Kauṭilya, out of whom Kauṭilya also recruits, as we have seen, the Ministers of different ranks, the High Officers of the State like the *Sannidhātā* (whom Megasthenes calls Treasurer), the Judges, the Heads of Departments (whom Megasthenes calls the Chief Magistrates) and other subordinate officers.

Other Officers. " Herdsmen and hunters, who alone are allowed to hunt, and to keep cattle, and to sell draught animals or let them out on hire. In return for clearing the land of wild beasts and fowls which devour the seeds sown in the fields, they receive an allowance of grain from the king."

" The armour-makers and ship builders receive wages and their victuals from the king, for whom alone they work."

"Of these, some are armourers, while others make the implements which husband-men and others find useful in their different callings. This class is not only exempted from paying taxes ; but even receives maintenance from the Royal Exchequer."

"Officers who superintend the rivers, measure the lands as is done in Egypt, and inspect the sluices by which water is let out from the main canals into their branches, so that everyone may have an equal supply of it."

"Fighting men who are maintained at the king's expense and hence they are always ready, when occasion calls, to take the field; for they carry nothing of their own with them but their own bodies."

"Officers who collect the taxes and superintend the occupations connected with lands, as those of the wood-cutters, the carpenters, the black-smiths and the miners."

"Officers who construct roads, and, at every ten *stadia*, set up a pillar to show the by-roads and distances."

"Officers in charge of the Royal Stables for horses and elephants and also the royal magazine for arms."

Further: "A private person is not allowed to keep either a horse or an elephant. These animals are held to be special property of the king and persons are appointed to take care of them. They are professional trainers of horses who break them in by forcing them to gallop round and round in a ring, specially when they see them refractory. Such as undertake this work require to have a strong hand as well as a thorough knowledge of horses. The great proficients test their skill by driving a chariot round and round in a ring; and in truth it would be no trifling feat to control with ease a team of four high mettled steeds when whirling round in a circle."

List of Officers. A study of these Greek accounts of Indian Administration will show that they notice a large number and variety of administrative interests, urban and rural, and of Officers, to deal with them in the different Departments of Administration. A list of these as mentioned by them includes the following :—

1. Ministers, Advisers and Councillors.
2. The Chief Magistrates (Heads of Departments, and City Magistrates.
3. Revenue and Taxes.
4. Irrigation.
5. Survey and Settlement (Land Revenue Administration).
6. Agriculture.
7. Forestry.
8. Timber Factories.
9. Metal Foundries.
10. Mines.
11. Urban Factories.
12. Foreigners in cities.

13. Inns (urban).
14. Vital Statistics.
15. Care of the Sick.
16. Control of Market.
17. Weights and Measures.
18. Controllers of Public Works.
19. Priests.
20. Overseers.
21. Treasurers.
22. Judges.
23. Herdsmen and hunters.
24. Armament Manufacturers.
25. Ship-builders.
26. Manufacturers of agricultural implements.
27. Superintendents of rivers and canals for distributing water for irrigation.
28. Horses, elephants, chariots.

It will be seen that while the Greek writers could only make a mention of the various administrative officers and indicate generally their functions, it was left to Kauṭilya to give detailed descriptions of these functions and of the working of the various Departments administering the manifold interests committed to their care.

Kautilya's Scheme of Administration: The Province (*Janapada*). The unit of administration in the Kauṭilīya scheme [II. 1] was the *Janapada* or Province which normally consisted of at least 800 villages with 100-500 families (*Kulaśatāvaraṁ pañcha-śatakulaparam*) to each village. If the normal family which was a joint family (*Kula*) be regarded as consisting of 10 members with three brothers and their children, then the total population under each provincial administration would number 40 lacs The provincial Governor (*Rājūka*) under Asoka is stated in his Inscription [Pillar Edict V] to be ruling over "many hundreds of thousands of souls."

The villages were situated or planted within a convenient distance of each other so as to afford protection (*Krośa-dvikrośa-sīmānamanyo-nyārakshum*). Natural boundaries were availed of as far as possible to separate them, e.g., a river, a mountain, a forest, and the like (*nadīśailavana*).

Defences. The provincial defences were well organized. The approaches to the Province were protected by frontier pickets under the Warden of the Frontiers called *Antapāla* (*Janapada-dvārāṇ-yantapālādhishṭhitāni sthāpayet*,) while the interior was protected and policed by a special staff recruited from deer-trappers, Śabaras ('born of Śūdra father and Bhil mother'), Pulindas ('born of Nishṭi Mlechchha father and Kirāta mother'), Chaṇḍālas (in charge of cremation grounds *śmaśānapālāḥ*) and Foresters (*teshāmantarāṁiVāgurika-Śabara-Pulinda-Chaṇḍālāraṇyacharāḥ raksheyuḥ*). In the four extremities of the Province [II. 3] (*chaturdiśam janapadānte sāmparāyikaṁ daivakritaṁ durgaṁ kārayet;* again [II. 1] : *Anteshvantapāla-durgāṇi*) were constructed four forts which utilized the natural fortifications afforded by water or mountain, desert or forest (*nadī-parvatadurgaṁ janapadārakshasthānaṁ dhānvanavanadurgaṁ*).

Centres of Administration. Administrative head-quarters or civil stations were located at the centres of 800, 400, 200, and even 10 villages and were called respectively (1) *Sthānīya* (2) *Droṇamukha* (3) *Kārvaṭika* and (4) *Saṅgrahaṇa.* Of these, a *Sthānīya* was the centre of wealth in the locality (*samudayasthānaṁ dhanotpattisthānabhūtaṁ* in II. 3), a sort of a provincial capital in those days.

Provincial Head. (Collector-General, '*Samāhartā*'): **District Collector** (*Sthānika*). The Head of the Provincial Administration was the *Samāhartā*, the Collector-General, who controlled [I. 1] a number of district Collectors in his Province. Each Province was in fact divided into four Districts [II. 35] (*samāhartā chaturdhā janapadaṁ vibhajya*), each of which was placed under an officer called the *Sthānika* who was responsible for the affairs of his District (*evaṁ cha Janapada-chaturbhāgaṁ Sthānikaḥ chintayet*).

Sources of Revenue. The Collector-General was responsible for the realisation of the provincial Revenue. The Revenue was derived from a variety of sources, each of which required a special administrative Department for its utilisation and expansion. Thus an account of the sources of Revenue will supply the key to administrative organisation and machinery brought into being.

The duty of the *Samāhartā* was to see to (*aveksheta*) the collection of Revenue due from the following sources, viz., (1) Towns (*Durga*) (2) the country side or rural parts (*Rāshṭra*) (3) Mines (*Khani*) (4) Plantations (*Setu*) (5) Forests (*Vana*) 6) Cattle (*Vraja*) and (7) Communications (*Vaṇikpatha*, 'roads of traffic').

Durga. The Revenue to be derived from the Towns or urban areas (*Durga*) was the Revenue to be collected from a number of sources, each of which was separately administered by a Department under its special Head called *Adhyaksha* assisted by a suitable staff. These administrative Departments were those of (1) Customs (*Śulka*) (2) Police (*Daṇḍa*) (3) Weights and Measures (*Pautava*) (4) Municipalities (*Nāgarika*) (5) Boundaries (*Lakshaṇa*) (6) Passports (*Mudrā*) (7) Excise (*Surā*) (8) Slaughter-house (*Sūnā*) (9) Cotton Industry

(*Sūtra*) (10) Oil Industry (*Taila*) (11) Dairy (*Ghṛita*) (12) Sugar Industry (*Kshāra*) (13) Gold (*Svarṇa*) (14) Warehouse (*Paṇyasaṁsthā*) (15) Courtesans (*Veśyā*) (16) Gambling (*Dyūta*) (17) Buildings (*Vāstuka*) (18) Arts (*Śilpa*) (19) Crafts (*Kāru*) (20) Religious Institutions (*Devatā*) (21) Octroi (*Dvarādeyam*) and (22) Amusements (*Bāhirikādeya*, 'amusements like Acting, Dancing, etc.') [II. 6.]

All these twenty two Departments were administered by as many Heads or Superintendents (*Adhyakshas*) and made up the city's general and municipal administration.

Rāshṭra. Much of the Revenue of the State was derived from the countryside through which its sources lay scattered. Each such source had to be carefully tapped and administered by a separate Department under a Head or Superintendent with a special staff. These sources of Revenue are thus enumerated:

(1) *Sītā*, Crown Lands.

(2) *Bhāga*, the share of agricultural produce payable to the State as Land Revenue.

(3) *Bali*, a general Land-Tax.

According to Megasthenes [Frag. I], "the Husbandmen pay a land-tribute to the king, besides paying a fourth part (*Bhāga*) of the produce of the soil." The usual sense of *Bali* in Sanskrit is a religious offering or voluntary contribution.

It may be noted that the village Lumbini (*Luṁmini-gāme*) was rendered *ubalike* and *aṭhabhāgiye* (*udbalika* and *ashṭa-bhāgika*) by Asoka out of regard for it as the native place of the Buddha (*hida Bhagavaṁ jāte ti*), as recorded in his Rummindei Pillar Inscription. Thus the State in Asoka's time imposed a *Bali* or Tax on all land in addition to its usual share of agricultural produce called *Bhāga* which was reduced by half, from $\frac{1}{4}$ to $\frac{1}{8}$, for this village. In Kauṭilya's language [II. 35], Lumbini thus became a *parihāraka* village.

(4) *Kara*, Tax on Orchards (*phalavṛikhsādi-sambandhaṁ Rājadeyam*).

(5) *Vaṇik*, Tax on merchandise at source (*Vaṇigdvāreṇādeyam*).

(6) *Nadīpāla*, Tax payable to Superintendent of Rivers at the landing places leading to centres of pilgrimage (*Tīrtha-rakshaka-dvāreṇādeyam*).

The Greek writers also tell of the Superintendents of Rivers.

(7) *Tara*, Ferry charges (*Nadītaraṇavetanam*).

(8) *Nāva*, Tax payable to the Superintendent of Shipping (*Nāvadhyakska-dvāralabhyam*).

(9) *Paṭṭana*, Taxes payable at market towns.

(10) *Vivīta,* Tax on Pasture-lands.

(11) *Vartanī,* Road-cess payable to the *Antapālas,* the Wardens of the Marches (*Antapāladvāralabhyam*).

(12) *Rajjū,* Cess payable for Settlement to the rural officer called *Vishaya-pāla.*

(13) *Chora-Rajjū,* Chowkidārī or Police Tax to be collected at the village and levied for expenses for catching thieves (*Choragrāha-kāya grāmadeyam.*)

Khani. The Superintendent of Mines is to collect the imposts payable by Mines such as those of "silver, diamond, gems, pearls, corals, conch-shells, metals, salts, and other minerals extracted from earth, stone, or oil-fields ((*rasa*) like mercury" (*Suvarṇa—rajata—vajra—maṇi-muktā-pravāla-śaṅkha-loha-lavaṇa-bhūmi-prastara-rasa-dhā-tavaḥ Khaniḥ*).

Setu. This term indicates the collection of Taxes levied on cultivated fields or gardens producing (a) Flowers (*Pushpa* like *Kuṅkuma*) (b) Vegetables (*phala-vāṭa vārtāku-urvārukādi*) like 'Brinjals, Cucumber and the like' (c) Sugarcane (*Vāṭa ikshu-vāṭa*) (d) Plantains and Betel-nuts (*Shaṇḍa*) (e) Crops like Rice (*Kedāraḥ dhānyakshetram*) (f) Spices such as 'ginger, turmeric and the like' (*Mūlavāpa*).

Vana. Tax on Forests of which four classes are mentioned, viz., those of (1) Cattle (2) Deer (3) Commercial products like timber or rubber (*dravya*) and (4) Elephants.

Vraja. Taxes levied on Cattle-breeding-or Stud-Farms for the rearing of domesticated animals such as "Cow, Buffalo, Goat, Sheep, Ass, Camel, Horse and Mule."

Vanikpatha. Taxes levied on Roads of Traffic by Land or Water and collected at their ends or entrances.

The realization of provincial Revenue from such a large number and variety of sources called for an elaborate administrative machinery, a hierarchy of officers comprising the Minister in charge of the Revenue Portfolio at the top called the *Samāhartā,* Collector-General, the Heads of Departments, and any number of subordinate staff attached to each Department, making up what may be called the provincial Civil Service.

Kauṭilya in the second Book of his *Arthaśāstra* gives an account of the working of the following Departments, viz. those of

(1) Accountant-General (*Akshapaṭalādhyaksha*).

(2) Mines (*Ākara*).

(3) Gold (*Suvarṇa*).

(4) Stores (*Koshṭhāgāra*).

(5) Commerce (*Paṇya*).
(6) Forest Products (*Kupya*).
(7) Armoury (*Āyudhāgāra*).
(8) Weights and Measures (*Tulāmānapautava*).
(9) Customs (*Śulka*).
(10) Spinning and Weaving Industry (*Sūtra*).
(11) Agriculture (*Sītā*).
(12) Excise (*Surā*).
(13) Slaughter House (*Sūnā*).
(14) Courtesans (*Gaṇikā*).
(15) Shipping (*Nau*).
(16) Cattle (*Go*)
(17) Horses (*Aśva*).
(18) Elephants (*Hasti*).
(19) Chariots (*Ratha*).
(20) Infantry (*Patti*).
(21) Passports (*Mudrā*).
(22) Pastures (*Vivīta*).
(23) Metals (*Loha*).
(24) Mint (*Lakshaṇa*).
(25) Treasury (*Kośa*).
(26) Elephant forests (*Nāga-vana*).
(27) General trade (*Saṁsthā*).
(28) Religious Institutions (*Devatā*).
(29) Gambling (*Dyūta*).
(30) Jails (*Bandhanāgāra*).
(31) Ports (*Pattana*).

It will be seen from the above list of Departments that all are not necessary for the collection and administration of Revenue, while some are Departments connected with the administration of cities or Municipalities. These may be taken to be Nos. (10), (12), (13), (14), (29), (30) and (31). Some again are Departments belonging to the capital and royal Palace. These are Nos. (1), (3), (4), (7), (8), (24) and (25). Some of these Departments again such as Nos. (4), (6), (25) are Departments placed in charge of the Minister of Revenue and Stores (*Sannidhātā*) whose business is to receive the Revenue gathered in by the Minister of collections (*Samāhartā*). Thus these two officers are the most important in the entire Civil Service, most of whose offices are subordinate to them. There is a third officer of the same high status, the Accountant-General to whom the different departments have to submit their accounts. Nos. (17), (18), (19), (20), together with No. (7), would be under the *Senāpati*, Commander-in-chief.

It is hardly necessary to repeat that most of these Departments and officers are mentioned by the Greek writers and the correspondence of their observations to the account of Kauṭilya is very close and striking so as to establish the trustworthy character of both.

Samāhartā. The *Samāhartā* is so-called because he gathers in the Revenue of the State from different sources and realises it fully without allowing arrears of collection (*Śarvāyasthānebhyaḥ Rājārthānāṁ samyak samantāt vā āhartā*). His duty is further defined to be *Samudaya Prasthāpanam* [I. 1], to establish ways and means of obtaining and increasing Revenue (*Samudayo dhanotthānaṁ tasya prasthāpanaṁ mārgaparikalpanaṁ Samāhartā kayā kayā vidhayā samudayaṁ prasthāpayet ityetat*). This shows that the *Samāhartā* like the Chancellor of the Exchequer was empowered to initiate new schemes of taxation and levy new taxes as sources of additions to Revenue.

Sannidhātā. The officer complementary to *Samāhartā* was the *Sannidhātā* who took charge of the Revenue as it was gathered in and received into the State Treasury. While the *Samāhartā* was an executive and spending authority, the *Sannidhātā* was in charge of saving and accumulating revenue. He had to store up the revenue by constructing buildings and chambers appropriate to the kind of things in which revenue was received (*Nichaya-karma dravyasaṁgraharakshaṇa-karma*). For that reason he had to construct (1) a *Kośagṛiha*, the State Jewellery House, for storing up 'precious stones, gold and the like' in which revenue was paid; (2) *Paṇyagṛiha* where was housed the merchandise for sale (*Vikraya-dravya*); (3) *Koshṭhāgāra*, the State Granary for storing 'articles of food, grain, oils and the like', (4) *Kupyagṛiha*, store-house for forest-produce of all kinds by which Revenue was realised in kind; and (5) *Āyudhāgāra*, the royal Armoury.

Treasury-House, The *Kośagṛiha* is to be built in two parts: (1) the subterranean chamber, *Bhūmigṛiha*, to be built of three storeys (*tritalaṁ*) with flooring and walls of stone, many rooms constructed in a framework of timber (*anekavidhānaṁ sāradārupañjaraṁ*), provided with a mechanical moveable staircase (*yantrayuktasopānam*), carvings of images of gods on the wooden covering (*devatāpidhānam*) and only one door; (2) the upper part, the Treasury-house proper (*Kośagṛiha*) to be built like a *prāsāda* or palace, with its outer and inner door fitted with bolts (*ubhayatonishedhaṁ bahirantaśchārgala-yuktaṁ*) and provided with a hall of entrance (*sapragrīvaṁ mukhaśālayā sahitam*) and furnished with rows of vessels (*bhāṇḍavāhinī-parikshiptam*) for holding the precious articles.

Besides the Treasury-house at headquarters, the *Sannidhātā* was also to build on the borders of the country (*janapadānte*) against emergencies palatial mansions by employing as builders criminals condemned to death (*abhityaktaiḥ purushaiḥ vadhyaiḥ*), who are to die after the completion of the building, so that their designs and plans by which its treasures are stored will remain a secret.

Other Buildings. The house of merchandise (*Paṇyagṛiha*) will be one of four buildings round a quadrangle (*chatuḥ-śālam*) and with many rooms (*anekasthānatalam*).

The Granary House (*Koshṭhāgāra*) should be similarly built.

The store-house of forest produce (*Kupya-gṛiha*) must be more commodious, made up of many spacious buildings, each with rows of rooms along its walls.

The Armoury (*Āyudhāgāra*) should be similarly built, but it is to be provided with an underground chamber (*bhūmigṛihaṁ*).

Courts, Secretariat, and Prison. The *Sannidhātā* is also charged with the duty of constructing three other important government buildings : (1) Courts of Justice with accommodation for litigants, and lock-up for accused (*Dharmasthīyaṁ tatra dharmasthā vyavahāranirṇetārah tatsambandhi dharmasthīyaṁ vyavahārārthaṁ āgatānāṁ avasthityarthaṁ vyavahāra-parājita-nirodhārthaṁ cha sthānam*) ; (2) Secretariat Buildings, with accommodation for (*a*) Offices of Ministers who are Heads of Departments like the *Samāhartā* and *Sannidhātā* ; (*b*) for Ambassadors ; and (*c*) for persons secured in the course of war (*viśvāsādhitvena gṛihītānāṁ yuddha-parigṛihītādīnām*) ; (3) Prison-House (*Bandhanāgāra*) with separate accommodation for Male Wards and Female Wards, and with cells (*kaksha*) whose exits are well guarded (*vibhakta-strīpurushasthānaṁ apasārataḥ suguptakakshyaṁ*).

It is interesting to note that some of these buildings had shrines in which Deities connected with their business were installed. For instance, god *Dhanada* was installed in the *Kośagṛiha*, goddess *Śrī* in the Commercial Building and Store-house, god *Viśvakarmā* in the *Kupya-gṛiha*, god *Yama* in the Armoury and *Varuṇa* in Jail [Commentator].

The *Sannidhātā* will thus discharge his responsibility for the revenues of the State with the assistance of his own staff of trustworthy officers (*āptapurushādhishṭhitaḥ*). He should have a knowledge of the resources of the State, the sources of its revenue from both urban aud rural areas (*Bāhya-abhyantaraṁ āyam*) for a period of last 100 years so that he may answer questions about it without any difficulty. He should also always be able to show the surplus revenue of the State in the Treasury.

Accountant-General (*Akshapaṭalādhyaksha*). Like the *Samāhartā* and the *Sannidhātā*, there was another officer at the Centre to control the Departments and District Officers. He was the Accountant-General who was in charge of the two offices of Currency (*Akshapaṭala*) and Accounts (*Gaṇanā*) The term *Aksha-paṭala* means the *paṭala* or office where visible objects like coins are counted (*Akshā gaṇana-yogyāni rūpyakādīni teshāṁ paṭalaṁ sthānaṁ Aksha-paṭalam*) [I. 1]. His first duty is to bring together the Heads of different Departments (*tattadadhyakshāṇāṁ sambhūya sva-sva karmānushṭhānādeśaṁ kārayet*) [Commentary on II. 7], and then to provide for them necessary office accommodation. He is to arrange for different rooms for different Departments and for their Heads in accordance with their rank (*vibhaktopasthānaṁ vibhaktāni uttama-madhyama-adhamānāmadhyakshāṇāṁ pṛithak-sthityanukū-latayā vibhajya*). He is also to fit up the rooms with accommodation for the books of accounts and records (*nibhandha-pustakasthānaṁ*).

He will have the number and names of different Departments (*adhikaraṇānāṁ saṁkhyā nāmataḥ parigaṇanam*), their localities (*prachāro janapadaḥ*), and the total (*agram*) of revenue produced by each in relation to its administrative area, entered in their respective account-books.

He should also enter in the books particulars showing how different Departments, in respect of different works undertaken by them (*karmāntaḥ* 'such as Mines, Rice-fields, Commercial products, Currency and the like'), invest their resources (*dravyaprayoge*) with reference to (1) profit (*vṛiddhi*), (2) employment of paid labour (*kshayaḥ yugyapurushaviniyoga*), (3) cost in grain and cash (*vyayaḥ dhānyahiraṇya-viniyoga*), (4) quantity produced or the demand for it (*prayāmaḥ*), (5) amount of *vyājī* (premia in cash or kind) realised, (6) adulteration (*yogo dravyāpadravyamiśraṇam*), (7) locality of production, (8) wages, (9) retained labour (*vishṭi*, denoting labourers not working on hire but retained on terms of domestic service).

The Accountant-General is also to record in his books particulars as to the following.

(1) The religious practices (*dharma*), laws (*vyavahāra*), and customs (*charitra-saṁsthānam*) observed by different regions (*deśa*), villages (*grāma*) castes (*jāti*), and families (*kula*).

(2) The privileges (*pragraha*), residences (*pradeśo vāsasthānam*), gifts (*bhoga-upāyanam*), remissions of taxes (*parihāra*), provisions for horses, elephants, and troops (*bhaktaṁ aśva-gaja-padāti-abhyavahāraḥ*) and salaries (*vetanam*) enjoyed by State-officials (*rājopajīvi*), such as 'Mantrī, Purohita, etc.'

(3) Special allowances given to the king, queen, and the princes (*nirdeśam*), special allowances for festivities (*autpādikalābhaṁ utsavādibhavaṁ dhanalābhaṁ*) and for ceremonies to ward off evils like diseases (*pratīkāralābham*).

He will also have recorded in his books the following particulars to be supplied by the Heads of different Departments (*Sarvādhikaraṇānām*): (1) the work to be done, (2) the work done, (3) cash balance, (4) revenue and expenditure, (5) statements of accounts (*nīvī*), (6) the time for submission of their reports of work by the scribes (*upasthānaṁ kāyasthānāṁ svasvakārya-darśanārthasannidhānakālam*) and (7) the locality concerned, its customs, and previous systems followed in it.

He is to assign to Superintendents of different grades, high, middle, and inferior, works suitable to their qualifications. The Commentator instances Superintendents of Works of three grades concerning (1) Treasury (2) Granary and Armoury and (3) Wines and Meats. For these bodies of officers (*Sāmudāyikeshu*), persons of special fitness are to be appointed, who can be punished without causing any remorse to the king. This rules out officers 'who are Brahmins or friends or intimate relations of the king.'

The Chief Accountants (*Gāṇanikyāni gaṇanāḥ tatpradarśakāḥ Adhyakshāḥ*) of different Departments are to come to headquarters to present their accounts in the month of Āshādha, the last month of the financial year.

They are to assemble in one place in the Accountant-General's office with sealed boxes containing their books of account (*Samudra-pustabhāṇḍa*) and the net balances of revenue. They are to remain in the hall without talking with one another (*ekatrāsambhāshāvarodhaṁ kārayet*). They are first orally to explain the accounts relating to receipts, expenditure, and the total of revenue (*nīvī*) before the net revenue is received into the Treasury. The account orally given is compared with that written in the books. If the amount of income stated is less than the amount of the books, or if the stated amount of expenditure is less than the amount entered in the written account; or if the stated cash balance (*nīvi*) is in excess of what is written; the Accountant in each case will have to pay 8 times the amount of the difference as a penalty for false accounting, Conversely, if there is a difference between the Central Account books and those of the Districts as to the amounts of Income, Expenditure, and Cash Balance, the difference is not to be made good.

The Chief Accountants who do not present themselves at headquarters in time (i.e., in the mouth of Āshāḍha) with their books of account and cash balances of revenue will have to pay a penalty.

Conversely, when they so present themselves (*Kārmike adhyakshe upasthite*) but are not attended to by Accountants (*Kāraṇika gaṇanādhikṛita*) of the Central Office, these are to be fined.

The ministers in a body (*samagrāḥ Mahāmātrāḥ*) are to bring together the Heads of Departments in the Districts in a meeting and explain to them the general revenue position of the Province with reference to revenue receipts, expenditure, and surplus (*Prachārasamaṁ Mahāmātrāḥ samagrāḥ śrāvayeyuḥ avishamamātrāḥ, prachāro janapadaḥ jānapadān sadasi melayitvā bodhayeyuḥ ityarthaḥ*). A minister keeping aloof or misrepresenting accounts is punishable.

Accounts are to be posted daily (*ahorūpahara.*)

The cash balance and daily account submitted by the Accountant are to be checked by the Chief Accountant who is to see how far they correspond to (1) religious injunctions (*dharma*), (2) law (*vyavahāra*), (3) custom (*charitra*), (4) precedence (*saṁsthāna*), (5) total of revenue receipts (*saṅkalanaṁ sarvadhanaikīkāra-gaṇanā*), (6) the work accomplished (*nirvartana*), (7) estimate of revenue (*anumāna*) and (8) report of informers on the revenue realized (*chāraprayoga*).

Abstracts of accounts shall be prepared (*pratisamānayet*) every 5 days, fortnight, month, four months, and per year.

Failure on the part of a *Kāraṇika* to enter revenue realized (*Rājārthe apratibadhnataḥ rājārthaṁ pustakeshu alikhataḥ* or to follow instructions (*ājñāṁ pratishedhayato*), or to write accounts of income and expenditure according to prescribed forms (*nibandha*) is punishable.

Not writing accounts in the proper order (*kramāvahīnaṁ avalikhataḥ*), writing accounts inverted order (*utkramaṁ avalikhataḥ*) writing accounts in a manner not comprehensible (*avijñātaṁ avalikhataḥ vedituṁ anarhayā rītyā likhataḥ*), or entering the same item again (*punaruktaṁ*), all such wrong accounting (*avalikhanaṁ*) will be punishable.

Making wrong entries of cash balance (*nīvīmavalikhato*), embezzlement (*bhakshayato*) or causing loss of revenue (*nāśayataḥ*) are punishable [II. 7].

Superintendents or Heads (*Adhyakshas*) **of Departments in the Districts.** We shall now consider the duties assigned to the *Adhyakshas* in charge of different Departments, and of productive or profitable works and concerns in the Districts, as sources of revenue to the State.

Their salary and Grades. As has been stated above, the salary attached to the grade of *Adhyakshas* or Superintendents is 1000 *paṇas.* Government servants of grades (*varga*) from 100 to 1000 are to be placed under *Adhyakshas* who are empowered to fix their subsistence (*bhukta*), salary (*vetana*), emoluments (*lābha*) instructions (*ādeśa*) and assignment of work (*vikshepa*). In case there is no work for them (*avikshepe*), the *Adhyakshas* will depute their respective staffs to take charge of royal property (*rājaparigraha*), fortifications, and Law and Order in the country (*Rāshṭrarakshāvekshaṇa*). The subordinate staffs must always work under the Heads of their respective sections (*nityamukhyāḥ*), and will also be under the many Heads above them (*anekamukhyāḥ*) [V. 3].

Nationalisation of Industries. It will also be observed that the Kauṭilīya polity was based on a considerable amount of socialism and nationalisation of industries. A large part of the administrative machinery is employed in the management and exploitation of State property of various kinds administered as business concerns. There were large royal estates and forests. The State had a monopoly of Mines. It carried on both Export and Import Trade and appropriated the profits of middlemen. It established factories for working up of raw materials of different kinds into finished products. Besides, as revenue was payable in kind, large establishments had to be maintained all over the country for dealing with vast quantities of agricultural products tendered in payment of taxes, as well as the products derived from the crown estates. Again, a Central Store at headquarters was necessary for several purposes, as a reserve against famine, as provision for the royal household, as a source of raw material for the royal manufactories, and, lastly, as the means of paying salaries to officials in kind.

Department of Agriculture. We shall now describe the working of the principal Departments of Administration.

Director of Agriculture (*Sītādhyaksha*). The Director of Agriculture (*Sītādhyaksha*) [II, 24] was in charge of the cultivation of crown lands or of Government Agricultural farms.

Supply of Seeds. His duty was to have a collection of seeds of the various crops to be grown such as Grain (*dhānya*), Flowers, Fruits, Vegetables (*śāka*), Herbs (*kanda*), Roots, Fibre-producing plants (*kshauma*) and Cotton (*kārpāsa*).

Agricultural Labour. He was to employ in the work of cultivation the following classes of labourers, viz., (1) Serfs (*Dāsa*) (2)

Hired Labourers (*Karmakara*) and (3) Convicts condemned to labour (*Daṇḍapratikartā*).

Appliances for Cultivation. He is to supply these labourers with all things necessary for the work of cultivation such as implements (*karshaṇa-yantra*) like 'plough, rope, sickle, together with bullocks.' Peasants must also be supplied with the supplementary assistance of Artisans (*Kāru*) such as the Blacksmith (*Karmāraḥ Ayaskāraḥ*), Carpenter (*Kuṭṭākaḥ Takshā*), the Digger (*Medaka* or *Khanaka* or *Bhedaka*), Rope-maker (*Rajjuvartakaḥ*) and destroyer of pests (*Sarpagrāhādi*).

Records of Rainfall. A meteorological forecast of the different countries seems to have been attempted. The Western coast [(beyond the Ghats), *Aparānta*] and the Himalayan tarais (*Haimanya*) were singled out, as now, for the heaviest rainfall, the country of the Aśmakas on the Godāvarī (or *Āraṭṭhas* of the Punjab and Avanti for moderate rainfall, and the deserts (*Jāṅgala*) for the lowest. We may note that arrangements for recording rainfall were known in those days. "In the central Store-House (*Koshṭhāgāra*), there was to be kept a vessel (*kuṇḍa*) whose mouth should be 1 *aratni* wide, to serve as rain gauge (*varsha-māna*)" [II. 5]. It may be noted that 1 *aratni* = 24 *aṅgulas* = 1½ ft. [II. 20]. Countries irrigated from artificial canals (*Kulyāvāpa*) were of course in no want of water.

Means of Irrigation. Fourfold means of artificial irrigation are mentioned, viz., manual irrigation, irrigation by water carried on the shoulder, irrigation by pumps (*sroto-yantraprāvartima*) and irrigation by letting in water from streams, lakes or wells, with the fourfold water-rates of $\frac{1}{5}$, $\frac{1}{4}$, $\frac{1}{3}$, and $\frac{1}{4}$ of the total produce respectively.

Megasthenes also, as we have seen, confirms Kauṭilya in his mention of "the sluices by which water is let out from the main canals into other branches so that everyone may have an equal supply of it," while the care which the empire of Chandragupta bestowed on irrigation is proved, as we have seen, by the inscription of Rudradāman I.

Agricultural Seasons. The seasons for crops are also stated to be those for (1) wet crops, (2) winter crops (*haimanam*), (3) summer crops (*graishmikam*).

Variety of Crops. The wet crops are mentioned as Rice (*Śāli* or *Vrīhi*), Coarse grain (*Kodrava*), Sesamum (*Tila*), Pepper, and Safforn (*Priyaṅgu*). These ought to be sown first in the rains (*Pūrvavāpaḥ*). Next come pulses called *mudga*, *māsha*. The last to be sown are *Kusumbha* (Saffron), *Masūra, Kuluttha, Yava* (Barley), *Godhūma* (Wheat), *Kalāya, Atasī* (Linseed), and *Sarshapa* (Mustard).

Food Crops. It is also pointed out that the Rices (*śālyādi*) are the most important crops (*jyeshṭha*) because, as the commentator points out, these are the principal food crops which are grown with the least cost and trouble and yield a good harvest.

Next come fruits like plantains (*Shaṇḍah Kadalyādi*).

Sugarcane. The worst crop is sugarcane (*Ikshu*) because, as the commentator points out, 'it is exposed to many pests like rats, it involves large outlay, and a vast amount of labour in cutting the canes, crushing them, and in boiling the extracted juice on pans'.

Varieties of Lands and Crops. It is also stated that lands that are 'beaten by foam' (*phenāghāta*), i. e , those on the banks of rivers or marshy lands, are suitable for growing *Vallīphala* such as pumpkin, gourd and the like. The flooded lands (*parivāhāntāḥ*) are suitable for sugarcane (*Ikshu*), pepper (*Pippalī*) and grapes (*Mṛidvīkā*). Lands depending on wells (*Kūpa-paryantāḥ*) are good for vegetables (*śāka*) and roots (*mūla*). Lands in the vicinity of canals, lakes, or tanks (*haraṇīparyantāḥ*) are good for fodder (*Haritaka*). Lands between cultivated plots may be utilized to grow cloves, medicinal herbs and fragrant plants.

Medicinal Plants. Medicinal plants are to be grown on different kinds of lands, marshy and dry, as required.

Wages. Labourers (*Vishṭi*) in charge of orchards (*Shaṇḍa*) and gardens (*Vāṭa*) and of cattle, whether serf or hired, will be given food and the monthly wages of 1¼ *paṇa*.

Cultivators were given half-share of the produce (*ardha-sītikāḥ*) and were to supply their own seeds and bullocks. But those who could not supply these but only their labour will have their share of produce reduced to ¼ or ⅕.

It is stated that the Director of Agriculture must be proficient in *Kṛishitantra* (Agricultural Science), *Śulba-śāstra* (Mensuration), and *Vṛikshāyurveda* (Science of plant life).

Superintendent of Store-House (*Koshṭhāgārādhyaksha*) [II. 15]. State Store-or Ware-houses were set up at different centres under the system which permitted payment of taxes and dues to the State in kind. The Director of Agriculture had to despatch to the Superintendent of Store-house the agricultural produce of the crown lands of different localities (*sītā*). Next, he had to receive payments in kind of various dues levied by the State. These are thus enumerated: (1) *Piṇḍa-kara*, village cess (2) *Shaḍbhāga*, the State's share of ⅙ of agricultural produce, (3) *Senābhakta*, military cess in the form of provisioning the army on march through the areas concerned (4) *Bali*, an extra impost of 10 to 20 *paṇas* levied on the village (5) *Kara*, State's share of fruits grown (6) *Utsaṅga*, presents to king on festive occasions such as birth of a child (7) *Pārśva*, an emergency tax (8) *Parihīṇaka*, compensation for loss to crops caused by cattle (9) *Aupāyanika*, presents to the king (10) *Kaushṭheyaka*, tax on lands irrigated by the State tanks.

All these heads of revenue paid in kind come under the general name of *Rāshṭra* as the revenue derived from the country side or rural tracts. The Superintendent had also to collect the dues payable to government from the sale of its agricultural products.

Of the Store thus accumulated, half will be devoted to expenditure by Government and half will be kept in reserve as an insurance against afflictions to the country (like famines) (*Tato ardhaṁ jānapadānāṁ sthāpayet*). The Store will be replenished by new supply.

It is also the duty of the Superintendent of Stores to personally supervise the increase or decrease caused to the grains as they are pounded (*kshuṇṇa*), frayed (*ghṛishṭa*), reduced to flour (*pishṭa*), or fried (*bhṛishṭa*) or dried after being soaked in water.

Kauṭilya also gives calculations of the amounts of food obtainable from given quantities of grain of different kinds as they are cooked or treated in other ways, of oil that can be pressed from the different oil-seeds, and of thread that can be spun from given quantities of cotton (*Kārpāsa*) and flax or jute (*Kshauma*) fibre.

Rations are prescribed for different classes of persons, men, women and children, soldiers, commanders of the army (*pattīnāṁ mukhyānām*), queens and princes (*devikumārāṇām*). They are also prescribed for different domestic animals.

These regulations and details only show the amount of control which the officer in charge of State properties of so many kinds had to establish to ensure that there is no loss of income to the State from the various uses to which they are to be put.

Lastly, one can have an idea of how the Store-house will look like when one goes into it. He will fiind grain stacked up higher and higher without contact with the ground; jaggery bound round in ropes of grass; oils kept in vessels of earth or wood; and salt heaped up on the surface of the ground.

Superintendent of Mines (*Ākarādhyaksha*) [II. 12]. The Mining Superintendent should be a scientific expert on his subject, with a knowledge of sciences called (1) *Śulba-śāstra* (2) *Dhātu-śāstra* (3) *Rasa-pāka* (4) *Maṇi-rāga*, a knowledge of Mines, a knowledge of seams and veins of ores (*bhū-śirāvijñāna*), Metallurgy, Science of Mercury, Gems, and precious stones. He was to prospect new mines and discover old ones by the signs of slags, ashes and the like, and ascertain the value of ores from their mechanical and chemical properties. Various kinds of ore are mentioned as being worked in those days, viz., those of Gold, Silver, Copper, Lead (*Sīsa*), Tin (*Trapu*), Iron (*Tīkshṇa*), Bitumen (*Śilājatu*). Various metallurgical processes were employed for treating the ores and purging them of impurities by use of alkalies and for softening metals.

Commerce in commodities manufactured from mineral products was centralised (*ekamukham*). Manufacturers, buyers and sellers of such commodities outside the prescribed locality (*anyatra*) were liable to punishment. Thus the State had a monopoly in the working of Mines, and in trade in their products. But Mines requiring a heavy capital outlay and much enterprise (*vyaya-kriyā-bhārikamākaram*) may be leased out to private persons on the basis of a share of the output (*bhāgena*) or a fixed royalty (*prakrayeṇa asyākārasya etāvat suvarṇādikaṁ rājārthe deyamiti paripaṇya*). Mines requiring small outlay are to be worked directly by the State (*lāghavikaṁ ātmanā kārayet*).

The Superintendent of Mines was associated in his work with a few other officers in charge of allied work.

Superintendent of Metals (*Lohādhyaksha*). He was entrusted with the work of manufacturing vessels (*karmāntān tadbhāṇḍa-ghaṭana- karmāṇi*) of such materials as Copper, Lead, Tin, Brass, Bell-metal and the like, and of business (*vyavahāra*) in such manufactures.

Superintendent of Mint (*Lakshaṇādhyaksha Taṅkaśālādhyaksha*). He is to manufacture the following classes of coins: (1) *Rūpyārūpa* (silver coins) made up of 11 parts of silver, 4 parts of copper and one part of any of the metals, iron, tin, lead or antimony (2) *Tāmrarūpa* (copper coins) 'made up of 4 parts of silver, 11 parts of copper, and 1 part of *Tīkshṇa* (iron or any other metal).' Each of these classes of coins was made in four denominations, e.g., 1, $\frac{1}{2}$ $\frac{1}{4}$ and $\frac{1}{8}$ *paṇa* for silver and 1, $\frac{1}{2}$, $\frac{1}{4}$ and $\frac{1}{8}$ *māsha* for copper, the last two of the copper coins being also named *kākaṇī* and *ardhakākaṇī*.

According to the Commentator, *Rūpyārūpa* is the same as *Kārshāpaṇa*. It was of an alloy mainly composed of Silver and was acceptable to the government treasury (*Kośapraveśya*).

The *Tāmrarūpa* was of an alloy mainly composed of copper and formed the coins of general currency (*vyāvahārika*).

It may be noted in this connection that the earliest indigenous coinage of India was represented by the standard coins (1) of gold called *Suvarṇa* (2) of silver called *Purāṇa*, or *Dharaṇa* and (3) of copper called *Kārshāpaṇa*. The coinage was modelled on the native system of weights as given by Manu [VIII. 132 f]. The basis of the system is the *ratti* (*raktika*) or guñja berry weighing on an average 1·83 grains or 0·118 grammes. The *Suvarṇa* was of 80 *ratis*=146·4 grains=9·48 grammes. No specimens of *Suvarṇa* have been traced. The silver *Purāṇa or Dharaṇa* weighed 32 *ratis*=58·56 grains=3·79 grammes and the copper *Kārshāpaṇa* was of the same weight as *Suvarṇa*. Vast hoards of these silver and copper coins and of their various multiples and subdivisions have been discovered all over India. These old coins are shaped like square or oblong. The silver coins appear cut from a flat sheet of metal and the copper ones of a bar. They are little more than weights of metal on which was stamped from time to time the symbol of the authority responsible for their genuineness and purity.

There was, again, an officer charged with the regulation of currency, the *Rūpadarśaka*. He had to realize the following Mint charges, viz., *Rūpika*, a seignorage of 8 per cent; *Vyājī*, 5 per cent, the profit accruing to government from the use of special weights and measures for the public; *Pārīkshika*, an assaying fee of $\frac{1}{8}$ *paṇa* per cent.

In commenting on these important Departments of Government, Kauṭilya says: "Mining is the source of the wealth (*Kośa*) of the State; wealth is at the root of the State's military power; the earth is attained by the combination of both (*Ākaraprabhavaḥ Kośaḥ Kośāt Daṇḍaḥ prajāyate*).

Another Superintendent of Mines (*Khanyādhyaksha*). There was another Superintendent of Mines called *Khanyādhyaksha* who had a more limited jurisdiction. He had to look after the business (*Karmāntān*) connected with conch-shells, pearls and coral, diamonds, and precious stones, and salts, and the trade in such articles.

Salt Superintendent (*Lavaṇādhyaksha*). The manufacture of salt was a government monopoly administered by the Salt Superintendent called *Lavaṇādhyaksha*. It was worked under a system of licences, on payment of a fixed fee, or a share of the output. Lessees of salt-fields had to pay rent (*prakraya*) and $^1/_6$ of the salt (*Lavaṇa-bhāga*) manufactured by them. This salt the Superintendent sold at full market rates, and realized in addition a supertax of 5 per cent called *Vyājī* (derived from the difference between government and public measure), together with the extra tax of 8 per cent (*mūlya*) and the assaying fee of 1/8 *paṇa* (*rūpa*).

Imported (*Āgantu*) salt was more heavily taxed. It had to part with a sixth and on this portion, when sold, were levied the premium of 5 percent (*pañchakaṁ śataṁ vyājīṁ*) *Vyājī*, and 8 per cent *Rūpika*, besides a toll (*śulka*) and compensation (*vaidharaṇa*) for loss to revenue from salt imported and not home-made (*kretā śulkaṁ rāja-paṇyāchchhedānurūpaṁ cha vaidharaṇaṁ dadyāt*).

Adulteration of salt, and its manufacture without licence (*vilavaṇaṁ anisṛishṭopajīvī*) were punished except in the case of hermits (*vānaprastha*). Persons given to sacred learning (*śrotriya*), ascetics (*tapasvī*), and labourers not engaged on hire (*vishṭi*) are to get salt free of cost, provided it is for food and not trade (*bhaktalavaṇa*). Thus the salt-tax did not press heavily on the poor.

Gold Superintendent (*Suvarṇādhyaksha*). There was an officer called *Suvarṇādhyaksha* who was in charge of the working of gold and silver in separate compartments, with his office located in a special building called the *Askhaśālā* [II. 13]. This was meant for manufacture of artistic works of gold and silver. But for the public, a shop was established on the high road (*viśikhāmadhye*) under an approved goldsmith. According to the Commentator, "his duty is to help the people in selling and buying gold, silver, and jewels." In this chapter, the *Arthaśāstra* gives instructions as to the methods of testing and distinguishing different qualities of gold, processes of manufacture of articles of gold and silver, of setting of jewels, and elaborate safeguards against fraud and theft on the part of workmen in the factory. The rule is that no one who is not an employee at the *Askhaśālā* can have admission into it. A trespasser will be beheaded (*Akshaśālāmanāyuto nopagachchhet abhigachchhan uchchhedyaḥ*). All workmen are also to have their body and dress searched before they enter or leave the factory (*vichita-vastrahasta-guhyāḥ . . . praviśeyuḥ nishkāseyuścha*).

State Goldsmith (*Sauvarṇika*). There is also a Chapter [II. 14] called *Viśikhāyāṁ Sauvarṇikaprachāraḥ*, "The goldsmith on the high road." It prescribes that the State goldsmith (*Sauvarṇika*) is to employ artisans (*āveśanibhiḥ śilpiśālīyaiḥ suvarṇakārādibhiḥ*) to work up the gold and silver of the town and country people. He is to see that the same quality and weight of the material are returned to the customer as are received by him.

As regards coinage, it is laid down that in getting a *suvarṇa* coin (of 16 *māshas*) manufactured out of gold bullion, one *kākaṇī* (¼ *māsha*) weight of the metal is to be allowed as loss involved in the manufacture.

Manufacture of gold and silver articles was not permitted in a shop not licensed by the State goldsmith (*Sauvarṇikenādriśhṭamanyatra vā prayogaṁ kārayato*).

Conservator of Forests (*Kupyādhyaksha*) [II. 17]. There was a Superintendent in charge of State Forests and forest-products (called *Kupyādhyaksha*). He was to collect timber and other woods by employing the Forestguards (*Vanapāla*) and supervised the manufacture of works of wood ('such as houses, carts and the like'). He was to employ on wages (*vetana*) foresters who knew intimately all parts of trees, top, trunk, branches, roots (*vrikshamarmajña*) so as to decide which part might be cut off without damage to the tree for purposes, say, of fortifications (*durgatāraṇārthe*). Wood-cutting against instructions was punishable except against emergencies where wood was required e.g., for a cart that broke down (*anyatra āpadbhyaḥ* as explained by the Commentator).

The Forests are thus described with reference to their produce :

(1) *Dāru-varga*, Timber such as *Sāla*, *Śimśapa*, etc. ;

(2) *Veṇu-varga*, bamboos of different kinds ;

(3) *Vallī-varga*, different kinds of creepers like canes (*vetra*) ;

(4) *Valkala-varga*, fibres of different kinds such as hemp (*śaṇa*) ;

(5) *Rajju-bhāṇḍa*, material for ropery, such as *muñja* ;

(6) Leaves (*patra*) for writing, such as palm-leaves ;

(7) Flowers as materials for dyeing, 'such as *kiṁśuka*, *kusumbha*, and *kuṅkuma*' ;

(8) *Aushadha-varga*, medicinal plants yielding herbs, roots, and fruits used as medicines (*kanda-mūla-phala*) ;

(9) *Visha-varga*, poisonous trees.

It may be noted that Asoka in his Rock Edict II states that he made arrangements for the cultivation of plants as sources of wholesome drugs obtained from their roots (*mūlāni*), and fruits (*phalāni*), and that where these medicinal herbs (*aushadhāni*) were not available, they were to be imported (*hārāpitāni*) and planted (*ropāpitāni*) in the State Botanical Gardens. In this way, he was ministering to the relief of human suffering (*Manushyachikitsā*) and also to that of the animal kind (*Paśuchikitsā*) by instituting measures of medical treatment, general, and veterinary.

Among forest-produce are also mentioned hides, skins, sinews (*snāyu*), bones, teeth, horns, hoofs, and tails of animals, like crocodile, leopard, tiger, lion, elephant, buffalo, yak, or porpoise, and of birds and snakes.

Forest products also include materials for making baskets of bamboos and cane (*vidala*) or utensils of earth (*mṛittikābhāṇḍa*).

They also include things like charcoal, bran, ash, firewood, and fodder.

Forest products are useful for certain necessaries of life (*ājīvārthāḥ*) as 'materials for making ploughs, mortar, pestle, carts, and the like' and also for defensive purposes (*purarakshārthāḥ*) as materials for making implements (*yantra*) and weapons (*āyudha*).

Superintendent of Slaughter-house (*Sūnādhyaksha*). There was the allied Department of the Superintendent of Slaughter-house (*Sūnādhyaksha*) [II. 26], some of whose regulations are connected with those for forests. It appears that there were certain 'protective' forests (*abhayavana*) the denizens of which were protected against violence by declaration (*pradishṭābhayānāṁ*). These were animals like 'deer, rhino, bisons, and buffaloes, birds like peacocks, and fishes.' There were other animals and birds protected on the principle that they were not killed according to custom (*apravṛittavadhānām*). Thus violence against such non-violent creatures was punishable.

Of such violent creatures which were killed as being not owned by any one (*aparigṛihīta*), the State was to have a sixth ; of fishes and birds, a tenth, and of harmless animals, a toll of tenth or more.

Of the harmless beasts and birds captured, a sixth would be taken by the State and let off in the reserved forests.

The *Arthaśāstra* gives a long list of animals, fishes, and game-birds (*vihāra-pakshiṇo*) which are protected against violence or capture (*hiṁsā-vādhebhyo rakshyāḥ*). There is a special declaration for the protection against slaughter (*avadhya*) or slaughter by torture (*klishṭaghātaṁ ghātayataścha*) of the milch cow, the calf, and the stud-bull.

Sale of meat from unlicensed slaughter-houses (*parisūnaṁ*) was not permitted. Nor was the flesh of remnants of animals found killed in the forests, with their head and leg lost, nor flesh rotten and smelling foul (*vigandham*), nor the flesh of creatures dead of disease (*svayaṁ mṛitaṁ roga-mṛita-māṁsam*).

It may be noted that Asoka also in one of his Edicts [Pillar Edict V] proclaims the protection of certain animals and birds mentioned in its list which is similar to that of Kauṭilya. Asoka's principle of protection is that 'the living must not live on the living' (*jīvena jīve no pusitaviye*), but his actual ordinance is based on Kauṭilya's principle in limiting protection to the harmless and non-violent creatures. In general, Asoka also protects "all quadrupeds which do not lend themselves to any use nor are eaten" (*Paṭibhogaṁ no eti na cha khādiyati*). The creatures mentioned in common for protection are *Haṁsa*, *Śuka*, *Śārika*, *Chakravāk*, and *Palasate* (Rhino). Kauṭilya has another principle of protection: it is to be extended to all creatures which are considered auspicious (*maṅgalyāḥ*).

Superintendent of Cattle (*Go'dhyakshaḥ*) [II. 29]. The State was to have the care of the cattle or the livestock of the country upon which depended so much its national key-industry of Agriculture. The cattle committed to the care of *Go'dhyaksha* included cows, buffaloes, goats, asses, mules and sheep, pigs and dogs. He was in charge not merely of the State Cattle but also private herds which sought his protection against cattle-lifters in return for a share of their dairy produce.

The Department dealt with the following:

(1) Herds of 100 heads of cattle each, which were looked after by a group of five classes of workers, namely (a) the cowherd (*gopālaka*), (b) the herdsman in charge of buffaloes (*piṇḍāraka*), (c) the milker (*dohaka*), (d) the churner (who prepared curds; *dadhimathanakarmā*), and (e) the hunter (*lubdhaka*) who was to protect the cattle against wild animals. Kauṭilya [XIV, 3] also mentions dogs (*śunakāḥ*) keeping watch in the village (*grāme kutūhalāḥ*). All these were employed on the basis of fixed wages paid in kind (*hiraṇyabhṛitā*). They were not paid in shares of milk or clarified butter 'lest the calves are deprived of the milk that sustains them'.

(2) Herds of 100 heads each (*rūpaśatam*), composed of equal number of aged cows, milch-cows, pregnant cows, heifers, and calves, which could be looked after by a single herdsman who was paid by a share of the dairy produce. The arrangement is called *Karapratikara*.

(3) Herds of 100 heads of afflicted or crippled cattle, or cattle, that can not be milked by anyone other than the accustomed person, cattle that are not easily milked (*Durdoha*), or cattle that bring forth dead off-spring (*Putraghni*). Such a useless and abandoned herd (*bhagnotsṛishṭa*) may be looked after by one person and paid by a share of the dairy produce.

(4) Herds which are committed to the care of the State cattle-farm for protection against cattle-lifters on the basis of a fee of a tenth part of the dairy-produce. This arrangement is called *Bhāgānupravishṭaka*.

The Superintendent of cattle under his care classified them as calves, steers, tamed cattle, draught oxen (*vāhinaḥ*), stud-bulls (*vṛisha*), bullocks which are yoked to carts, buffaloes whose flesh is eaten, and buffaloes which carry burden.

Killing or stealing cattle is liable to extreme punishment.

Cowherds were expected to treat the diseases of cattle.

They could sell meat raw (*āmam*) or cooked or dried.

They fed their dogs and boars with butter-milk (*udaśvit*).

Milking is to be done twice a day in *Varshā*, *Śarat* and *Hemanta* seasons, and only once in *Śiśira*, *Vasanta* and *Grīshma*.

Once in six months, sheep and goat will be shorn of their wool (*ūrṇā*).

All cattle should be provided with 'abundance of fodder and water'.

Superintendent of Pastures (*Vivītādhyaksha*). In association with the Superintendent of cattle, there was a Superintendent in charge of the pastures (*Vivītādhyaksha*) [II. 34] who made arrangements for their grazing. He was to establish the pastures for cattle in places 'secure from risks from cattle-lifters and snakes to which the low-lying forests are specially exposed.'

He is to establish new pasture grounds in waterless tracts by endowing these 'with wells, tanks, embankments for storing water (*setu-bandha*) as well as small sources of water (*utsa*) which will also grow gardens of flowers and orchards.' The Superintendent is to employ a body of hunters (*Lubdhaka*) who, with their hunting hounds (*Śvagaṇa*), will be moving through the forests to guard them. They are also mentioned as entrapping tigers with their hounds [IV. 3].

Lastly, his duty is to utilise the surpluses (*ājīva*) left over in the timber-and elephant-forests (*dravya-hasti-vana*) for the following purposes, viz., (1) provision of facilities for transport (*vartanī*), (2) protection against thieves (*chora-rakshaṇam*), (3) escorting caravans (*sārthātivāhyam*), (4) protection of cattle (*go-rakshyam*) and (5) dealings in these goods (*vyavahāra*).

Superintendent of Passports (*Mudrādhyaksha*). There was a Superintendent of Passports (*Mudrādhyaksha*) who issued passes to every traveller on a fee of one *Māsha*. Travelling without a pass was punished with a fine of 12 *paṇas*.

Superintendent of Shipping (*Nāvadhyaksha*) [II. 28]. He had to control all traffic and transit by water ways, riverine as well as oceanic, from the sea to its coast (*samudra-saṁyāna*), or where the river falls into the sea (*nadīmukha*), or on lakes (*devasara*) and tanks (*visara*), wherever situated, at the centres of administration and population of the provinces.

He also policed the rivers and sea-shore, provided State boats and ships, received the fares of all passengers (*yātrāvetanam*), collected all tolls (*śulkabhāga*) payable according to the custom of the harbour (*pattanānuvṛittam*) at the ferries, cess (*Klṛiptam*) on river-side and sea-side villages, and $\frac{1}{6}$ of the proceeds of all fisheries as shipping charges (*naukābhāṭaka*).

Fishing pearls and conch-shells was taxed except where one's own boats were used.

Crossing rivers without permission (*anisṛishṭatāriṇaḥ*), and from places, and at times, other than those fixed by Government (*akāle atīrthe cha taraṇam*) was punished with fines. Criminals, suspects, persons trying to avoid payment of tolls, or carrying poison (*vishahastam*), secret weapons (*gūḍhaśastra*), and explosives (*agniyogam*) were arrested.

Free passage was allowed to fishermen (*Kaivarta*) : carriers of firewood and grass (*Kāshṭhatṛiṇabhāra*) ; watchmen of flower-and fruit-gardens (*pushpaphala-vāṭa*) ; herdsmen looking after cows and bulls (*shaṇḍa-go-pālaka*) ; to policemen in pursuit of criminals; spies and men carrying provisions to the army; to persons carrying seed (*bīja*), food for labourers (*bhakta*) and plant-products such as flowers, fruits, vegetables etc. (*dravyaṁpushpa-phala-śākādi*) ; people residing in marshy areas (*ānūpa-grāmāṇām*) ; and also Brāhmans, ascetics, childern, the ages and afflicted, and pregnant women.

The Superintendent should extend his fatherly protection (*piteva anugṛihṇīyāt*) to such ships as are weather-beaten (*vātāhata*) or have lost their way (*mūḍha*), and also reduce by half (*ardha-śulka*) or forego (*aśulka*) customs charges on merchant vessels damaged by water (*udaka-prāpta*).

Ships touching at harbours in their course (*saṁyātīrnāvaḥ*) are to pay harbour dues.

Piratical ships (*hiṁsrikāḥ*) and those bound for the enemy's country (*amitravishayātigāḥ*) or violating harbour-regulations (*paṇya-pattana-chāritro-paghātikāḥ*) were captured.

At the ferries of large rivers and small, State-vessels were always ready for traffic, manned by an adequate crew consisting of the Captain (*Śāsaka*), the Steersman (*Niyāmaka*), the crew in charge of the ship's implements (*Dātra-grāhaka*) and rigging (*Raśmigrāhaka*) and those who are to bale out water (*Utsechaka*).

Ferry fees were fixed and varied with the nature and weight of the load carried, e.g. camels, buffaloes, bullockcarts, etc.

Superintendent of Port-Towns (*Pattanādhyaksha*) [II. 28]. It was his duty to lay down regulations (*nibandha*) for the control of port-towns (*paṇya-pattana-chāritram*) which were binding on the Superintendent of Ships.

Superintendent of Commerce (*Paṇyādhyaksha*) [II. 16]. He was in charge of the control of supply, prices, purchase, and sale of commodities. Sale of home products owned by the State (*sva-bhumija-rājapaṇya*) is to be made through one market (*ekamukham*) and centralised, and imports through many markets (*aneka-mukham*).

There was also provision for State control of sale and purchase of commodities and of prices under the Superintendent of Commerce. He should be conversant with the prevailing prices of commodities (*arghavit*). He controlled stocks of grain and other merchandise by issuing licences (*anujñātāḥ*) to traders.

Unauthorised stocks were liable to forfeiture.

When the licence to trade is granted to a body of traders, it should not be issued to others, so long as the goods in stock remained unsold.

This provision was meant to prevent competitive reduction of prices.

The Superintendent could also regulate sale through one centralised market (*ekamukhaṁ vyavahāraṁ sthāpayet*), until his stocks were disposed of. Till then, others will not be allowed to sell the same goods.

The Superintendent also controlled prices by checking profiteering. This he did by fixing the *whole-sale* price, and a margin of profit (*ājīva*) above it to settle the *retail* prices. It was 5 per cent in the case of home-made goods (*svadeśīyānāṁ paṇyānām*) and 10 per cent for foreign goods.

Any attempt to realise profits in excess of the scale of prices fixed is punishable with a minimum fine of 200 *paṇas* which was proportionately increased.

The object of this wholesome regulation was ultimately to benefit the consumers (*anugraheṇa prajānām*) by limiting strictly the margin of profit to what should be the dealer's legitimate earning per day (*divasavetanam*) [II. 16; IV. 2].

Prices should not be oppressive to the people (*anugraheṇa anupapīḍayā*). Nor should the State profiteer at their expense (*sthūlamapi cha lābhaṁ prajānāṁ aupaghātikaṁ vārayet*).

Commodities that are necessaries of life, for which there is no limit as to demand or supply (*ajasrapaṇya* 'such as milk and vegetables'), are to be sold at any time and place.

The State many employ private traders as agents for the sale of its goods, provided it is compensated against loss (*chhedānurūpaṁ vaidharaṇaṁ*). But such sale must be permitted at many markets (*bahumukham*) instead of a centralised one.

The State should encourage imports by concessions (*anugraheṇa*), such as freedom from molestation by frontier police, foresters, and the like, and also from imposts like *vyājī*. Imports by sea are to be specially favoured (*nāvika-sārthavāha*).

Merchants coming from foreign countries (*āgantūnām*) are not to be sued for debts (*anabhiyogaśchārtheshu*), but they should fulfil their obligations to those who help them in business (*Anyatra sabhyo-pakāribhyaḥ tadupakāri-karma-karān-apahāya*).

The Commercial Superintendent will export commodities, provided it is profitable (*udayaṁ paśyet*) after paying the various charges such as toll (*śulka*), road-cess (*vartanī*), escort charges (*ātivāhika*), military cess (*gulmadeya*), ferry-charges (*taradeya*) and the like.

He should also push the sale of goods within the country by advertising them properly, and sending specimens to different markets through agents who may also, in need, sell them duty-free, and cheap. Such travelling agents should carefully study the markets for goods, specially on occasions of pilgrimages.

It may be noted that Megasthenes speaks "of the great Officers of State of whom some have charges of the market." These correspond to *Paṇyādhyakshas*.

Superintendent of Trade-Routes (*Saṁsthādhyaksha*) [IV. 2]. In association with the *Paṇyādhyaksha* worked the *Saṁsthādhyaksha* who superintended the trade of the country and controlled its routes (*Vipaṇimārgādhyaksha*, as the commentator explains the name).

Merchandise for sale was to be first deposited for examination in the Government warehouse (*paṇyasaṁsthāyām paṇya-śālāyām*).

The Superintendent will allow sale or mortgage of old goods if their ownership is proved.

He is to examine the weights and measures used by the merchants so as to punish flagrant differences from the legal standard.

Adulteration of all kinds was fined heavily. It is described as passing what is inferior and artificial (*asāraṁ kṛitrimam*) for superior and natural; wrongly describing the origin of articles; selling artificial stones described as natural ones (*rāḍhā śobhā tayā yuktam kṛitrima-mauktādikam*) or mixing pure with impure things (*upadhiyukta*).

Adulteration was practised in regard to the following articles: timber, iron, precious stones ; rope, leather, earthenware; thread, bark (*valka*) and wool; grain, oil, sugar, salt, scent, or drugs.

Superintendent of Customs (*Śulkādhyaksha*) [II. 21]. He had an Office (*Śulka-śālā*) marked by a flag (*dhvaja*) at the main gate of a town. There would be four or five collectors of customs or tolls at the office, who registered full details of answers to their queries: "Who the merchants are, whence they come, with what quantity of merchandise, and where it has been *visaed*" (*ke kutastyāḥ kiyatpaṇyāḥ kva chābhijñānamudrā vā kṛitā*).

Absence of trade-marks, or tampering with them, was penalised, sometimes with detention or confinement in a special room (*sthāna*) of the Customs Office for three *ghaṭikās*, (*ghaṭikāḥ* meaning *ghaṭikātraya-kāla* as explained by the commentator with the help of the *Kapiñjala-nyāya*). When goods were brought thither, their owners publicly offered them for sale (*eṭat pramāṇenārgheṇa paṇyamidaṁ kaḥ kretā*), and the tolls were levied on the basis of the prices they realised. In case of prices being pushed up by the bidding of buyers (*kretṛisaṁgharshe mūlya-vṛiddhiḥ*), the excess of the price and the toll were received by the State, while a fraudulent under-statement of the quantity or the price of goods was penalised by the levy of 8 times the proper toll. The same punishment was imposed on merchants showing inferior samples (*hīna-prativarṇakena*) to conceal the true worth of their goods (*nivishṭa-paṇyasya bhāṇḍasya*).

The fixing of the prices of goods beyond their proper value was punishable. To ensure this, the sale of goods was allowed after they were weighed (*dhṛita*), measured (*mita*) or numbered (*gaṇita*).

There was a wholesome regulation making merchants combining (*vaidehakānāṁ sambhūya*) to dictate prices of commodities and also to corner them (*paṇyamavarundhatāṁ anargheṇa vikrīṇatāṁ krīṇatāṁ vā*) liable to a fine of 1000 *paṇas* each [IV. 2.]

Similarly punishable were also craftsmen combining (a) to strike work (*karma-guṇāpakarshaṇa*) and to raise their wages (*ājīvam*) or (b) to raise the prices of things they have to sell and reduce those of things they have to buy (*sambhūya vikraya-krayopaghātaṁ samutthāpayatām*) [*Ib.*].

Articles such as weapons, armour, metals, carriages, precious stones, grains, and quadrupeds, trade in which was banned (*anirvāhya*) by declaration, if sold, would be confiscated (*paṇyanāśa*) by the State, and a fine would be imposed on the dealers. If any of the prohibited articles were imported, they would be sold outside the Customs House or the Town, free of toll (as they will be purchased by the State). Articles for marriages (*vaivāhika*), dowry goods (*anvāyanam*), gifts to the king (*aupāyanikam*) and commodities for religious purposes (*yajña-kṛitya-devejyā* etc.) and the requisites for Midwifery (*prasavanaimittikam*) were admitted free of toll. False declarations on these were punished like theft (*steya-daṇḍa*).

The Officials levied fines for infringement of regulations, e.g., wice the toll for coming without a passport (*amudrāṇām*) ; eight times the toll for presenting a forged passport (*kūṭamudrāṇāṁ*) ; 1¼ *paṇas* per bullock-load for presenting a fraudulently altered pass (*rājamudrā-parivartane*) ; or for fraudulent description (*nāmakṛite kārpāsādi-dravyāṇāṁ tūlādināma-niveśena*) of goods. Smuggling was punished with forfeiture of goods smuggled (*tachcha tāvachcha daṇḍaḥ*).

To facilitate collection of tolls and prevent their evasion, it was laid down that commodities were to be sold only at the appointed place and could not be sold in the place where they were grown or manufactured (*Jātibhūmīshu cha paṇyānāmavikrayaḥ*) [II. 22]. But customs dues were not levied upon them until they were offered for sale. Thus purchase of goods direct from mines, fields, flower-, fruit-and vegetable-gardens was variously fined [II. 22].

Table of Tolls (*Śulka-vyavahāra*). There was framed a regular Table of Tolls (*Śulka-vyavahāra*) [II. 22]. Goods were classified according to the tolls charged on them. They might be of three descriptions :

(1) Grown on the country side (*vāhyam*).
(2) Produced within the city (*ābhyantara*).
(3) Imported from abroad (*ātithya*).

Tolls were levied on both imports (*praveśya*) and exports (*nishkrāmya*), when goods were entered for sale, and sent out on sale. Imports paid $\frac{1}{5}$ of their value in toll. Perishable goods (such as flowers, fruits, vegetables, fish, flesh etc.) paid $\frac{1}{6}$. Other goods such as clothes of cotton (*kārpāsa*), silk (*krimitāna, chīnapaṭṭa*), jute (*kshauma, sthūla-valkajam*), linen (*dukūla, sūkshma-valkaja*), wool, metals, dyes, ivory skin, etc., paid from $\frac{1}{10}-\frac{1}{15}$ and $\frac{1}{20}-\frac{1}{25}$.

Prohibited and Free Imports. It is finally laid down that goods which are harmful to people (*rāshṭra-pīḍā-karam* [II. 21]) 'such as poison or alcohol', or which are of little value such as vegetables, are not to be imported, while goods which are of benefit to the country (*mahopakāram*), 'goods like seeds of food-crops, or medicinal plants,' are to be imported free of toll.

Warden of the Marches (*Antapāla*). A Warden of the Marches (*Āntapāla*) [II. 21] policed the borders, issued sealed passports which had to be presented later to the Officials under the Superintendent of Customs, and levied a Toll upon all traffic passing the frontier viz., 1¼ *paṇa* on each load of merchandise as road cess (*vartanī*), 1 *paṇa* on each load of single-hoofed beasts, ½ *paṇa* per load of double-hoofed quadrupeds, and $\frac{1}{16}$ *paṇa* on each load carried on the head.

Road-Cess. The Road Cess or *Vartanī* (*mārgarakshābhṛitim*) was intended to meet the cost of protecting traffic along its routes which had to be rendered secure.

Superintendent of Excise (*Surādhyaksha*) [II. 25]. The Excise Superintendent controlled the manufacture and sale of liquor and intoxicating drugs. The manufacture was carried on by State Agency in Government Breweries and Distilleries and also by private persons under licence. Foreign liquor had to pay an Excise duty of 5 per cent on the sale-proceeds.

Extent of Prohibition. The Superintendent of Excise controlled the sale of liquor by restricting it as to time, place, quantity, and character of customers. Liquor could be sold only to approved parties (*jñātaśaucha*) on whom its effects would be the least deleterious.

It could not be sold outside the liquor-house.

It could not be taken out after the appointed hour.

It should be sold in quantities which customers can carry.

Drinking of alcohol outside the village (*grāmādanirṇayanam*) or home (*asampātam gṛihāt gṛihāntare janākīrṇe vā*) is prohibited lest there is over-indulgence without check.

Taverns: Restrictions on Sale of Liquor. Taverns (*pānāgāra*) were allowed only in towns and the quantity of liquor to be sold was restricted so as not to cause intoxication (*pramāda*) in workmen, undignified behaviour (*maryādātikrama*) among the gentry (*Ārya*) or want of sanity in violent people (*tīkshṇa*) who may use their arms out of rashness (*utsāha*) or fear (*bhaya*), without judging of time or place (*asthāne*).

Only sealed (*lakshitaṁ abhijñāna-mudrā-chihnitam*) liquor was to be sold. It was to be sold in small quantities and only to approved persons (*jñāta-śaucha*).

As to others, the liquor was to be drunk in the licensed taverns only. A person found to possess property not his own (*asvāmikam*) was handed over to the police and arrested (*grāhayet*) outside the liquor-shop.

Arrest of Drunkards. There was another hard regulation for the arrest of drunkards who were given to spending too much (*ativyayakartā*) or beyond their means (*anāyativyayam*).

Furniture at Taverns. At the same time, drinking was made pleasant by furnishing the tavern with any number of rooms, beds, and seats (*anekakaksha* and *vibhaktaśayanāsana*). Scents, garlands, and drinks further added to the comforts of the customers.

Espionage. At the same time, a careful watch was kept upon them as to their expenses and also on foreign customers (*āgantūn*).

A Staff of Spies was there to keep a watch on the ornaments, dress, and gold in the possession of the customers sleeping in drunkenness. The keeper of the tavern was held responsible for the loss of these valuables.

The keeper of the tavern had also to keep an eye upon the behaviour of the customers, whether native (*vāstavya*) or foreigners (*āgantū*) who lie down in drunkenness with their handsome mistresses in the guise of *Āryas*.

Medicinal Wines. The *Arthaśāstra* enumerates various kinds of liquors in use in the country in those days, including those which were not harmful, but medicinal, such as *Āsavas*, *Arishṭas* approved by physicians (*chikitsaka-pramāṇāḥ*), *Madhu* or grape juice (*mṛidvīkā-rasa*) of the varieties called *Kāpiśāyana* and *Hārahūraka*, i.e., the wine from Kāpiśa or northern Afghanistan and the wine which came from the country of the *Harahūras*, a people mentioned in the *Bṛihatsaṁhitā* as inhabiting a region to the west or perhaps north-west of *Bhāratavarsha.*

It may be noted that these wines were in use in earlier times. Pāṇini mentions them by the names *Kāpiśāyana* and *Kāpiśāyanī* in the sense that they were 'produced in' the country called Kāpiśī [IV. 2, 99]. Kapiśa (=modern Kafiristan) was the region lying between the Kunar river and Hindukush beyond which lay Bāhlīka.

The *Hārahūraka* was similarly the wine produced in the valley of the river called Harahvaiti (Avestan)=Harahuvatī (old Persian) =modern Helmand, as stated above.

Harahūrā is still the name used for black raisins, while *Kāpiśāyana*, as explained by Bhaṭṭoji Dīkshita, was a kind of *madhy* or wine (perhaps derived from the green grapes) and *Kāpiśāyanī* a kind of *drāksha*.

It is also to be noted that the regions producing these wines were parts of the Indian empire under Chandragupta Maurya.

Free drinking. Drinking, however, was permitted free and outside the licensed liquor-shops on occasions of festivals (*utsava vasantādi-utsaveshu*), social gatherings (*samājabandhujana-melaneshu*) and religious worship (*yātrā ishṭadevatāpūjā*), for a period of four days. But if this limit of licence was exceeded, the Excise Superintendent was to impose a daily fine on those who would drink beyond that time (lest 'as workmen, they cause loss of work').

It will thus appear that these various Excise Regulations were framed with a view to Prohibition as the ultimate aim of Government.

Megasthenes. We may note that Megasthenes has stated that the Indians drank wine at sacrifices and this statement agrees with what is mentioned by Kauṭilya regarding the issue of special liquor licences on such occasions.

Superintendent of Weights and Measures (*Pautavādhyaksha*) [II, 19]. He had these manufactured. Weights were made of the iron or stone of Magadha and Mekala or of such material as did not expand under heat nor contact in cold. Balances, with scale-pans, were made, with levers from 6 *aṅgulas* or inches in length, and upwards. The Superintendent also stamped the weights and measures used by private parties, and charged a fee of 4 *Māshas* for it. There was a periodical checking of weights and measures, once every 4 months, and its cost was met from a special tax of 1 *kākaṇī* per day. There were also the lineal and square measures of space and the measures of time determined by Government.

Superintendent of Spinning and Weaving (*Sūtrādhyaksha*) [II. 23]. There were Government factories for manufacture of yarn, clothing, mail-armour (*varma*) and ropes.

Female Labour. Female labour was employed in such factories for spinning (*kartayet*) yarn out of wool (*ūrṇā*), bark (*valka*), cotton, silk-cotton (*tūla*), hemp (*śaṇa*) and flax (*kshauma*).

Such women were employed as were without support, viz., widows, disabled women (*Nyangā*), girls, women-ascetics, convicts, aged *Devadāsīs* and the like.

Women in *purdah* (*anishkāsinyaḥ*) who could not come to work in the factory were supplied with work by its women-employees (*svadāsibhiḥ*). Yarn was received at the Ware-house called *Sūtraśālā*.

Wages. Wages were paid according to quantity or quality of work turned out. Delay of payment due was punishable (*vetana-kālātipātane madhyamaḥ sāhasadaṇḍaḥ*).

Manufactures. Yarn was woven (*sūtravāna-karma*) of various materials as *kshauma* (flax or jute), *dukūla* (silk), *kṛimitāna* (silk from cocoons), *rāṅkava* (wool of deer) and *kārpāsa* (cotton).

There were also manufactured garments, blankets (*āstaraṇa*) and curtains (*prāvaraṇa*) of new designs (*utthāpayet apūrvān nirmāpayet*).

The factories were also busy in making ropes of yarn and straps (*varatrā*) of cane and bamboo-bark, by which draught animals could be trained and tethered.

Department of Information and Criminal Intelligence [I. 11, 12; IV. 4, 5]. The Department was manned by what are called Secret Agents (*Gūḍha-Purushāḥ*) organised into special Service under its own Minister (*Mahāmātrāpasarpa* or *Mahāmātyāpasarpa*).

Recruitment. In view of the highly responsible character of their work, the members of the Secret Service were recruited from the tried men of the Civil Service, the *Amātyas*, whose purity and integrity were proved by all tests (*upadhābhiḥ śuddhāmātya-vargo gūḍhapurushānutpādayet*).

Two Branches of Service. The Service was organised into two branches, Stationary (*Saṁsthā*) and Touring (*Sañchāra*).

Stationary (*Saṁsthā*) **Branch.** The first Branch employed a variety of spies in all possible guises, those of student, recluse, householder, merchant, or ascetic. These were set to work among their respective classes.

Touring (*Sañchāra*) **Branch.** The Touring Section of the Service was also manned by spies of different classes called (1) *Satrī*, who were versed in palmistry, sorcery, and other arts of attracting the populace; (2) *Tīkshṇa*, comprising desperadoes who would employ themselves as menials of high officials; (3) *Rasada*, those who drug people, sometimes working in the guise of women, (4) *Bhikshukī* or women spies who quartered themselves on the households of Ministers (*Mahāmātra-kulāni*).

Salary. The salary of the first branch of the Secret Service was 1000 *paṇas* and that of the second 500 *paṇas*.

Greek References. The Greek writers are full of references to Informers whom they call "Overseers," as we have already seen. According to Megasthenes, they comprised an entire class of people whose business was to watch all that was going on and "make reports secretly to the king." What is a more interesting statement confirming Kauṭilya is that "the most trustworthy men are appointed to fill these offices." Arrian, speaking in the same strain, also states that "it is against use and wont for these to give in a false report."

Reporters of Asoka. It is interesting to note that Asoka also, in one of his inscriptions [Rock-Edict VI], refers to officers whom he calls *Prativedakas* whose duty was to report to the king to whom they had free access, at all hours, and places, on what was going on in the country (*athe me janasya paṭivedetha iti*).

Detectives. Detectives were liberally employed by the administration for the purpose of preventing and tracing crime. They were recruited from all classes of people in the country such as ascetics, jugglers (*chakrachara*), bards, diviners, fortune-tellers, physicians, traders, artists (*kāru-śilpī*), musicians, vintners (*śauṇḍika*), confectioners (*āpūpika*), and the like. If a person is suspected of criminal conduct, a suitable spy would be told off to shadow him.

Some of these spies were employed as *agents provocateurs*, inciting to crime of all kinds. They watched the suspects of the countiy and incited each to the crime to which he was prone.

If it was a judge (*Dharmastha* or *Pradeshṭā*), he would be tempted by offer of bribery and convicted as an *upadāgrāhaka.*

If it was a village headman (*Grāma-kūṭa*) or a magistrate (*Adhyaksha*), he was incited to extortion of rich citizens and punished as an *utkochaka.*

Or a person might be bribed to give false evidence, or poison people, or procure or corrupt women by charms and incantations, and be convicted as a *kūṭa-sākshī*, a *Rasada*, or *krityābhichāra-śīla* (sorcerers).

Or a spy may quarter himself as an apprentice in the service of a man suspected to manufacture counterfeit coins, and if it is found to be true, will have him apprehended and banished as *kūṭa-rūpa-kāraka* and *kūṭa-suvarṇa-vyavahārī.*

Young men given to robbery and adultery would also be entrapped by spies enrolling themselves as members of their gang whom they would lead to a village, and into its marked house, by a prearranged plan, and to commit there all crimes. As thieves, they would associate themselves with thieves to have them caught.

We are even told of detectives masquerading as brigands, going among criminal forest-tribes, and instigating them to attack caravans or villages stocked beforehand for the purpose with spurious gold and other goods. As the attack takes place according to plan, the assailants may be slain by armed forces posted there in advance to lie in wait for them, or they may be arrested while sleeping in intoxication from the effects of drugged food or drinks provided from them [IV. 4, 5].

Department of Embassies. [I. 16]. The Government maintained a Department of Embassies in charge of its foreign relations. Ambassadors called Dūtas were recruited from Ministers (*Amātyas* of full qualifications) and were of different grades : (1) *Nisṛishṭārtha*, Plenipotentiary (2) *Parimitārtha*, Envoy charged with limited mission and (3) *Śāsana-hara*, instructed emissary, the bearer of Royal Decrees.

The Ambassador was deputed to foreign States with due pomp and equipment as regards conveyance (*yāna*), horses and other animals as vehicles (*vāhana*), retainers (*purusha*) and provisions for food and rest (*parivāpa*) suitable for each journey. He is described as the mouthpiece of the king (*Dūtamukhāḥ rājānaḥ*). He must know how to behave in a foreign country. He must not be impatient but stay on till his mission is over and is asked to leave (*vasedavisṛishṭaḥ*). He must not be affected by honours shown to him (*pūjayā notsiktaḥ*).

He must live a strictly moral life, abstaining from women and wine (*striyaḥ pānaṁ cha varjayet*). He is charged with duties of great importance, delivery of his king's message, maintenance of treaties (*sandhipālatvam*), issue of ultimatum (*pratāpa*), acquisition of allies (*mitra-saṁgraha*), political intrigue (*upajāpa*), breaking enemy's alliances (*suhṛid-bheda*) and the like.

Superintendent of Religious Institutions (*Devatādhyaksha*). This officer is called by the apt name of *Devatādhyaksha* [V. 2]. He was in charge of all temples of towns and rural areas and their properties. He could also set up new shrines or *Śiva-liṅga* in an old temple and hold in its celebration religious processions and gatherings at which he would collect moneys offered by pilgrims in aid of the institutions (*yātrā-samājābhyāṁ ājīvet*).

A List of Chief Officers. Of these, Kauṭilya gives a list [I. 12] which includes the following : (1) *Mantrī* (2) *Purohita* (3) *Senāpati* (4) *Yuvarāja* (5) *Dauvārika* (Chamberlain) (6) *Antarvaṁśika* (7) *Praśāstā* in charge of military camping arrangements (8) *Samāhartā* (9) *Sannidhātā* (10) *Pradeshṭā* (11) *Nāyaka* (Commander) (12) *Pauravyāvahārika* (13) *Kārmāntika* (Mining Superintendent) (14) *Mantri-parishat-adhyaksha* (15) *Daṇḍapāla* (Chief Commandant as distinguished from the *Senāpati* who is the *Īśvara* or the Head of an *Akshauhiṇī*, an army of 21,870 chariots, as many elephants, 65,610 horse, 109,350 foot) (16) *Durgapāla* (17) *Antapāla* and (18) *Āṭavika* (*Aṭavīrājyādhipati*, 'Lord of the realm of foresters'). Kauṭilya also calls these eighteen chief offices *Ashṭādaśatīrthas*.

CHAPTER VII

LAND-SYSTEM AND RURAL ADMINISTRATION

Survey. The cultivated land was measured by the *rajju*=10 *daṇḍas*=40 *hands*, 1 *hand* being equal to 54 *aṅgulas*. Different standards of measurement were used for different kinds of land, such as military camping grounds, timber-forests, roads and wells, revenue-free lands, and the like.

The cost of Survey and Settlement was charged to the proprietor of the land benefiting by them.

Settlement. There are interesting injunctions regarding the duties of the State as landlord. First, a start was made with the establishment of villages of minimum sizes of 100 and maximum 500 families. The State would settle on these villages the peoples of other regions by their assisted emigration (*paradeśāpavāhanena*) or a part of its own population by transferring it from over-populated areas (*svadeśābhishyandavamanena*).

The villages are to be separated by well-defined boundaries such as river, hill, forest, shrubs (*grishṭi*), valley (*dārī*), embankments (*setubandha*) and trees like *śālmalī*, *śamī*, or *vaṭa*. The villages should not be too far apart. They should be within a *krośa* or two of each other, so as to be able to protect each other (*anyonyārakshaṃ*) [II. 1].

The rural collective life was promoted by organising every 10 villages under a common administrative centre called *Saṅgrahaṇa* ; every 200 villages under *Khārvaṭika* ; every 400 villages under a *Droṇamukha* ; till the culmination was reached in a Union of 800 villages called *Mahāgrāma* with its administrative centre called a *Sthānīya*, a centre of culture, trade, business and means of livelihood, where the villagers of the entire locality would meet and cultivate a corporate life [*Ib*.].

The State is to grant lands free of rents and taxes to those whose services the village needs, viz., (1) those who conduct religious ceremonies, (2) teachers, (3) priests and (4) men of learning [*Ib*].

Such grants of land were also made to village officers in lieu of salaries, but these were inalienable by sale or mortgage (*vikrayādhānavarjam*). The scale of salaries payable to the rural officers of different grades in the shape of grants of land is thus fixed in both

Manu-Smṛiti [VII. 119] and the *Mahābhārata* [XII. 87, 6-8] : The lord of 10 villages is to be given 1 *kula* of land, defined to be "as much land as can be cultivated with 12 oxen ;" the lord of 20 villages, 5 *kulas* ; of 100 villages, one entire village ; and of 1,000 villages, one entire town.

Land made fit for cultivation is to be settled on rent with its cultivator for life. Land not fit for cultivation is not to be taken away from those who are making it fit.

Non-cultivation of land will render it liable to forfeiture. The land thus released will be given to other cultivators in the village in the first instance. Failing that, the State is to settle it with more resourceful people who can make it profitable and can pay rent for it. These may be persons in the employ of the village itself (*Grāmabhṛitakas*) and even the local merchants (*Vaidehaka*). This shows that non-cultivating capitalists were entertained for promoting agriculture instead of depending solely on the actual cultivators or tillers of the soil.

The State should encourage cultivation by advance of seeds, cattle, and money (*hiraṇya*), so that cultivators may be enabled to make it profitable and afterwards (*anu*) pay back the agricultural loan and the dues to the State without difficulty (*sukhena dadyāt.*)

Favours and remissions of rent (*anugrahaparihāra*) cannot be granted to cultivators at the cost of the State [*Ib.*].

According to Kauṭilya, [VII. 11], a country the majority of whose population is of lower classes (*avaravarṇa-prāya*) is, from the economic point of view, better (*śreyasī*) than one of the four highest castes (*chāturvarṇyābhiniveśe*). The lower classes are capable of all work and hardship (*sarva-bhogasahatvāt*) such as agricultural needs. Agriculture further depends on cattle and the Śūdras are herdsmen and follow cattle-rearing as their profession (*paśupālya*). There are also needed the *Vaiśyas* who store up grain and supply agricultural loans on the basis of crops (*paṇya-nichayariṇānugrahāt*). Kauṭilya considers Agriculture as the best industry because it may be plied at most places (*bāhulyāt*) and is certain of results (*dhruvatvāt*). Thus, in his opinion, that *bhūmi* or country is the best which is (1) *karshaṇavatī*, suitable to agriculture ; (2) *gorakshakavatī*; full of herdsmen ; and (3) *vaṇigvatī*, full of merchants who finance agriculture. Kauṭilya's appreciation of the lower castes and his Indian economics are remarkable in a Brahmin of his aggressive orthodoxy.

Village Planning. Apart from its arable land, a village should have its uncultivated land (*akrishyā bhūmi*) distributed for purposes of (1) Pastures (*vivīta*) for the grazing of its cattle; (2) Sylvan retreats for religious study and practices (*Brahma-Somāraṇya*) and others for ascetics (*Tapovana*); (3) a reserved forest for royal hunt to be stocked "with tamed (*dānta*) animals like deer and elephant, and wild animals like tiger but with their teeth and claws cut off"; (4) ordinary forests for the shelter of all animals (*sarvātithi-mṛigam mṛiga-vanam*); (5) plantations of different kinds of forests growing different kinds of produce such as Timber-forests, Bamboo-forests, or forests of bark-producing trees; (6) factories for utilisation of forest-products (*dravya-vana-karmāntān*); (7) colonies of foresters and (8) forests for rearing of elephants beyond human habitation [II. 2].

Rural Development. The State must take charge of rural development under a programme comprising (1) Mining and Metallurgical works (*ākara-karmānta*), (2) Plantations of forests yielding timber and also valuable and medicinal woods like sandal-wood or scented wood, (3) Plantation of forests for elephants, (4) Grazing grounds for cattle, (*vraja*), (5) Roads for traffic (*vaṇik--patha-prachārān*), (6) Water-ways and land routes (*vāristhalapatha*) and (7) markets for commodities (*paṇyapattana*) [II. 1].

The State should also make provision for rural water-supply by construction of reservoirs (*setu*) filled from a river or by rain. It should also help private persons to construct tanks by free gifts of land, passage for water, timber, and other necessary materials.

The State should also make such gifts of land and material to private persons constructing places for worship (*Puṇya-sthāna*) and gardens or parks rest for the public, (*Ārāma*).

The State should enforce supply of stipulated contributions in the shape of labour and bullocks towards any co-operative undertaking decided on by the village. In lieu of stipulated contribution, the defaulter had to pay for it and his share of the cost of the undertaking (*vyaya-karmaṇi cha bhāgī syāt*).

The sovereign has rights over what grows in the tanks created by dams (*setushu*), whether fish, ducks, or aquatic plants.

A village must not be provided with pleasure-gardens or halls for purposes of dramatic performance, dancing, vocal music, concerts, buffoons, and bards, disturbing the work of helpless agriculturists.

The State must protect agriculturists from exacting fines, free labour, and rents or taxes.

A village had its flower-gardens, orchards (*pushpa-phalavāṭa*), clusters of trees such as lotus or bamboo (*shaṇḍa*), and paddy fields (*kedāra*) [II. 1; 6].

There are laid down a few other wholesome regulations for the growth of a healthy village life. The State must check indiscipline in the family and enforce the obedience of the dependants like relations, indentured servants (*āhitakas*) and hirelings [*dāsas* (by birth, *garbha-jāta* ; from birth, *griha-jāta* ; by purchase (*krīta*), by acquisition (*labdha*), or by debt, *dāyopagata*)] to their master.

The State is also to support the helpless in the village, the young, the aged, the diseased, the afflicted and the destitute, and the childless women.

The elders of the village (*grāma-vṛiddhāḥ*) are enjoined to protect the property of its minors and see to its improvement till they come of age, and similarly protect the properties of temples for all times (*bāla-dravya* and *deva-dravya*).

Again, failure to maintain one's children, wife, parents, minor brothers, daughters, sisters and widowed daughters, on the part of one who is able to support them, was fined, except in the cases of lapses from morality, but the mother is to be excepted under all circumstances.

Any person leaving home as an ascetic without providing for his son and wife was punishable ; so also any person who converts a woman to asceticism.

One could renounce the world only at the age fixed by the *Śāstras*. Otherwise he is to be imprisoned (*niyamya*) [II. 1].

Land Revenue. The administration of the Department of Land Revenue was under the control of the officer called *Samāhartā* whose functions have been already dealt with.

Its Sources. As we have already seen, the items of Land Revenue mentioned are derived from a variety of sources described under the term *Rāshṭra* which means 'the country side' or rural area, excluding the *Durga*. These are technically called (1) *Sītā* (Crown land) ; (2) *Bhāga* or the sixth part of agricultural produce payable to the State ; (3) *Kara*, or the levy of an impost upon the yield of orchards ; (4) *Vivīta* or a levy on pastures ; (5) *Vartanī* or road-cess ; (6) *Rajjū* or cess payable for settlement ; (7) *Chora-rajjū* or Chowkidari or Police cess ; (8) *Setu*, irrigated lands and tanks ; (9) *Vana* or forests ; (10) *Vraja* or Cattle-breeding Farms or Stud-Farms ; (11) *Bali*, presents to the king, a sort of abwabs ; (12) *Mines* such as those of "gold, silver, diamond, gems, pearls, corals, conch-shells, metals, salts and other minerals extracted from earth, stone, or oilfields (*rasa*) like mercury." [II. 6].

Administration : Revenue Officers. The Revenue Department comprised three grades of officials, viz,, (1) *Samāhartā*, Collector-general, the Head of the Department, (2) *Sthānika* and (3) *Gopa*. The Province (*Janapada*) was split up into four Circles or Divisions, each under a *Sthānika*. Each such Circle was subdivided into groups or Unions of 5 villages and 10 villages which were placed in charge of officers called *Gopas*. In addition to *Gopa* and *Sthānika*, the rural staff working in a village comprised the following officers : (1) *Adhyaksha*, like the officer in charge of gold and jewellery works (*suvarṇādhyaksha*) ; (2) *Saṅkhyāyaka*, the village accountant ; (3) *Anīkastha*, trainer of elephants (caught in the adjoining elephant-forests) ; (4) *Chikitsaka*, the village *Vaidya* or physician ; (5) *Aśvadamaka*, trainer of horses ; (6) *Jaṅghākarika* (*Jāṅghika*), a runner and carrier of messages (*dūradeśagatāgatajīvī*) and others [II. 1].

Villages in each of the four provincial Divisions were grouped under three classes in the order of the number of their population and the value of their resources (Commentator).

Records. Written records (*Nibandhas*) were prepared, counting villages of different descriptions such as (1) Revenue-free (*parihāraka*); (2) Contributing military service in lieu of taxes (*āyudhīyaṁ daṇḍakaradāyakaṁ grāmāgram* ; or (3) Contributing regularly as tax assessed (*pratihāraḥ pratiniyātaḥ karaḥ*) prescribed quantities of *dhānya* (grain or crops) ; number of animals of different kinds, whether beasts of burden, or those yielding milk or wool (*vāha-doha-lomādi-upakartṛīn paśūn iti paśukaraḥ*) ; assessed quantities of precious metals (*hiraṇya*), such as gold, silver, or copper, for purposes of coinage (*kośapraveśya*) ; of raw materials (*kupya*) ; and of labour (*vishṭi karmakarapurushāḥ*) [II. 35].

Thus the rural registers recorded the substance (*grāmāgraṁ*) of each village, its economic value and resources (*prātiśvikam*), the kind of contribution it made to the general welfare of the country, as also the collective substance of all the villages in a division (*sāmūhikaṁ cha parimāṇam*).

Details. After the villages were thus classified according to the kind of contribution they made to the revenue and resources of the State, each individual village was further studied with reference to the following particulars which the village officer in charge called the *Gopa* was to enter in his own Record (*Nibandha*), viz.

(1) Demarcation of villages by defined boundaries such as river, rock and the like and ascertainment of the exact area of each village thus demarcated (*sīmāvarodhena grāmāgram*) ;

(2) Measurement and description of plots (*kshetra*) as (a) cultivated, (b) uncultivated and waste, (c) high and dry, (d) paddy-fields (*kedāra*), (e) park (*ārāma*), (f) orchard (*shaṇḍa*), (g) plantations

of sugar-cane and the like (*vāṭa*), (h) wood (*vana*) for supplying the villagers with firewood, (i) inhabited, covered by dwellings (*vāstu*), (j) trees for worship (*chaitya*), (k) temples, (l) irrigation works (*setu*), (m) cremation grounds, (n) almshouses (*sattra*), (o) watering places (*prapā pānīyaśālā*), (p) places of pilgrimage, (q) grazing grounds (*vivīta*) and (r) roads;

(3) Preparation of Registers (*nibandhān*) recording (a) boundaries (*maryādā*) and areas (*pramāṇam*) of plots, (b) woods for common use (*araṇya*), (c) approaches to plots (*patha*) (d) plots acquired by gift (*sampradāna*), (e) plots acquired by sale (*vikraya*), (f) amount of loan advanced to agriculturists (*anugraha*) and (g) revenue remissions granted by Government (*parihāra*) ;

(4) Preparation of a Census of Households in the village (*grihāṇāṁ saṅkhyānena*) showing (a) the number of each house in the register; (b) whether it was taxed or tax-free (*karada* or *akarada*); (c) composition of each household as to number of Brāhmaṇas, Kshatriyas, Vaiśyas, and Śūdras living in it (*etāvat chāturvarṇyam*); (d) number of cultivators (*karshaka*), herdsmen (*gorakshaka*), traders (*vaidehaka*), artisans (*kāru*), workmen (*karmakara*), serfs (*dāsa*); (e) number of men and live-stock; (f) amount contributed by each household to the State in the forms of cash, labour, tolls and military service (*hiraṇya-vishṭi-śulka-daṇḍa*); (g) number of males and females and their ages (*strī-purushāṇām bāla-vriddha-vayaḥ-parichchhedam*) in each household (*kulānām*); (h) occupations (*karmāṇi*) according to *varṇa* (caste); (i) customs (*charitra*) of the village and the family concerned; (j) domestic budget of each family indicating its Income and Expenditure (*ājīva-vyaya-parimāṇa*) [II. 35].

The preparation of these village Records and Registers enabled government to have a complete grip upon the condition of the countryside in all its details, leaving no room for any speculation. Periodical Survey of rural conditions was obviated by the Census being kept up as a standing institution.

Besides the village officer at the bottom of the scale, thus keeping record for each village under his charge, the next higher Revenue Officer, the *Sthānika*, in charge of one of the four districts of the province (*janapada-chaturbhāgam*) was also to prepare similar records and registers for his circle.

Inspectors (*Pradeshṭāraḥ*). The Revenue Minister also enforced the working of this administrative system by appointing Inspectors to go about the country in disguise as Informers to inspect the Records and Accounts kept by the District and Village Officers regarding the cultivated fields, homesteads (*griha*) and families (*kula*) ; (a) fields under the heads of area and output (*māna-sañjātābhyāṁ kshetrāṇi*); (b) households under the heads of revenue assessed (*bhoga*) and remissions (*parihāra*); and (c) families under the heads of caste, occupation, number of members (*jaṅghāgra*, counted as per pair of feet and not per head), income and expenditure. They had also to inform themselves of the movements of the people, to and from the village, of doubtful characters (*anarthyānām*), "such as dancers, actors and the like," and of foreign spies.

Other classes of Inspectors will inspect the quantity and price of the various products due to the State, those from cultivated fields, orchards, forests, mines and factories.

Another set will examine the imports by land or water and the dues levied on these in the shape of toll (*śulka*), road-cess (*vartanī*), conveyance-cess (*ātivāhika*), military-cess (*gulma-deya*), ferry charges (*tara-deya*), 1/6 portion of their value payable by merchants (*bhāga*), the charges for their living (*bhakta*), and accommodation of their goods in government warehouses (*paṇyāgāra*) [II. 35].

Inspectors in the guise of ascetics were set to watch the activities of cultivators, herdsmen, merchants and Heads of Government Departments (*Adhyakshas*). "In places of trees worshipped, where four roads meet, at solitary places, in the vicinity of tanks, rivers, bathing-places, at centres of pilgrimage, at hermitages, in desert-tracts, on hills, and in thick forests, Informers in the guise of veteran thieves with their followers will be set to ascertain the causes of arrival and departure, and halt, of thieves, enemies and outlaws."

In addition to the subordinate Inspectorate, there were also *Pradeshṭās* of higher grade to inspect regularly the work of their subordinate Revenue Officers in the districts [II. 35 for above].

Land Transactions [III. 9]. Lands were as easily saleable as moveable properties. They were put up to auction publicly in the presence of forty persons who owned property in the vicinity of the land or the house on sale. They congregated before the land or in front of the house on sale and announced it as being such. The aged persons of the locality presided over the transaction. A description was given of the boundaries and other necessary particulars of the property. The auctioneer then loudly called out three times, 'Who will purchase the land or the house at such a price' (*anena arghena kaḥ kretā*)? The purchaser gets the land after this, if it is not objected to by any one (*avyāhatam*). But if, at this stage of the transaction, bidding commences, and the price is enhanced, the enhanced amount, together with the toll on the sale-value, was paid into the king's treasury. The purchaser, who enhanced the value by bidding, paid the toll. The seller of lands or houses, the owners of which were absent or unknown, had to pay a fine of 24 (*paṇas*) [III. 9].

Tax-paying cultivators could mortgage or sell their lands only among themselves. Persons who enjoyed revenue-free (*brahmadeyika*) lands could mortgage or sell such lands only to those who deserved or were already granted such lands. Otherwise the sellers were liable to a fine of first amercement [III. 10].

Similarly, a tax-payer had to live only in a village of tax-payers. A tax-payer living in a non-tax-paying village was punished with fines. A tax-payer acquiring property in a village of tax-payers had the same rights and privileges as the tax-payer replaced [*Ibid*].

In the case of a land-owner unable to cultivate his lands, another might do so on a five year's lease at the expiry of which he surrendered the land after obtaining a compensation for his improvements on the land. An absentee landlord in possession of rent-free land who was obliged to sojourn abroad for a time was entitled only to its usufruct (*bhoga*) and not the other gains from the land which accrued to the king [*Ib.*].

Assessment. The basis of assessment was, as we have seen, a share of the produce due to the State, usually 1|6. Irrigated lands paid in addition water-rates (*udakabhāga*) varying with the means of irrigation employed, amounting to 1|5 to 1|3, as has been already described. Any one constructing a new irrigation work like a tank will be entitled to a remission of tax for 5 years (*Taṭākasetubandhānāṁ navapravartane pāñchavārshikaḥ parihāraḥ*); for repairing such a work, remission for 4 years (*bhagnotsṛishṭānāṁ chāturvarshikaḥ*); for bringing new land into cultivation by clearing it of jungles, 3 year's remission (*samupārūḍhānāṁ traivarshikaḥ*) and 2 years for land in a better condition (*sthalam*) [III. 9].

To this basic revenue demand of a share of the produce (known as *Asal jumma* in Mogul times) were added then, as now, various additional demands (*abwabs*, as now called). The State in need (*kośamakośaḥ pratyutpannārthakṛichchhaḥ*) may claim 1|3 or 1|4 of bumper harvests reaped on well-watered lands (*deva-mātṛikān*). It may also claim 1|4 of grain (*dhānyānām*) and 1|6 of the following: (1) *Vanya* (forest produce), (2) *Tūla* (silk-cotton), (3) *Lākshā* (lac), (4) *Kshauma* (jute), (5) *Valka* (bark), (6) *Kārpāsa* (cotton), (7) *Rauma* (wool), (8) *Kauśeya* (silk), (9) *Aushadha* (drugs), (10) *Gandhapushpa* (flowers), (11) *Phala* (fruits), (12) *Śāka* (vegetables), (13) *Kāshṭha* (fire-wood), (14) *Veṇu* (bamboo); (15) *Māṁsavallūra* (dried meats) and also 1|2 of (1) *Danta* (ivory) and (2) *Ajina* (skins of animals like kine).

And again: "Fowls and pigs should pay 1|2, smaller beasts (like goat and sheep) 1|6, and cows, buffaloes, horses, mules, asses, and camels 1|10."

All this demand will be for once only, and never twice (*sakṛideva na dviḥ prayojyaḥ*).

But the *Samāhartā* would also raise money by appealing to the people of the town and country for donations in aid of a specific undertaking (*Samāhartā kāryamapadiśya paura-jānapadān bhiksheta*) [V. II]. We may add to these the extra taxes levied on the village like *piṇḍakara*, *senābhakta*, *bali*, *utsaṅga*, *pārśva* or *pārihīnaka* by the *Samāhartā*, as noticed before.

CHAPTER VIII

MUNICIPAL ADMINISTRATION

Scheme of Administration. Kauṭilya has a regular plan on the basis of which the administration of cities was modelled. It was designed to deal with the special problems and requirements of urban life [II. 36].

Mayor (*Nāgarika*). The Mayor or Prefect of the city which was normally the *Sthānīya* or town proper is called the *Nāgarika*. He is also called *Puramukhya* [II. 16]. It will be recalled that as an officer the *Nāgarika* was subordinate to the *Samāhartā* as the Minister whose portfolio included Municipal Administration as a subject along with several other subjects mentioned above. In the list of these subjects is mentioned the subject called *Durga* which again stands for a number of departments and interests among which the interests of cities are mentioned as being administered by the officer called *Nāgarika*.

Sthanika and **Gopa**. We are further told that the *Nāgarika* stands in the same relation towards the city as the *Samāhartā* towards the province (*Samāhartṛi-vannāgariko nagaraṁ chintayet*). Like the province, the town also was divided into four parts or wards each of which was placed under an officer called *Sthānika*, while each *Sthānika* controlled a number of subordinate officers called *Gopas* who were responsible for ten, twenty or forty households.

The *Sthānikas* or *Gopas* of each town in the *Kauṭilīya* scheme performed functions which very probably corresponded to those of Megasthenes's Committee No. 3, of which we have got only a partial view from Megasthenes.

Census. They acted as Census officers registering the number (*jaṅghāgram-janasaṁkhyāṁ*) and names of males and females of each household, their caste, *gotra* and occupations, as also their livestock and their income and expenditure.

Inns. Reports of all persons who came to or went out of the town had also to be sent up by the persons concerned. The managers of almshouses or *dharmaśālās* (*dharmāvasathinaḥ*) had to send up to the city officer beforehand information regarding the advent into their establishments of all travellers and heretics (like the *Pāśupatas* and *Śākyabhikshus* according to the commentator) and obtain permission of the civic authorities for their residence. They were, however, free to accommodate ascetics and divines in whom they had confidence (*sva-pratyayāḥ*).

Factories. Similarly, craftsmen and artisans could admit to their factories (*svakarmasthāneshu*) their own relatives.

Shops. Traders also could similarly admit to their shops men of their class but they had to report against those who sold any merchandise in forbidden place or time or those who possessed any merchandise not their own.

Restaurants. Similarly, vintners (*Śauṇḍikāḥ*) sellers of cooked meat (*Pākvamāṁsikāḥ*), and rice (*Audanikāḥ*), and women of ill-fame could allow persons well-known to them to stay with them, but they had to send reports about persons who were extravagant in their expenditure or who were of dangerous tendencies.

Some of the municipal regulations in fact were very strict but they were very necessary in the interests of public good. We may cite the following as additional examples :

1. **Guests.** Masters of households must make reports of their guests arriving or departing. Otherwise, they would be held responsible for any crimes committed during the night they accommodated the unknown persons, and, in the case of uneventful nights also, they were punished with fines as penalty for evading civic regulations.

2. **Liability of Surgeons and House-owners.** Surgeons treating patients suffering from suspicious wounds (*prachchhannavraṇa*), and masters of houses finding persons preparing dangerous or deadly drugs (*apathyakāriṇam roga-maraṇotpādaka-dravyam*) must always report the fact to the civic officials in charge, viz., the *Gopas* and *Sthānikas*. Otherwise, they were liable to the same punishment as the guilty persons themselves.

3. **Suspects: Fifth Column Activities.** Suspected characters and Fifth Column agents were held under check by a series of regulations. Way-farers along highways (*pathikā mahāmārgachāriṇaḥ*) or by-paths (*utpathikāvivītapatha-chāriṇaḥ*), either within or outside the town, were charged with the civic responsibility of arresting suspects or undesirable persons frequenting temples and holy places, forests and crematories. Under this description came persons who suffered from suspicious wounds (*savraṇam*) or carried harmful implements such as house-breaking apparatus (*anishṭopakaraṇam*), or were carrying a load beyond their capacity, or had a suspicious appearance, or were discovered sleeping beyond time (*atisvapnam*), too much fatigued from long journeys or were absolute strangers to the country. These signs marked out criminal persons.

Such characters were also spied out within the town in deserted houses (*āveśana*) and factories (*śilpa-śālā*), liquor saloons, restaurants supplying cooked rice and meat, gambling houses, and the abode of heretics.

4. **Curfew Order.** The movements of citizens were forbidden at night when it was 6 *nālikās* before dawn and 6 *nālikās* after sunset. A *nālikā* being equal to 24 minutes, the period of restriction was from 9 P. M. to 3-30 A. M. A trumpet (*yāma-tūryam*) was sounded to announce the hours when the curfew commenced and ended and all movements between these hours, especially in the vicinity of the palace (*rājño grihābhyāśe*), were punished with fines. Inconvenience to the public which was caused by this restriction upon movement was obviated by granting exemptions in the following cases where free movement was a necessity : (1) persons attending delivery cases (*sūtikānimittam*), (2) medical practitioners, (3) carriers of dead bodies (*pretanimittam*), (4) persons moving about with lanterns (*pradipayāna-nimittam*), (5) persons going in response to the summons by drum of the city magistrate (*nāgarikatūrya*), (6) persons going to a theatrical performance passed by the censor (*prekshānimittaṁ rājānujñāṭa-nāṭakādiprayoga-darśane nimitte*), (7) persons called out of their houses by emergencies such as outbreak of fire, (8) persons moving with passes after time (*mudrābhiścha agrāhyāḥ akshaṇachārino*) [I. 36].

Exemption. Movement was, however, declared free for festal nights (*Chāra-rātri*) but persons going about in veil, or in inappropriate dress, males in female's and females in male's dress (*prachchhannaviparītaveshāḥ*), ascetics, persons with lāthi or weapon in their hands (*daṇḍa-śastra-hastāścha*) are to be examined and, if found guilty, to be punished (*doshato daṇḍyāḥ*).

Police (*Rakshiṇaḥ*). The Police were to inform authorities of any mishaps occuring at night, affecting life and property (*chetanācheta-nikam rātridosham*).

They were to be punished for interfering with the movements of persons entitled to freedom of movement or omitting to interfere where such freedom was not granted (*avāryaṁ vārpayataṁ vāryañcha avārayatām*).

Arrest of persons who should not have been arrested and non-arrest of persons who should have been arrested was both punishable.

Policemen found guilty of violating women were severely punished, and in the case of a lady of a respectable family (*kulastrī*), with the extreme penalty of death. Laxity of control of Police over places of indulgence (*pramādasthāne*) was punished according to the gravity of the occasion. [*Ib.*]

Jail Code. The city had its Jail under its Superintendent called *Bandhanāgārādhyaksha* [IV. 9]. The Jail Code was quite strict and fair. The Jail proper is called *Bandhanāgāra* attached to the court of the *Pradeshṭā* and is distinct from the lock-up called *Chāraka* attached to the Court of the *Dharamasthīya*. An officer letting off an accused from the lock-up under a bribe (*nissārayataḥ lañchagrahaṇena*) is to be severely punished. Again, one who releases from a *Chāraka* a man against whom an action has been brought (*abhiyukta*) will be fined and made to pay the amount of the claim against him (*abhiyogadānam*). An officer (prematurely and improperly) releasing a convict from the Jail will forfeit his whole property (*sarvasvaṁ*) and may even suffer the extreme penalty (*vadhaḥ*).

Fines are imposed for other offences as follows: releasing from a lock-up a prisoner without the order of the Superintendent, 24 *paṇas*; putting a prisoner to unauthorised labour, 48 *paṇas*: removing a prisoner and depriving him of food and drink, 96 *paṇas*; torturing a prisoner, heavy fine; similarly, extortion (*utkocha*).

Jail-deliveries. There are to be limited gaol-deliveries on the following occasions: (1) the day of the lunar mansion (*Nakshatra*) in which the king is born; (2) the day of full moon, when juvenile prisoners, the old, the sick, and the destitute only will be released. There are to be general gaol-deliveries on occasions of national rejoicing such as (1) Conquest of a new country, (2) Installation of Yuvarāja, (3) Birth of a prince. There is also a jail regulation that everyday, or once in five days, account (*viśodhayet*) is to be taken of prisoners as to (a) prescribed lobour (*karma*); (b) bodily punishment (*kāyadaṇḍa*) in lieu of (a); and (c) fine (*hiraṇya*) in lieu of (b) [II. 36]. Persons of known good character (*puṇyaśīlāḥ*) (whose offence is accidental) or those imprisoned for non-fulfilment of agreement (*samayānubaddha*) may pay a ransom or fine according to offence (*dosha-nishkraya*) [*Ib.*].

Precaution against Fire. There were also many municipal regulations to prevent the outbreak of fire which was perhaps very common, considering the predominantly wooden material of the architecture of the period. The kindling of fire was prohibited in houses having thatched roofs during the second and third quarters of the day in summer, or cooking had to be done outside the house. Every householder had to provide himself under the penalty of fines with eightfold apparatus for control of fire (*agninirvāpaṇa- sādhana*) comprising (1) the *kumbha* (a kind of vessel), (2) the *droṇī*, a trough made of wood for storing water, (3) the ladder (*niḥśreṇī*) for climbing up to the top on fire, (4) the axe (*paraśu*) 'to cut off beams', (5) the winnowing basket (*śūrpa*) 'to blow off smoke' (6) the hook (*aṅkuśa*) for tearing away things burning, (7) pincers (*kachagrahṇī*), for pulling out burning straw from the thatched roof of houses and (8) the leather bag (*driti*) for sprinkling water. On the public highways, on cross-roads, at the gates of town, and in all government buildings, rows of vessels in thousands filled with water (*kuṭavrajāḥ*) were always kept in rows as safeguard against fire. Thatched houses made of straw were not allowed to be built in the summer months within the municipal limits. The masters of such house-holds had to remain within doors at night and they were liable to fines if they failed to run towards the scene of fire. Fines were also imposed upon shopkeepers for similar offence, though lighter than those of householders. Those who caused an outbreak of fire through carelessness had to pay a fine of 54 *paṇas* but those found guilty of deliberate incendiarism were themselves burnt to death (*prādīpiko agninā vadhyaḥ*). Lastly, those whose occupation was connected with fire (e.g. blacksmiths) had to live in a separate locality of the town (*agnijīvinaḥ ekasthān vāsayet*).

Sanitary Regulations. The sanitary regulations of the municipality were enforced with strictness. Throwing dirt (*pāṁśu-nyāse*) or causing mud and water to collect on the roads (*paṅkodaka-sannirodhe*) was punished with fines and the fine was doubled in the case of the Royal Road thus interfered with. Committing nuisance in places held sacred (*puṇyasthāna*), reservoirs of water, temples, and royal buildings was also punished but exception was made when it was not done deliberately but caused by medicine, disease, or fear. Throwing inside the city the dead bodies of snakes, and animals like the cat, dog or mongoose was punished with a fine of 3 *paṇas*; in the case of the carcases of the larger animals like an ass, camel, mule, or horse, the above fine was doubled, while in the case of human corpse, the fine was 50 *paṇas*. Carrying dead bodies along roads or through gates other than the prescribed ones was punished, while the guards who connived at that offence were also fined. The cremation or burial of dead bodies (*nyāse dahane cha*) in places other than the prescribed ones was similarly punishable [*Ib*].

Building Regulations (*Vāstukam*). Town-planning was, indeed, regulated by the needs of sanitation. Every house was to be provided with a privy (*avaskara*), drain (*bhrama*), and a well (*udapāna*), only at the prescribed place (*grihochitam*), except in the case of temporary pits to serve the place of confinement (*sūtikā-kūpa*) or needs of festivities, but these were to be filled up as soon as the need was over. There were also wholesome regulations for location of (1) *Chakri-Sthāna*, sheds for goats and draught animals, (2) *Chatushpada-Sthāna* (to accommodate big animals like elephants), (3) *Agnishṭha* (oven), (4) *Udañjara-Sthānam*, a place for keeping big jars for water, (5) *Rochanī* (cornmill) and (6) *Kuṭṭanī* (mortar) [III. 8]. The object kept in view was to reduce to the minimum the inconvenience to neighbours. In case of two houses of which the above parts touched, it was obligatory to allow some space between them.

There was to be left some open space between houses (*Sarva-vāstukayoḥ prākshiptakayor vā kishkurantarikā tripadī vā*). There should be windows in each house for ventilation (*prakāśārtham alpaṃ ūrdhvaṁ vātāyanaṁ kārayet*). The rules governing house-building could be determined by common consent so as to prevent mutual inconvenience (*Sambhūya vā gṛihasvāmino yatheshṭam kārayeyur anishṭam vārayeyuḥ*).

The construction of doors or windows facing those of another's house to cause inconvenience was punished except when houses were separated by the King's Road or other highways. If any part of a house caused inconvenience to another house by obstructing its water course and letting the collected water damage its foundations (*parakuḍyam udakena upaghnato*), the owner was fined. If it was caused by accumulation of excreta, the fine was doubled [*Ib.*].

House-owners in fact were bound to keep the gutters of their houses in such condition as to allow easy passage to gutter-water. They had also to construct raised platforms in front of their houses and to leave open in perfectly communistic spirit for public use the places where fire was worshipped or grain was grounded. Violation of the above rules was punished with various kind of fines [*Ib.*].

Epidemics (*Upanipāta-pratīkāra*). Special measures were adopted in the time of epidemic outbreaks. Physicians went about the town distributing medicines (*aushadhaiḥ chikitsakāḥ*), while saints and ascetics were busy adopting religious remedies. The same measures were adopted in respect of cattle-plague (*paśu-vyādhi-marake*) [IV. 3.].

Rats. The danger from rats was recognised and measures were taken to destroy them. Cats and mongooses were let loose with penalty to those who would catch them. Poisoned food for rats was also widely distributed. In cases of virulent outbreaks of the plague epidemic, a 'rat-cess' (*mūshika-kara*) was imposed, requiring the owner of each house to trap a fixed number of rats per day [*Ib.*].

Medical Regulations. There were also rules regulating medical practice in the land. Dangerous diseases were always to be reported. Physicians were fined if the patient died of disease that was not previously reported. Error of treatment (*karmāparādhena*) causing death (*vipatti*) was more heavily punished. A surgeon was to lose the limb which he causes a patient to lose by his wrong operation (*marmavedha-vaiguṇya-karaṇe marmaṇi śastrakriyā anyathā-karaṇe daṇḍapārushyaṁ vidyāt bhishakkriyā-dosheṇa rogiṇo yad aṅgam upahataṁ tad bhishaja uphanyāt*) [IV. 1].

The medical profession comprised the following classes of specialists: (1) the ordinary physicians (*Bhishajaḥ* or *Chikitsakāḥ*), (2) those who treated cases of poison (*Jāṅgalīvidaḥ*), (3) those who specialised in midwifery (*garbhavyādhi-saṁsthā* and *Sūtikā-Chikitsakāḥ*), (4) the surgeons who accompanied the army with the surgical instruments and appliances, oils and bandages (*Chikitsakāḥ śastra-yantrāgada-snehavastra-hastāḥ*), together with Nurses who carried the necessary food and beverage for the sick and the wounded *striyaśchānnapāna-rakshiṇyaḥ*) and (5) the Veterinary surgeons who treated the diseases of cattle, horses, and elephants, of whom we have already given an account [X. 3].

Snake-bite. It may be noted that cases of snake-bite were so successfully treated that it drew the attention of Alexander who always consulted the Indian Vaidyas in preference to his Greek experts whenever such cases occured [Arrian].

Supply of Medicines. The towns had also hospitals with medical stores containing sufficient quantities of medicines which could last for years and were constantly replenished by fresh supplies (*navena anavaṁ śodhayet*). In the king's household, the medical store contained specially all the medicines that were required for midwifery, and medicinal plants and herbs were grown in pots in the hothouses. Indeed, the State maintained at its own expense gardens for the cultivation of medicinal plants and herbs [II. 4].

Washermen (*Rajakāḥ*) The dirt of clothes was attended to by the washermen who had to do the washing in fixed places on wooden planks or stones of smooth surface. Washing elsewhere was punished with a fine. There were various rules framed to secure honest dealings by washermen. Their own clothes were marked with a *mudgara* in order to distinguish them from others. They were fined if they used clothes other than those so marked, or if they sold, mortgaged or let out on hire the clothes of others. The substitution of one's clothes for another's was also punishable. Making delay in washing was also punished with fines. Washing was to show four degrees of whiteness in the stuff washed. The time allowed for washing corresponded to the degree of whiteness required. For example, 4 nights were allowed for best washing showing the utmost whiteness. Only a night was allowed for simple washing and removal of dirt, 5 nights were allowed for simple colouring (*tanurāgam*) ; 6 nights for colouring with indigo (*nīlaṁ*), saffron flowers (*pushpa*), lac (*lākshā*), and *mañjishṭhā* flowers. Costly clothes (*jātyaṁ vāsaḥ*) which required much skill, care, and labour (*guruparikarma yatnopa-chāryaṁ yatnasaṁskāryam*) were to be returned after 7 nights [IV, 1].

General Duties of the Mayor. There are prescribed certain daily duties to be discharged by the Chief Executive Officer of the city. He is to inspect (1) the sources of the city's water supply (*Udaka-sthānaṁ*) ; (2) the state of its roads (*Mārga*) ; (3) its grounds (*Bhūmayaḥ*) ; (4) its subterranean passages (*Chhannapathāḥ*) ; (5) the city's defences such as *Vapra* (battlement), *Prākāra* (wall), *Rakshā* such as *Aṭṭālaka* (tower) or *Parikhā* (moat).

He is also to keep charge (*rakshaṇam*) under proper Municipal arrangements of things lost (*nashṭa*) by carelessness or forgetfulness of the owners (*prasṛita*), and also of cattle that have strayed away (*apasṛitānām svayaṁ apagatānāṁ dvipada-chatushpadānām*) [II. 36].

Adulteration Lastly, public health was sought to be protected by punishing adulteration (*Samavarṇopadhānaṁ tulyavarṇaiḥ hīna-mūlyaiḥ dhānyādibhiḥ miśraṇe*) of food products of all kinds e. g. grains, oils, alkalies, salts, scents and medicines [IV. 2].

Control of Morals. The city's morals were protected by regulations regarding its public women (*gaṇikā*) under the control of a special officer called *Gaṇikādhyaksha* [II. 27]. He controls their earnings and properties. Their relations with their customers are regulated by law. Their incomes are taxed at the rate of two days income to be paid per month.

Amusements. There was no dearth of amusements and recreations in the city. These were provided by bands of (1) Actors (*Naṭas*), (2) Dancers (*Nartakas*), (3) Musicians, (4) Artists giving instrumental music (*Vādaka*), (5) Story-tellers (*Vāgjīvana*), (6) Nautch-girls (*Kuśīlavāḥ nartakīpradhānāḥ*), (7) Experts in exercises with ropes (*Plavaka rajjvārohaka*), (8) Magicians (*Śaubhika*), (9) Minstrels (*Chāraṇa*), and (10) Pimps.

Schools of Art. The city also provided for institutions for teaching the arts such as (1) Vocal Music (*Gīta*), (2) Instrumental

Music (*Vādya*), (3) Story-telling (*Pāṭhyam ākhyāyikādi*), (4) Dancing (*Nrittaṁ padārthābhinayaḥ*), (5) Acting (*Nāṭyaṁ vākyārthābhinayaḥ*), (6) Writing (*Lipi*)), (7) Drawing and painting (*Chitraṁ ālekhya-karma*), (8) Playing on harp (*Vīṇā*), flute (*Veṇu*) and tabor (*Mṛidaṅga*), (9) Thought-reading (*Parachitta-jñānam*), (10) Making scents (*Gandha*), (11) Making garlands (*Mālya*), (12) Massage (*Saṁvāhana*) and (13) Captivating (*Vaiśika*) (the art of the courtesan taught by the teacher, Dattaka).

Summary: Growth of Towns. We shall now in a summary try to obtain a view of life in the towns of India in those days. A standardised municipal administration was itself the outcome of a considerable development of urban life.

Evidence of Megasthenes. We have it on the authority of Megasthenes [Frag. XXVI] "that the number of cities in India is so great that it cannot be stated with precision, cities on the "banks of rivers or on sea coasts," or "on commanding situations, or on lofty eminences."

Kautilya on Towns or Forts. The location of cities as thus described by Megasthenes correspods closely to what Kauṭilya recommends for them (*Nadīparvatadurgaṁ nadīsaṅgame hradasya vā antardvīpaṁ sthalaṁ prāstaraṁ pārvatam*) [II. 3]. Kauṭilya here mentions all varieties of forts, such as those built (1) on the bank of a river, (2) at the confluence of rivers, (3) on a lake, (4) in an island, (5) in a desert (*dhānvana*), (6) in a forest (*vana*) and (7) on a hill in stone (*pārvataṁ prāstaram*). Of all these forts, Kauṭilya prefers the fort on a hill as being defended by nature (*svāraksham*), difficult to besiege (*duruparodhi*), and to climb up (*kṛichchhrārohaṇam*), while it can be further defended by hurling down blocks of stones and trees (*śilā-vṛiksha-pramokshaścha*) at the invaders (*mahāpakāriṇām*). He does not approve of a fort on a river (like Pāṭaliputra), as the river lends itself to crossing by bridges of wood, elephants and boats (*hasti-stambha-saṅkrama-setubandhanaubhiḥ sādhyam*), while it may also be drained of its writers (*anityagāmbhīryaṁ avasrāvyudakam*) or rendered shallow [VII. 10]. Like the Greek writers, Kauṭilya, as a native of Taxila, shows his preference for a hilly fort from his personal experience of the heroic defence offered by rock-citadels like Massaga or Aornus against the seige of Alexander. He also must have seen how Alexander was easily crossing the rivers by his 'bridges of boats'. By thus crossing the Jhelum, he was able to defeat his most powerful foe, Porus. In VII. 12, he definitely prefers a hill-fort to a fort on a river, and the latter to an inland frot (*sthala-durga*). In VIII. 1, he mentions the isolated fort on a hill, promontory (*antarīpa*), or island (*dvīpa*) as insecure for its paucity of population.

Numbers of Towns. The Greek writers further tell us that the territories of Porus comprised "5000 considerable cities, and villages without number" [Plutarch, Alexander LX]. The republican people called *Glauchukāyanika* (Glaussaii) boasted of 37 towns within their small territory. Megasthenes ascribes some 30 towns to the Āndhra country alone [Frag LVIX].

Grades of Towns. The town covered a wide range from the smallest called *Saṅgrahaṇa* as the centre of a circle of 10 villages, the country towns called *Kārvaṭaka* and *Droṇamukha* serving a group of 200 or 400 villages, the provincial town, *Sthānīya* (modern *Thānā*), the great city (*Nagara* or *Pura*) or port-town (*Paṭṭana*) up to the royal capital (*Rājadhānī*). We have to add to these the forts on the frontiers in charge of the *Antapālas* or located in special situations in the interior, in the midst of a desert, what Kauṭilya calls *Dhānvana*, or in a forest (*Vanadurga*), or swamps and lowlands (*Nimnāvaruddhamaudakam*).

Art of Fortification. The development of towns implied that of the art of fortification for which there is a standard plan handed down from earlier times. The descriptions of the Greek writers of what they had seen of the Indian fortifications at the cities like Pushkalāvatī, Maśakāvatī, or Varaṇā (Aornos) and at Pāṭaliputra, and the prescriptions laid down in the *Kauṭilīya* apply also to the cities described in the Epics. The Epic city was protected by ditches and battlemented towers, covered ways, water-gates, and portcullises.

These descriptions also correspond to what we see depicted on the monuments of Bhārhut and Sanchi in their sculptures of nearly the same age.

Buildings at the Capital. The *Kauṭilīya* city or the royal capital must have been known for its variety of buildings such as the State Treasury Building (*Kośagṛiha*), the State Granary (*Koshṭhāgāra*), the State Storehouse (*Bhāṇḍāgāra*) the State Arsenal, (*Āyudhāgāra*), the House of Merchandise (*Paṇyagṛiha*), the Courts of Justice (*Dharmasthīya*), the Council House (*Upasthāna* or *Mantrabhūmi*), the administrative offices or Secretariat buildings (*Mahāmātrīya*), the Jail (*Bandhanāgāra*), and the industrial factories (*Karmāntas*). It is interesting to note that the State Jewellery House was an under-ground building with three storeys (see references already given).

Its Amenities. The city offered considerable amenities of life to its ordinary citizens under the regulations of its municipality already described. Every street had its water-courses serving as house drains and issuing ultimately into the moat. Their obstruction by deposit of rubbish or any other article was punished. The law of easement was known. Houses could not have windows overlooking each other except across the street. Instead of a mechanised Fire-Brigade, there was a standing provision of vessels of water kept "in thousands" in the streets. Protection of property was further assured by a curfew order prohibiting movement at night in the interval announced by the trumpet. The Mayor of the city had to report all incidents and take charge of all lost and ownerless property. The security of the city, the problems of its Law and Order, were further secured by the Municipal Regulation that all inns, hostelries, sarais and places of entertainment should be under surveillance and should send reports of new arrivals.

The city had also its gay side represented in its inns, restaurants, eating houses, sarais, gambling houses, taverns, slaughter houses. The city had also its public dinners and its theatrical performances. The physician was also abroad. Royal processions were very spectacular.

Agreements of Kautilya and Megasthenes. It will also appear from the above account that the details of administration given by Kauṭilya are quite in keeping with the general description left by the Greek writers. But this subject may be examined a little more closely as providing evidence to show that the *Arthaśāstra* gives a picture of India under the Mauryas.

Town Officers. Megasthenes refers to the town official called *Astonomoi* as performing functions of which the details are given by Kauṭilya. Among these he mentions 'Supervision of Factories.' Kauṭilya states that these factories in the cities represented the Cotton Industry, the industry of Spinning and Weaving, the manufacture of gold, silver and jewellery which was pre-eminently a city industry and also the working of metals other than gold and silver, the armament industry, the building industry, the State-mint, the manufacture of dairy products and of forest products. According to Megasthenes, the factories of the cities were under government 'supervision'. Kauṭilya describes how this supervision was exercised by the Government Superintendents in charge of these factories such as the *Sūtrādhyaksha*, the *Sauvarṇika*, the *Lohādhyaksha*, the *Lakshaṇādhyaksha*, the *Kupyādhyaksha* and the like.

Megasthenes next refers to a group of town officials whose duties included control of the inns, care of strangers, and their medical treatment. Kauṭilya describes in detail how the city Administration took charge of these and many other duties as described above. Megasthenes has taken a special note of the duties of the city with reference to its "strangers" or foreign population, being himself a foreigner. Kauṭilya only includes this among other allied functions of the City Administration.

The third class of functions mentioned by Megasthenes concerns the registration of births and deaths. Kauṭilya mentions the officers called the *Sthānikas* and *Gopas* whose duty was to keep a complete register of the population and prepare a regular Census, besides a record of vital statistics. This work required the visits of officers from house to house for which the city was divided into a number of wards.

The fourth class of functions noticed by Megasthenes is described by him as "the control of the market." For this Kauṭilya provides a special officer called *Paṇyādhyaksha* whose duties have been already elaborated.

Next, Megasthenes mentions the city's "inspection of weights and measures." Kauṭilya shows that this was the charge of a special officer called *Pautavādhyaksha.*

The fifth class of functions mentioned by Megasthenes is described as "the inspection of manufactured goods, provision for their sale with accurate distinction of new and secondhand articles."

All these functions were exercised by the officer named *Paṇyādhyaksha* by Kauṭilya. As we have seen, he was the controller of prices, of markets for both home, and foreign, products, for food-products, imports and exports.

Lastly, Megasthenes mentions the duties connected with the collection of taxes charged on sales. Both he and Kauṭilya refer to an *ad valoren* tax on sales. Only while Megasthenes mentions the rate to be tithe, the *Arthaśāstra* mentions a variety of rates ranging from 4 to 20 per cent. The collection of these taxes was the charge of the officer called the *Śulkāḍhyaksha.*

As regards Megasthenes's reference to "accurate distinction of new and second-hand articles," it was secured by the *Śulkādhyaksha* of Kauṭilya. As we have seen, this officer was authorised to penalise fradulent understatement of the quantity or price of goods, or showing inferior samples to conceal the true quality of their goods in order to avoid taxation. We have also seen how fines were imposed on adulteration.

According to Strabo, these duties of the town officials were discharged by Boards of Five numbering six Boards in all. As F. W. Thomas point out [*Camb. Hist.*, I 489] : "No doubt, the system varried from place to place, and it may have differed according as the city was capital or provincial, subject to a sovereign or independent. We may think of the difference between a royal borough and a free town in our own middle ages."

District Officers. In this connection, we may also notice the correspondence between Kauṭilya and Megasthenes as regards the District Officials or the *Agronomoi*, most of whom were controlled by the *Samāhartā* at headquaters.

Agreement of Kautilya and Megasthenes : Irrigation. The first of their functions Megasthenes describes as relating to irrigation and land-measurement. We have already seen that in the *Arthaśāstra*, irrigation constitutes one of the charges of the *Samāhartā*. It is indicated in a number of terms such as *Nadīpāla* (the Superintendent in charge of rivers and their landing-places), *Tara*, *Nāva*, *Setu* and *Sītā*. It will be further seen that while the *Samāhartā* was the chief controlling officer or the Head of the Department, he had under him a number of departmental heads in the districts, one of whom, the *Sītādhyaksha*, Director of Agriculture, was in charge of irrigation and the revenue due from it. We have already seen how the water-rates varied with the means of irrigation employed.

Megasthenes has a further statement regarding "Officers who superintend the rivers, measure the land, and inspect the sluices from which water is let out to its branches from the main canal, so that every one may have an equal supply of it." The Superintendent of rivers is called by Kauṭilya by the appropriate name of *Nadīpāla*, as we have seen. The *Sitādhyaksha* is also described, we have seen, as "letting in water from river (*Nadī*), lake (*Saraḥ*), reservoir (*Taṭāka*) and wells (*Kūpa*) by regulation by sluice gates" (*Udghāṭam udghāṭyate nissāryate jalaṁ aneneti udghāṭo araghaṭṭakādi-yantram*) [II 24]. There is also a regulation that "letting out water and receiving it out of turn (*avāre*) or obstructing its flow into a field which should get it by its turn (*vāre*) is a punishable offence" [III 9]. This shows that (a) distribution of water from a canal was made by turns among its consumers, the cultivators, and (b) the distribution was effected by the operation of a sluice-gate. Cultivated fields irrigated by canals are described as *Kulyā-vāpa* [II. 24]. There is also a reference to a process of irrigation called *Srotoyantra prāvartimam* which means the arrangement or appliance by which the irrigation officer distributes the water among the fields by bringing it from flowing streams (*sāraṇīpāyitajalanishpannaṁ udakabhāgam*) [*Ib.*]. As regards the statement of Megasthenes that the distribution of water should be such that "every one may have an equal supply of it", it may be noted that the equality of the supply of water for irrigation is ensured by Kauṭilya. All are taxed equally and pay equally for the water they choose to make use of for their respective irrigation needs. The irrigation office had also to settle disputes as to distribution of water among different fields (*kedāra*) situated at different levels. A reservoir constructed later at a lower level (*paśchānnivishṭamadharataṭākam*) must not be allowed to flood a field irrigated by a pre-existing tank at a higher level (*udakena āplāvayet*). Nor should the flow of water from a new and higher to an older and lower tank be stopped, except where it is not required for cultivation [III. 9].

As regards the last point regarding the measurement of land, we have already described the details of Land-Revenue administration based on Survey and Settlement.

Hunting. The next class of duties Megasthenes assigns to District Officials concerned supervision of hunting. In connection with these duties, Kauṭilya provides for a regular Department of Forests under an officer called *Kupyādhyaksha* who was, as we have seen, in charge of the conservation of forests and its products by the employment of forest guards (*Vanapāla*), foresters who knew every inch of a tree, and could. gather in the various forest products. Associated with the *Kupyādhyaksha* was the *Vivītādhyaksha* whose duty was to secure the grazing grounds of cattle against the attack of wild animals. As we have seen, he had to employ a staff of hunters (*Lubdhakas*) who with their hunting hounds (*Śvagaṇa*) would keep the forests clear of all sources of mischief.

We have also seen that both Megasthenes and Kauṭilya are at one in describing how hunting was preeminently a royal pastime. As has been already noted, Kauṭilya is in favour of hunting as a healthy and useful sport for the king, but he provides for his safety by the employment of hunters (*Lubdhakas*) who, with the hounds of the royal kennels, would keep the forests free of ferocious animals like tigers, so that the king might learn in safety the difficult art of shooting at a moving mark like deer.

Forestory and Mining. Megasthenes mentions that the District Officials were in charge of the various industries connected with Agriculture, Forestry, Work in Timber, Metal Foundries and Mines. These duties Kauṭilya distributes among different Departmental Heads such as *Śītādhyaksha*, *Kupyādhyaksha*, *Ākarādhyaksha*, *Lohādhyaksha*, *Suvarṇādhyaksha*, and *Khanyādhyaksha* who are to render the accounts of their respective departments to their chiefs, *Samāhartā*, and *Sannidhātā*, at headquarters.

Roads. Lastly, Megasthenes refers to the duties of these officials to maintain the roads. We have already seen that the maintenance of the roads of Traffic (*Vaṇikpatha*) was one of the main duties of the *Samāhartā* in the administrative scheme of Kauṭilya. Kauṭilya refers to various classes of roads in the country which he calls (1) *Rājamarga* [I. 21; II. 4], (2) *Rathyā* or the provincial roads leading to the district headquarters, (3) roads leading to elephant-forests, (4) the by-roads leading to the fields (*utpatha*) and other by-ways, (5) and the roads meant for vehicular traffic.

The many agreements between Kauṭilya and Megasthenes are thus summarised by a classical scholar of repute, H. G. Rawlinson [*India and the Western World*, p. 67]: "Megasthenes' account of the constitution of Chandragupta finds close confirmation in many details in the *Kauṭilīya Arthaśāstra*. In this book, we find the king's palace described very much after the manner of Megasthenes, with its moats, ramparts, and towers. The king is surrounded by a body-guard of 'women armed with bows' [*Strīgaṇaiḥ dhanvibhiḥ* of *Arthaśāstra*, II. 3].

"The *Arthaśāstra* describes the highly organized bureaucracy in terms very similar to those employed by Megasthenes but in great detail. Thus Megasthenes tells us that the District officers were in charge of the forests, temples, harbours, mines, roads etc. He also describes the Six Boards who managed municipal affairs. But the general duties assigned to them are nearly the same. Thus Kauṭilya describes a Superintendent of Commerce and a Superintendent of Warehouses, who between them managed the markets, fixed the market-prices, regulated the trade in agricultural produce, levied the subsidies for provisioning the army, and collected the royal tithes on goods bought and sold. These were almost precisely the duties assigned to the first, fourth, fifth, and sixth Boards in the polity described by Megasthenes.

"The *Arthaśāstra* mentions a Superintendent of Courtesans and of Public Gambling, two functions of the police department not occurring in Megasthenes. But Megasthenes tells us how the king's agents employed the courtesans to obtain information. This ancient profession was treated as a recognised trade, taxed, inspected, and utilized by Government.

"On one important point Kauṭilya supplies information which supplements Megasthenes very considerably. This is with regard to the Board of Shipping. The Port Commissioner supervised sea and river-traffic, and ferries. Fishermen, merchants, and travellers, were all subjected to taxation and the ferries were in the hands of the Government. The fords were guarded by pickets who prevented suspects from entering or leaving. It was the duty of the Harbour Masters to assist ships in distress, and of those in charge of the ferries, to see that they were not used when the river was in a dangerous state.

"On the whole, the two accounts supplement one another in a remarkable manner."

CHAPTER IX

LAW

Sources of Law. Kauṭilya [III. 1] mentions four Sources of Law in an ascending order of validity viz., (1) *Dharma* [sacred precept based on Truth (*satye sthito dharmo*)] (2) *Vyavahāra* (agreement), (2) *Charitra* (custom) and (4) *Rājaśāsana* (royal decree).

It is further stated that the king is to administer that Law (*anuśāsat*) in accordance with (1) *Dharma*, (2) *Vyavahāra*, (3) *Saṁsthā* (*Lokāchāra*) and (4) *Nyāya*.

It will thus appear that *Rājaśāsana* or the royal edict which is mentioned as the fourth source of Law is really based on *Nyāya* or what is right in the view of the king. The *Rājaśāsana* or the king's application of the law, or what may be called the judge's decision or judge-made law, will be determined by *Nyāya* or Right.

Nyāya thus stands out as the ultimate source of law. It is explained that where there is a conflict in a case (*arthe*) between established custom, *Saṁsthā*, and *Dharmaśāstra* ('such as that of Manu') or between the king's decree (*Śāstraṁ rājaśāsanam*) and what is established by evidence (*Vyāvahārikaṁ Sākshivachanam*), the conflict is ultimately to be solved in the light of *Dharma*, i.e., *Dharmaśāstra*. In such a case, neither the evidence of witnesses nor the opinion of the king will count. When, however, there is a conflict between *Śāstra* or *Dharma-Śāstra* and *Nyāya* supported by local *dharma* and *āchāra* or custom, then *Nyāya* is to prevail. In such a case, the maxim of a *Dharmaśastra* will have no effect (*tatra pāṭho hi naśyati*). For instance, as the commentator points out, there is a maxim of the Dharma-śāstra that if there is a breach in the embankment, and in its neighbourhood a man is found with a spade in his hand, he is to be taken as the man who committed that breach (*Kuddālapāṇirvijñeyaḥ setubhettā samīpagaḥ*). But this decision will not be accepted in case the holder of the spade is a child incapable of committing that offence.

Kauṭilya emphasises the conception that the king stands for *Daṇḍa* which upholds *Dharma*, the law that governs the four castes and *āśramas* or stages of life, and also the customs of the people based on it. It is this *Rāja-dharma* which protects all other *dharmas* that will decline without this protection (*Chaturvarṇāśramas-*

yāyaṁ lokasyāchārarakshaṇāt| naśyatā ṁsarvadharmāṇāṁ rājadharmaḥ pravartakaḥ). Thus *Daṇḍa*, which enforces Dharma equally among all, whether son, or enemy, and is no respecter of persons, will ensure happiness in this world and pave its way for the next world too (*Daṇḍo hi kevalo lokaṁ paraṁ chemaṁ cha rakshati|Rājñā putre cha śatrau cha yathādoshaṁ samaṁ dhṛitaḥ*).

Courts of Justice. Persons well-versed in Dharma as expounded above are to be appointed as Judges called *Dharmasthas*. They are to be recruited from officers of the rank of *Amātyas* and *Amātyas* who are further qualified by the tests of *dharma* or righteousness (*dharmopadhāśuddhān dharmasthīyakaṇṭakaśodhaneshu sthāpayet*) [I. 10]

A Court is constituted by six Judges, three who are specialists in law, and three *Amātyas*. It is to be established at the different administrative headquarters both within the country (*janapada*) and also on its borders under the jurisdiction of the *Antapāla* at its towns (*durga*). In the country it will be established at the centres called *Saṅgrahaṇa*, *Droṇamukha*, and *Sthānīya* (*Janapadasandhyādishu janapadasandhau antapāladurge saṅgrahaṇa-droṇamukhasthānīyeshu*).

The Court used to sit in the morning.

Civil Law. It is described under the heads of marriage and dowry, inheritance, housing and neighbourhood (including trespass), debt, deposit, slaves, labour, contract, sale, violence, and abuse, gaming and miscellanea.

Validity of Agreements. There are rules pointing out the circumstances which invalidate agreements (*vyavahāra*) such as (1) *Tirohita*, where the agreement shows lapses due to its execution (a) without owner's consent (*svāmitirohita*), (b) in an improper place (*deśatirohitaḥ parokshisākshikaḥ*) where there were no direct eyewitnesses (c) after lapse of proper time (*kāla-tirohita*), (d) by improper transaction (*kriyātirohita*), and (e) with reference to parts of immovable property which are not visible objects (*dravyatirohita*) ; (2) *Antaragāra* (made in a secret chamber) ; (3) *Nakta* (made at night) ; (4) *Āraṇya* (made in a forest) ; (5) *Upadhi* (*chhadmakṛitaḥ*) (made by fraud) ; and (6) *Upahvara* (made in secret by the two parties to the agreement.).

Exceptions are, however, allowed under each case, specially when witnesses are available or where an agreement made in the privacy of home concerns women who are in *purdah* (*strīṇāṁ anishkāsinīnām*) or the sick, or those of unsound mind, who can not execute the agreement out of house.

Kauṭilya mentions different categories of valid and invalid agreements (*vyavahāras*) which seem to have been mixed up.

An exception is made in favour of agreements of class (1) (b) described above, which were entered into by a couple contracting a *gāndharva* marriage (*mithaḥ samavāye*) or of class (3) made by foresters (*araṇyacharāṇāṁ*), whether merchants (*Sārtha*), cowherds (*Vrajāḥ goshṭhavṛittayo gopālāḥ*), denizens of forests (*Āśramo vanakuṭumbinaḥ*), hunters (*Vyādhāh Kirātāḥ*) and wandering acrobats (*Chāraṇāḥ laṅghanaplavanādijīvinaḥ*).

Agreements made by unauthorised persons are invalid.

Hearing. There are rules of procedure laid down, allowing plea, counterplea, and rejoinder.

Procedure. The hearing of the case is to be preceded by registration (*abhilikhya niveśayet*) of the date of agreement, the names, place of residence, caste, *gotra*, and the substance (*kṛitasamarthāvasthayoḥ*) of the parties to the suit.

Statements of the plaintiff (*vādi*) and the defendant (*prativādi*) are also to be duly written and recorded.

The recorded statements are to be carefully scrutinised (*nivishṭāṁścha aveksheta*).

Recording Clerk A clerk (*Lekhaka*) of the Court not writing statements as they are made, writing what is not stated and not writing what is stated (*uktaṁ na likhati anuktaṁ likhati*), adding words of his own to what is stated to make it unobjectionable (*duruktaṁ upalikhati*), or objectionable, (*sūktaṁ ullikhati*), and thus alters the grounds of the suit (*arthotputtim vā vikalpayati sādhyasiddhiṁ anyathayati*) is fined according to the gravity of the offence (*yathāparādham*).

Quick Justice. There was not much of Law's delay. The Defendant is allowed 3 to 7 nights to file his defence. Delay will be fined. The Plaintiff must submit his rejoinder (*pratyuktaḥ saḥ abhiyuktadattottaraḥ pratibrūyāt*) the very day the defendant submits his answer (*pratyukta*). Otherwise he will be fined [III. 1].

Local Courts. The Law's delay was further reduced by decentralising the administration of justice. "Cases were commonly disposed of locally by reference to a body of arbitrators, permanent or constituted *ad hoc*, or by the officials of various grades ; and there was a system of appeals as far as the king, who was regularly present in Court or represented by a Minister (*Prāḍvivāka*). Offences against caste or religion were tried by committees called *Parishads*" [*Cambridge History*, I. 485].

For instance, disputes about boundaries (*sīmāvivāda*) in the villages were decided on the spot by the elders and wise men of the neighbouring 5 or 10 villages (*pañchagrāmī daśagrāmī vā*) [III. 9].

Or the elders among the cultivators and herds-men (*Karshaka-gopālaka-vṛiddhakāḥ*) or those who were the previous owners of the fields involved in the dispute (*pūrvabhuktikāḥ*), will be assisted by one or more other persons who are not non-residents of that locality (*abāhyāḥ*) and who have personal knowledge of the disputed boundaries ('such as the hunters of the neighbourhood'). They will lead them to the spot and point out the correct boundaries, wearing their distinctive dress different from that of others (*viparītaveshāḥ*). The hunters and such other persons having personal knowledge of the disputed boundaries may be associated with the judges of the dispute as a body or by one representative (*bahava eko vā*).

Disputes about the ownership of fields (*Kshetra-vivādam*) are to be decided by the elders of the adjoining villages (*Sāmanta-grāma-vṛiddhāḥ*). In case they differ (*dvaidhībhāve*), the decision will be according to the opinion of the majority of persons known for their piety and popularity (*yato bahavaḥ śuchayo anumata vā tato niyach-chheyuḥ*) [III. 9].

In a similar manner, by bodies of local abitrators, disputes are to be settled regarding (1) *Tapovana*, habitations of hermits (2) *Vivīta*, pasture lands (3) *Mahāpatha*, the highways (4) *Śmaśāna*, cremation grounds (5) *Devakula*, temples (6) *Yajñasthāna*, places for sacrifice and (7) *Puṇyasthāna*, sacred places.

The evidence of men on the spot counts most in justice (*Sarva eva vivādāḥ sāmantapratyayāḥ*) [III 9].

This principle of neighbourhood and local knowledge is accepted by all the later law-givers, such as Manu [VIII. 62; 258; 262; 259; 260]; Yājñavalkya [II. 150-2]; Bṛihaspati [1. 25-7]; and *Śukranīti* [IV. 5, 24; stating that 'foresters are to be tried with the help of foresters, merchants by merchants, soldiers by soldiers']. Each group was thus self-governing in the matter of its disputes and judging them.

Examples of Law : Marriage. Kauṭilya mentions eight kinds of marriage, *Brāhma*, *Prājāpatya*, *Ārsha*, *Daiva*, *Gāndharva*, *Āsura*, *Rākshasa*, and *Paiśācha*. In *Brāhma* marriage, the dowry of the bride is a free and loving gift to her of her father. *Ārsha* marriage is marked by the gift of a couple of cows (*go-mithuna*) to the bride's father. That it was a very common form of marriage in those days is evident from the statement of Megasthenes that the Indian's marriage was marked by a gift of "a yoke of oxen" [Frag. XXVII]. In *Āsura* marriage, the father receives a consideration (*Śulka*) in return for which he gives away his daughter in marriage to the bridegroom (*Śulkādānādāsuraḥ*) [III. 2].

Property and Rights of Married Women. *Strīdhana* may consist of *vṛitti*, or means of subsistence, or *ābandhya*, such as ornaments. *Vṛitti* thus includes *bhūmi*, agricultural land, and cash (*hiraṇyādi*), above a minimum of 200 *Kārshāpaṇas*, which will produce an income from its investment. The minimum is mentioned because an amount below it will be too small to produce a living income. There is no minimum limit mentioned for jewellery.

It is lawful for the husband to make use of his wife's property against emergencies like disease, scarcity, or calamity, and also in warding off dangers, and for a religious purpose. In the case of the first four approved kinds of marriage, when the husband and wife have become parents of two children, then the amount of *strīdhana* spent by them up to a limit of 3 years will not be required to be repaid.

A widow devoid of issue may remarry the brother of her husband with the consent of her father-in-law.

She forfeits her property given by her husband and father-in-law if she re-marries any one against the consent of the latter. If, while her husband is alive, she leaves him and re-marries another (*jñātihastād abhimṛishṭā*), the second husband must return the property given her by her first husband and father-in-law.

A widow with a son has to pass her property to him in case she re-marries [III. 2].

Re-marriage. Kauṭilya is for monogamy. He permits a second wife for the sake of an issue and a son]*Ib.*].

Marriage is dissoluble by prolonged absence, except in the case of a government servant (*rāja-purusham*) sent abroad [III. 4].

Re-marriage is allowed in the case of husbands turning ascetics, or being dead and leaving no issue. Even if there is issue, prolonged absence will be a cause for re-marriage.

But re-marriage is restricted to the relations of the husband, preferably brothers in order of age, and, failing them, a person of the same *gotra* and a nearest relation. In case of her marriage (*vedane*) with one who is not a kinsman of her previous husband, the man who gives away the bride in marriage (*dātṛi*) and also he who marries her (*vetṛi*) are both punishable.

If she lives with another man in an unlawful manner (*jāra-karmaṇi*), both (*jāra-strī*) will be proceeded against on a charge of adultery [*Ib.*].

A girl attains majority (*prāptavyavahārā*) at 12 and a boy at 16 [III. 3].

Inheritance. Sons as such have no right to property (*anīśvarāḥ*) when their parents are alive.

Sons only will inherit their father's property, and not daughters, except where there are no sons. In that case, brothers will have a share in inheritance with the daughters [III. 5]. Megasthenes also states : "The sons succeed the father" [Frag. XXVII].

A person dividing his property while living should not favour one son (*naikaṁ viśeshayet*) but should treat all sons equally. He should not also disinherit a son without sufficient reason. This points to the right to disinherit.

Sons of different kinds. Sons are described as of different varieties: (1) *Aurasa,* natural legitimate son: (2) *Putrikā-putra,* born of a girl appointed to raise male issue for him by a father who has no sons, (3) *Datta,* a son given away by his parents according to prescribed ceremony to another person who adopts him as his son; (4) *Upajata,* one who offers himself as a son to a person who adopts him, (5) *Kṛitaka,* one who is affectionately adopted as a son without any ceremony; (6) *Krīta,* one who is obtained by purchase from his parents and adopted as a son; (7) *Kshetraja,* son begotten on one's wife by another appointed by him for the purpose (*niyuktena*); (8) *Gūḍhaja,* a son begotten on one's wife in secret in the house of relatives, without appointment by her husband; (9) *Apaviddha,* a son disowned (*utsrishṭa*) by his parents and adopted by another by ceremony (*saṁskāra*); (10) *Kānīna,* son born to a maiden before marriage; (11) *Sahoḍha,* son of a girl carrying at the time of marriage; (12) *Paunarbhava,* son of a remarried woman [III.7].

A natural son born after the adoption of other classes of sons will be entitled to two-thirds of his father's property. The other sons of the same caste (*Savarṇa*) will be entitled to 1/3 and sons of other castes will be entitled only to subsistence and clothing i.e., livelihood. A *Savarṇa* son is defined to be one belonging to the next lower caste, a son, for instance, who is born of a Brāhmaṇa father and a Kshatriya mother, while an *Asavarṇa* son is born of a mother of the next lower caste, *Vaiśya.*

The marriage of a man of higher with a girl of a lower caste is *anuloma* marriage. The marriage of a man of lower caste with a girl of higher caste is *pratiloma* marriage. *Pratiloma* marriage is against *Dharma* (*dharmātikrama*) and should not be allowed by the king. Otherwise he will go to hell (*narakamanyathā*).

Offspring of mixed castes (*antarālas*) will have equal shares of inheritance, [III. 7].

Laws of Co-operation. Rural life is regulated by a body of wholesome regulations.

Persons failing to make their stipulated contributions to work for the village are fined. The cultivator not making his contribution in labour (*akurvato*) has to pay as fine double the amount of wages (*karmavetana*) payable to him. One who does not make his contribution in the form of capital or cash as per stipulation will have to pay double the amount as fine. One whose contribution is to be in kind, in food and drink, will have to supply double the stipulated quantities at the village communal dinners (*pravahaṇeshu goshṭhī-bhojanādishu*) for which they were required and promised.

Any one not paying his share of contribution towards the expenses of public amusements (*prekshā*) arranged by the whole village, such as Music, Dance, and the like, is not to be allowed admission to them by himself and with his relatives (*sasvajano na preksheta*). If he still tries to enjoy the performance by surreptitious means (*prachchhannaśravaṇekshaṇe*), he will be fined double the amount of contribution expected from him.

Any one not contributing to works for the good of the whole village (*sarvahite karmaṇi nigraheṇa*) will have to pay a fine double the contribution fixed per head.

A person acting for the welfare of the whole village (*sarva-hita*) is to be obeyed. Disobedience is punished with a fine of 12 *paṇas*.

There is also a provision that in the event of the village Headman (*Grāmika*) being away on public duty (*grāmārtha*), his responsibility in the village for its agricultural operations would be taken over by turns by those who owe their living to the village as its employees (*upavāsāḥ*).

Lastly, it is laid down that it is the duty of the king to grant concessions to organisations of villagers who by mutual agreements (*samaya*) carry out works of public utility (*deśahitān*) in the villages, snch as extension of cultivation (*setu* as defined in II. 6), bridges on roads (*pathi saṅkramān*), or decorative and protective works (*grāmaśobhāścha rakshāścha*).

The concessions granted by the State included the appropriation of the amounts of fines imposed on the above classes of defaulters, wanting in the spirit of co-operation and in the civic sense, by the village itself and not by the State [III. 10].

Debt and Interest. The legal (*dharmya*) rate of interest is stated to be 15% per annum. This rate probably applied to debts secured by mortgage (*bandhādhānapūrvā*), as the commentator suggests. This explains the great difference in rates. 5 per cent per month is stated to be commercial (*vyāvahārika*) interest; 10 per cent prevailing among traders dealing in goods brought from out of the way places difficult of access (*kāntāragāṇāṁ durgamamārgapaṇya-vāhināṁ vaṇijām*); and 20 per cent among merchants engaged in sea-borne trade (*Sāmudra*).

Charging interest in excess of prescribed rates is punishable. Witnesses of such usurious transactions (*srotṛīṇām*) are also to be fined [III, 11].

Agricultural Loan. Interest on grains lent (*dhānya-vṛiddhi*) is not to exceed half of the quantity lent if it is repaid at harvest (*sasya-nishpattau*).

If the interest is paid after the harvest, the account of the loan will be converted in terms of money (*mūlya-kṛitā*).

The amount of the interest on the loan under the new arrangement (*prakshepa-vṛiddhi*) is not to exceed half the money value of the principal (*udayād-ardhaṁ*).

If the creditor abstains from asking for repayment of the loan (at the time of the harvest) (*sannidhāna-sannā*), when the debtor can conveniently pay it, the creditor will be entitled to interest for one year only after which no interest will run on the loan (*vārshikī deyā*).

Interest on debts due from persons who are engaged in sacrifices taking a long time (*dīrgha-satrāḥ*), or who are suffering from disease, or students staying away for their education in the homes of their teachers (*gurukuloparuddha*) or who are minors or devoid of substance (*asāra*) shall not be added to principal so as to increase the principal (*ṛiṇam na vardheta*).

Limitation. A debt is barred by limitation if it is not recovered within ten years. This law of limitation is however relaxed in the case of a creditor who is not able to proceed for the recovery of the debt, for instance, a minor, a person too old or sick, or who has gone abroad (*proshita*), or has left the country (*desatyāga*), or in times of civil commotion (*rājya-vibhrama*) [III. 11].

Cultivators and government servants (*Rāja-purushāḥ*) are not to be arrested for debt while at work (*karmakāleshu*) [*Ib.*].

Deposits. If a deposit (*upanidhi*) is lost under circumstances for which the holder of the deposit is not responsible, it is not to be reclaimed. These are stated to be (a) conquest of the country with all its towns and rural areas by the forces of the enemy or by wild tribes (*Āṭavikas*), (b) destruction wrought by outlaws (*pratirodhaka*) on a village, on its stores of merchandise (*sārtha or vaṇik-sangha*), and its cattle farms (*vraja*), (c) practice of fraud or financial ruin, (d) loss (*ābādha*) caused to the village by fire or flood, and (e) sinking of a ship laden with goods or its plunder by pirates. [III. 12].

Prescription. Prescriptive rights to property are governed by certain laws. A ten years' enjoyment and possession of property neglected by its owner will make him forfeit it, unless the owner is a minor, or too old, or living abroad, or has left the country in consequence of civil disturbance. Twenty years' possession is required to acquire title to immovable property [III. 16].

Defamation. Crimes under this head are described as *Upavāda* (defamation), *Kutsana* (contemptuous talk or insult), and *Abhibhartsana* (abuse or threat). All abusive expressions, whether true or false, are actionable.

Threat. Threatening with an injury renders one liable to half the penalty for inflicting the same injury [III. 8].

Slander. Reference is made to calumnies regarding the learning (*Śrutopavāda*) or calling (*Vrittyupavāḍa*) of persons such as Rhapsodists and Story-tellers (*Vāgjīvana*), Craftsmen (*Kāru*), or Artists and Dancers (*Kuśilava*) respectively. A cause of action may also arise from defaming a person as the native of a notorious place (*Janapadopavāda*). As examples of countries and subjects of contemptuous reference, Kauṭilya cites *Prāghūṇakas* and *Gāndhāras*. Prāghūnaka is the name of a country which is to the east of the country called *Hūṇaka* for which there is another name *Chaṇḍālarāshṭra* in popular language, according to the commentator. The reference to Gāndhāra and to a country beyond it is another proof of Kauṭilya's knowledge of that region of which he is a native [III. 18].

Miscellaneous Offences: Feeding a Buddhist. Among these, Kauṭilya counts the offence of feeding on occasions of the performance of worship or *Śrāddha* (*devapitṛi-kāryeshu*) Śākyas (Buddhists), Ājīvakas, Śūdras and wandering ascetics (*pravrajita*), and makes the offence penal [III. 20].

Criminal Law. The administration of Criminal Law is described by the technical term *Kaṇṭaka-Śodhana* [IV. 1]. Among the cases contemptated we may mention theft, murder, burglary, or forcible entry, poisoning, coining, injury to property, criminal negligence, contumelious violation of caste-rules, boycott and other acts of employees, combinations to control prices, or fraud in regard to weights and measures. In all these matters, the magistrates (*Pradeshṭā*) or revenue and police officers, were assisted by an army of spies, and *agents provocateurs*, as we have already seen.

Examples. Some special laws may be cited.

Arrest. No suspect (*Śaṅkitaka*) is to be arrested after an interval of three days from his supposed commission of an offence, except on strong proof of his guilt. Arrest on mere suspicion was not allowed (*trirātrād ūrdhvaṁ agrāhyaḥ*). The idea is that an interval of 3 days would lose much necessary evidence, rendering useless the later interrogation of the suspect, and would give time for the removal of incriminating implements, etc. to the custody of innocent persons (*prichchābhāvādanyatropakaraṇadarśanāt*) [IV. 8].

Abetment. Abetment was punished, such as supplying a murderer or thief with food, clothing (*bhaktavāsa*) and materials like fire, or giving information and advice [IV. 11].

Sale of goods without licence (*anujñā*) was punished. Stocking of goods in unauthorised places for sale was punished by confiscation of the stock [IV. 2].

Adulteration. Adulteration of goods of all kinds was also punishable, as we have seen, such as passing off old for new things [IV. 2 and 6]; impure, artificial, inferior, and foreign things for pure, natural, superior, and indigenous ones; and especially adulteration of food-products [IV. 2].

Protection of Merchants [IV. 2]. Merchants travelling in caravans (*Sārthikāḥ*) should camp in a part of a village allotted to them and should make known the value of their goods to the headman of the village (*Grāmamukhya*). If any of the goods be stolen or lost, the village headman (*Grāmasvāmī*) must make good the loss. If the theft or loss occur outside the village on its borders, the loss is to be made good by the *Vivītādhyaksha*. If it occurs in a place not within his jurisdiction, then the officer called *Chorarajjuka* is to compensate the loss. If the loss takes place where there is no such officer, even in that unprotected locality, the responsibility for the loss must rest on some one in charge of this "No Man's Land," who is called *Sīmā-svāmī*. Failing him, the people of the neighbouring five or ten villages must pay for the loss. This provision therefore, acted as a sort of Punitive Tax for the security of life and property [IV. 13].

Thus long trains of caravans of traders could slowly wend their way, by day, and by night, in assured safety from Pāṭaliputra to Gandhāra through different regions under changing guards transferring their charge from one to the other. This security of transport must have built up the trade of the country.

Traffic Regulations. There is an interesting traffic-regulation: the charioteer who gives the warning to a passer-by by shouting

" Get out ! Get out !" (*Apehi! Apehi !*) is not punishable in case of a collision (*saṅghaṭṭane*) [IV. 13]. The same is the case with one driving an elephant.

Blocking roads and flow of water for cultivation (*karmodakamārgaṁ rundhataḥ*) was punishable [III. 10].

Security against Thieves. Pocket-picking (*granthibheda*) was known and severely punished [IV. 10].

Security of life and property was the charge of a Department of which the head is called *Pradeshṭā.* His subordinate staff comprised the two classes of officers known as *Gopa* and *Sthānika.* Their duty is to detect thieves on the countryside (*bāhya*), just as it is the duty of the Mayor of the city (*Nāgarika*) to guard its interior (*antardurga*) against such thieves [IV. 4].

Law and Order : Greek evidence. The general conditions of Law and Order then prevailing in the country as a whole are thus reported by Megasthenes. In commenting on the rarity of law-suits among Indians as evidence of their frank dealing, he goes so far as to say that " an Indian has never been convicted of lying " [Frag. 35]. He also says : " Indians are not litigious. Witnesses and seals are unnecessary when a man makes a deposit. He acts in trust. Their houses are usually unguarded."

Strabo [XV. i. 53] says: "Megasthenes who was in the camp of Sandrokottos (Chandragupta), which consisted of 400,000 men, says, that he found that the thefts reported on any one day did not exceed the value of 200 *drachmai* (=about £ 8 or Rs. 100).

According to Onesicritus, in Sind, no legal action could be taken, except for murder and assault. 'We cannot help being murdered or assaulted, whereas it is our fault if we give our confidence and are swindled. We ought to be more circumspect at the outset and not fill the city with litigation" [Strabo, XV. c. 702]. Absence of facilities for litigation is an index to the high standard of morals prevailing in the country. Strabo [*Ib.*] says: "The simplicity of their laws and their contracts is proved by the fact that they seldom go to law." And again: "They dislike a great undisciplined multitude and consequently they observe good order."

Megasthenes has a further statement [Frag. XXVII]: "The Indians neither put out money at usury, nor know how to borrow. It is contrary to established usage for an Indian to do or suffer a wrong and therefore they neither make contracts nor require securities."

Penal Code. A general sense of Law and Order was, however, consistent with, and was perhaps maintained, by a severe Penal Code.

Mutilation of limbs was the punishment for certain crimes. Strabo says: "A person convicted of bearing false witness suffers a mutilation of his extremities. He who maims another not only suffers in return the loss of the like limb, but his hand also is cut off. If he causes a workman to lose his hand or his eye, he is put to death." The *Arthaśāstra* [IV. 8 and 10] has two Chapters dealing with various forms of torture (*Śaṅkārūpa-karmābhigraha*) and mutilation of limbs (*Ekāṅgavadha*), but treats the provision for mutilation as a dead letter by the substitutes prescribed in the shape of fines in lieu of such physical penalties.

Purity of Justice. This was secured by a close inspection of judicial administration under the chief Officers, *Samāhartā* and *Pradeshṭā* [IV. 9].

Offences of Judges. A Judge (*Dharmastha*) showing temper (*vākpārushya*) on the Bench by browbeating (*tarjayati*), rebuking (*bhartsayati*), expelling (*apasārayati*), or snubbing, or defaming and abusing the suitor, is punished.

If he does not put the question which should be put, or asks what should not be asked, or does not take note of the answer given to his own question, or tutors, prompts, and hints to a witness (*pṛichchhyaṁ na pṛichchhati apṛichchhyaṁ pṛichchhati pṛishṭvā vā visṛijati śikshayati smārayati pūrvaṁ dadāti veti*) he is also punished.

A graver offence for a Judge would be to put irrelevant questions to the witness (*adeyaṁ deśaṁ pṛichchhati*); to decide the issue without reference to him (*kāryaṁ adeśena ativāhayati sākshiṇaṁ vinaiva nirṇayati*); to mislead a truthful witness (*chhalena atiharati satyavādinamapi sākshiṇaṁ chchalavākyena aparādhayati*); to tire out the patience of litigants and force them to leave the court by making delay (*kālaharaṇena śrāntam apavāhayati*); to cloud the issue by not taking the statements of the witness in the order in which they are given (*mārgāpannaṁ vākyaṁ aparityakta-kramaṁ sākshivākyaṁ utkramayati*); or to have a collusion with the witness by helping him with hints and clues (*mati-sāhāyyaṁ sākshibhyo dadāti*); and finally, to take up again a case previously disposed of (*tāritānuśishṭaṁ kāryaṁ punarapi gṛihṇāti*). Repetition of such offences will be visited by dismissal (*sthānād vyavaropaṇam*) [IV. 9].

Tampering with deposition. Taking liberties with the statements of witnesses by not recording them faithfully or tampering with the records of depositions will make the Clerk of the Court concerned liable to punishment varying with the gravity of the offence, as we have already seen.

Priority of the Laws of Kautilya to those of Manu and other Smritis. It will appear that Kauṭilya legislates for a society which is much older than that to which the Smṛitis of Manu and Yājñavalkya are related. The most vital and fundamental factor of a social system is the laws governing marriage and the position of women.

As we have seen, the Laws of Kauṭilya in this respect are based on social customs which approximate to Vedic Society rather than to the later type of society reflected in the Smṛitis of Manu and Yājñavalkya.

Divorce. For instance, while divorce is unthinkable in the Smṛitis, Kauṭilya allows it under certain circumstances. No doubt, Manu allows the husband to divorce his wife and re-marry, but the woman is denied this privilege. According to Manu, "a wife who drinks spirituous liquors, who acts immorally, who shows hatred to her husband, who suffers from an incurable disease, who is mischievously inclined, or who wastes his property, may be divorced by her husband who may replace her by another wife" [IX. 80]. Manu also mentions certain conditions under which the husband can desert his wife for a temporary period. But the above Smṛitikāras are unanimous in confining these rights of divorce and desertion to husband and denying them to woman who is enjoined to offer unquestioning and unconditional obedience and fidelity to her husband in both life and death [Manu, V, 151, 154 ; IX, 77-78 ; V, 148 ; Yājñavalkya, I. 75, 77]. Kauṭilya, however, is more rational and human by allowing women equal rights with men. He allows the woman to divorce her husband under specified conditions. One of these is that both must consent to a divorce on the ground of their standing mutual enmity (*Parasparaṁ dveshāt mokshaḥ*) [III. 3], so that they may start afresh in their matrimonial career. But Kauṭilya does not allow divorce when either party is against it. According to him, a woman, even if she is full of hostility against her husband, cannot seek divorce unless he consents to it. Nor can a husband seek it against his unwilling wife, however much he may dislike her.

At the same time, Kauṭilya does allow the wife to separate from her husband where her position is insupportable due to the husband being "of mean morals (*nīcha*), tainted by the commission of the worst sins (*patitaḥ mahāpātakadūshitaḥ*), or a murderer (*prāṇābhihantā*), or impotent (*klība*), or afflicted by consumption (*rājakilbishī*), or accused of bribery, or of treachery to the king, or where he is away in a foreign country [III. 2].

Kauṭilya, however, does not depart altogether from the ideals of conservatism and orthodoxy when he does not allow a divorce in the case of the first four approved kinds of marriage, as we have seen (*amoksho dharmavivāhānām*) [II. 3].

Re-marriage. There is, again, a difference between Kauṭilya and the later law-givers in regard to remarriage of woman. According to Manu, the sacred texts do not allow remarriage of widows, and it is condemned by the learned as fit for animals [IX, 65, 66]. He also states emphatically that a maiden can be given in marriage only once [IX, 47]. He does not allow a widow even to mention the name of another man in connection with marriage [V, 157].

Again, the period of absence of her husband, however prolonged, is no excuse for the wife to choose a second husband [IX, 76, 78; Yājñavalkya, I, 89]. While Yājñavalkya considers it to be a crime on the part of a man not to remarry after his first wife is dead [I. 89], he would not allow a woman to remarry under similar circumstances. This means further that a widow could not find relatives to associate themselves with the impious undertaking of giving her away for her second marriage, and, if she remarried by herself, she would be branded as a *svairiṇī* [I, 63, 64, 67]. The ideal laid down for a wife was even her self-immolation as a *satī* [I, 86].

Manu contemplates the case of a woman who, abandoned by her husband, or as a widow, of her own accord, marries a second husband, in which case the son born of such marriage is called a *Paunarbhava*, 'the offspring of lust' [IX, 175]. But he evidently allows the virgin widow to remarry [*Ib.* 176].

Kauṭilya treats the absence of husband as a cause for his wife's remarriage, as has been stated above. The time of such absence differed according to circumstances such as caste, whether the woman was a mother or not, or whether she was provided with maintenance (*aprajātā*, or *prajātā*; *prativihitā apratvihitā*). In the case of the husband being a Brahmin student who is absent for study abroad, the period of waiting was extended to 10 years, and, if she is a mother, to 12 years. Remarriage was not permitted where the husband is an officer of the State and is sent abroad on public duty. Where the aforesaid periods of waiting were exceeded, the wife was permitted to take to a second husband of the same caste to prevent the extinction of her family. The wife might also remarry a second husband after her liking (*yatheshṭaṁ vindet*) where due to the absence of husband, she lacks maintenance and is not maintained by her relations, and is thus compelled to remarry as a means of livelihood, or of saving herself against difficulties [III. 4]. In the case of the approved marriages of four kinds aforesaid (*Dharmavivāha*), remarriage is allowed to the wife who is a *Kumārī* or a virgin, in case her husband has gone abroad, after waiting for his advent for the prescribed period varying from three months to one year. But the dissolution of the marriage was to be formally effected with the permission of the Court (*Dharmasthairvisṛishṭā*).

Remarriage is also allowed to women whose husbands have been abroad too long (*dīrghapravāsīnaḥ*) or have turned ascetics (*pravrajita*) or are dead (*preta*) [III. 4], or where the wife was left without issue (*Kuṭumbakāmā*), in which case she was entitled to the *Strīdhana* given to her by her former father-in-law and husband [III. 2].

Post-puberty Marriages. These marriages are allowed both by Kauṭilya and Smṛitikāras, but they differ in their attitude towards it. The adult bride loses all her claims upon her father when she chooses for herself a husband of her own choice [Manu IX, 90, 91; III, 27-30, 35; IX, 93, III. 36, 40; Yājñavalkya, I, 64; II, 287; etc.,]. Kauṭilya's position is that any kind of marriage is to be approved if it is a source of satisfaction to all concerned (*Sarveshāṁ prītyāropaṇam apratishiddham*) [III. 2].

Anuloma Marriages. Both Kauṭilya and the Smṛitis are at one in allowing *Anuloma* marriages [Yājñavalkya I. 57; Manu III. 14-19]. But, unlike Kauṭilya, the *Smṛitis* do not allow the marriage of a man of the three higher castes with a Śūdra girl. Kauṭilya is more liberal in not recognising any difference between the three higher castes and the Śūdra in this respect. The only distinction that Kauṭilya makes is as regards the division of inheritance. As we have already seen, the son of a man's Brahmin wife is entitled to four shares; that of his Kshaṭriya wife three shares; that of his Vaiśya wife two shares; and the son of a Śūdra wife one share [III. 6]. Then, again, while Manu will not give any share in his peternal propery to the son begotten of a Śūdra woman who is not legally married by the man of the upper classes, Kauṭilya would grant such a son a third share of the property [Manu IX. 155: *Arthaśāstra*, III, 6.].

Other features of Mauryan Society. Mauryan society as depicted by Kauṭilya was different in other ways from the society of the Smṛiti times. We have seen that Āryas were in the habit of drinking wine provided it was of prescribed quantity [II. 25]. On the other hand, Yājñavalkya will not allow even taking meals at the house of one who lives by selling liquor (*Surājīva*) [I. 164]. Again, Mauryan society saw Brahmins freely taking to a military career. The Mauryan army had its Brahmin regiment, as we have already seen [IX. 2].

It may be noted in conclusion that the *Ṛigveda* knows of post-puberty marriages, has no idea of the custom of *Satī*, and knows of widow-marriage. In the funeral hymn of the *Ṛigveda*, the widow is stated to lie by the side of her husband only for a moment. She is asked "to come unto the world of life" [*Rv.* X. 85, 21-22; 18, 8]. In the Epics also we see that the marriage of girls after puberty was a prevailing custom along with that of *Svayaṁvara.*

Thus the legal data and material furnished by the *Arthaśāstra* of Kauṭilya constitute valuable evidence proving its antiquity [See H. G. Narahari, *Society in Mauryan India.* in the *New Indian Antiquary* for February, 1940 for a good discussion of this topic].

CHAPTER X

THE ARMY

Chandragupta's Army. We have now considered the various aspects of Mauryan Civil Administration. We shall now give an account of the Mauryan Military administration. Chandragupta must have built up a powerful military force by which he was able not merely to overthrow the Greek rule in the Punjab and the powerful empire of the Nandas, but also to "overrun the whole of India," in the words of Plutarch. The Greek account of Nanda's Army estimates it at 2,00,000 infantry, 20,000 cavalry, 3,000 elephants, and 8,000 four-horsed chariots. Nanda, therefore, is called in the *Purāṇas* a *Mahāpadmapati*, 'the Lord of an infinite host.' Chandragupta must have mustered a larger and more powerful army to break this host. His army is computed by Pliny at 6,00,000 infantry, 30,000 cavalry and 9,000 elephants [*Natural History*, IV. 22]. Pliny does not mention the number of his war-chariots which may be taken as the same as that of Nanda, namely, 8,000 chariots. If, as Arrian has pointed out, each chariot carried two soldiers, besides the driver, and an elephant carried three archers, besides the Mahout, then the total number of men in Chandragupta's army would be 6,00,000 infantry, 30,000 horse-men, 36,000 men with the elephants, and 24,000 men with the chariots, totalling 6,90,000 in all, excluding followers and attendants.

A Standing Army. This vast army was not of the nature of a militia or a citizen's army but a regular standing army in receipt of due remuneration paid by the State, supplied by the State with necessary equipment such as horses, arms, elephants, and stores, and always remaining at its disposal and command. Kauṭilya considers it essential that the army should always be in a state of readiness instead of being distributed among different centres on prescribed missions from which they cannot free themselves to join colours at call (*vikshiptasainyaṁ netarat kārya-vyāsaktaṁ pratisaṁhartumśakyam*) [VII. 9.] In that view, Kauṭilya also prefers the tried troops serving at provincial garrisons to mercenary troops, because the former are habitually bound to their master in ties of service and loyalty (*Nityasatkārānugamāchcha maulabalaṁ bhṛitabalāchchhreyaḥ*) [IX.2]

Account of Megasthenes: War-Office. According to Megasthenes, the army was controlled by a War-Office constituted by thirty members distributed among six Boards of five members each. The six Boards were in charge of the following departments of the army viz. I. The Infantry II. The Cavalry III. The War-Chariots IV. The Elephants of War V. Transport, Commissariat, and Army Service, including the provision of drummers, grooms, mechanists, and grass-cuttets VI. The Board "to co-operate with the Admiral of the Fleet."

The duties of Board V are thus described: "They arrange for bullock-trains which are used for transporting engines of war, food for the soldiers, provender for the cattle, and other military requisites. They supply servants who beat the drum and others who carry gongs; grooms also for the horses, and mechanists for other assistants. To the sound of gongs they send out foragers to bring in grass, and by a system of rewards and punishments ensure the work being done with despatch and safety" [Megasthenes, Frag. XXXIV].

Constituents of the Army: *Mahābhārata.* The traditional description of the Hindu Army is that it is made up of four limbs. It is always described in the Arthaśāstra as *Chaturaṅgabala* [e.g. II. 33; IX. I, 2, etc]. Megasthenes mentions two other constituents of the army and these also are recognised from very early times. For instance, the full complement of an army, according to the *Mahābhārata*, comprises (1) the chariot, (2) the elephant, (3) the horse, (4) the foot, (5) the general labourers for transport, commissariat, and other services (*vishṭi*), (6) the navy, (7) the spies and (8) the *Deśikas*, meaning probably scouts and topographic leaders. It is apparent that numbers, (5), (6), (7) and (8) correspond to the supplementary components of the army noticed by Megasthenes.

Kautilya: Medical and Ambulance Arrangements. It is also interesting to note that Kauṭilya also refers to these subsidiary divisions of the army. "The work of scouts such as examination of camps, roads, rivers and digging of wells, landing places on rivers and preparing these for use; the transport of machines, weapons, armour, instruments and provision; carrying away from the battle-field men that are knocked down, along with their weapons and armour—these constitute the work of a special set of labourers (*śibira-mārga-setu-kūpatīrtha-śodhankarma yantrāyudhāvaraṇopakaraṇa-grāsavahanam āyodhanāch-cha praharaṇāvaraṇa-pratividdhāpanayanam iti vishṭi-karmāṇi*)' [X.4]. The other necessary aids to the army mentioned by Kauṭilya which Megasthenes has failed to observe are medical and ambulance arrangements thus described by him: "Surgeons carrying in their hands surgical instruments (*śastra*), apparatus (*yantra*), medicines (*agada*), healing oils (*sneha*), and bandages (*vastrāṇi*), and nurses with prepared foods and beverages, should always be in attendance and encourage the soldiers to fight" [XI. 3].

This is certainly a most creditable anticipation in that age of the work of the Red Cross Society which is as essential for the efficiency of the army as any of its four arms. The reference of Megasthenes to grooms, mechanists and grass-cutters is also supported by Kauṭilya who states that 'the captain with his retinue comprising mechanists (*vardhaki sthapati*) and labourers (*vishṭi*) should march in advance, preparing the path beforehand, digging wells of water [X. I]' and that 'supplies of grass, firewood and water should be previously known' [X. 2,] and "food-stuffs and provisions should be carried in double the quantity that may be required in any emergency" [X. 2]. Finally, Kauṭilya also mentions trumpets, flags and ensigns [X. 6].

Camel Corps. It is noteworthy that Kauṭilya [IX. I] provides for a supplementary force of Cavalry and Camels aided by Asses for operating in dry weather and on non-marshy ground (*kharoshṭrāśvabalaprāyaḥ*).

Senapati. In the Kauṭilīya scheme, the entire War-Office with all its departments is placed under the supreme control of the Commander-in-Chief known as the *Senāpati* who is to be possessed of all military qualifications. He should be proficient in all modes of warfare (*sarvayuddha*), in the art of handling all kinds of weapons of war (*praharaṇa*), a man of high general education (*vidyāvinīta*) and capable of controlling all the four Divisions of the army. Each of these Divisions will have its own chief under the control of the Commander-in-Chief at the top. He is to maintain the discipline of the army at peace (*sthāne gamananivrittau*), on the march (*yāne*), and in attack (*praharaṇe*). He is also to divide the army into *Vyūhas* or regiments with their distinctive marks in regard to trumpets (*tūrya*), ensigns (*dhvaja*), and flags (*patākā*) [II. 33].

Other Officers. The list of salaries given above shows that the War-Office comprised the following Chief Officers :

1. *Senāpatī*, with a salary of 48,000 *paṇas* (the highest salary in the Service).
2. *Praśāstā*, drawing 24,000 *paṇas*.
3. *Nāyaka*, drawing 12,000 *paṇas*.
4. *Mukhya*, getting 8,000 *paṇas*.

We shall now discuss the details of administration relating to each of the divisions of the army.

Infantry: Six classes of troops. We have already seen how Chandragupta's army was recruited from a variety of sources and composed of various classes of men. Kauṭilya describes them as follows :

(1) *Maula*: troops in charge of the *Mūla*, the root, or centre of provincial administration known as *sthānīya*, a provincial garrison (*mūla-rakshaṇam* in IX. 2.);

(2) *Bhṛita*, mercenary troops engaged on pay ;

(3) *Sreṇī*: gild-levies, troops recruited from the warrior clans belonging to countries such as Kāmboja, Surāshṭra and the like [XI. 1] ; and also interpreted to mean soldiers pursuing the military art as a means of livelihood in the province (*Janapadavartyā-yudhīyagaṇaḥ*) [I. 33 ; IX. 2, and X. 1] ;

(4) *Mitra-bala*: army supplied by an ally ;

(5) *Amitra-bala*: troops recruited from the enemy country ;

(6) *Aṭavī-bala*: the troops recruited from the forest tribes under the Warden of the forests (*Aṭavīpāla*) [*Ib.*].

Sreni-bala. Of these classes of soldiers, those coming from warrior-clans took to arms as a profession and are called by Kauṭilya *Śastropajīvinaḥ* [XI.1]. As just stated, Kauṭilya mentions the Kāmbojas and Surāshṭras as examples of such military clans. He also mentions a class of *āyudhīya* villages which were like colonies of professional soldiers censussed by the rural officers [II. 35]. It is interesting to note that Pāṇini mentions military communities called *Āyudhajīviśaṅghas*.

Atavikas. The importance of the wild tribes as the source of a gallant soldiery is adequately recognised by Kauṭilya. He says [VII. 10]: "The country full of forts, clans of robbers (*Chora-gaṇa*), Mlechchha people (like the *Kirāta* highlanders), and wild tribes (*Aṭavī*) is always a menace." Again, a king in despair (*utsāhahīna*) is advised to turn as a last source of strength to an army recruited from the fearless soldiers (*pravīra-purushāṇāṁ*) of the warrior-clans (*śreṇī*), gangs of brigands (*choragaṇa*), the foresters (*Āṭavika*), and the *Mlechchha* tribes (like the Kirātas) [VII. 14]. Among these again Kauṭilya [VIII. 4] values the *Āṭavikas* more than the *Choras* or *Pratirodhakas*. These are used to nocturnal operations, hiding in forests (*rātri-satra-charāḥ*), and to petty plunder of rich individuals (*pradhānakopakāścha*). The *Āṭavikas*, on the other hand, are a settled people, proud of their country (*svadeśasthāḥ*), operating openly and in day-light (*prakāśā dṛiśyāścharanti*), engaging in open warfare (*prakāśayodhinaḥ*) and publicly plundering property and killing people (*apahartāro hantāraścha*) like independent sovereigns (*rājas-*

adharmāṇaḥ), are many in number (*prabhūtāḥ*), and invincible (*vikrāntāḥ*). The *Āṭavikas* are also counted by Kauṭilya as a source of external danger (*bāhyakopa*) to the State along with the *Rāshṭra-mukhyas* (the provincial governors) and *Antapalas* [IX. 3]. These soldiers are best paid in kind (*kupya*) and in loot obtained in the enemy's country [IX. 2].

In one sense, Kauṭilya says that the mercenary troops are better than the troops recruited from the warrior clans. They are always ready for action and more at command (*vaśya*).

Caste. Kauṭilya preserves the tradition that the army could be recruited from all the castes, Brāhmaṇa, Kshatriya, Vaiśya, and Śūdra. But Kauṭilya does not think much of Brāhmaṇa soldiers, as they are forgiving to the prostrate enemy. The Kshatriya soldiers are more proficient in the military arts. The other classes of soldiers are useful for their strength of number [IX. 2].

Officering : Padika-Senapati-Nayaka. The officering of the army for field operations was according to a traditional plan. For every 10 elephants and 10 chariots accompanied by 50 horsemen and 200 foot-soldiers, there was a commander called *Padika* ; for every 10 *Padikas* or 100 elephants with 500 horsemen and 2,000 infantry, or 100 chariots with the same number of horsemen and infantry, there was a commanding officer called *Senāpati* (like the Commander of a Division). Over 10 such *Senāpatis* was an officer called the *Nāyaka* [X. 6]. It is apparent that the officering and command were based on the decimal system of computation. The entire infantry force was under the control of the officer called *Pattyadhyaksha* [II. 33]. His duty is to distribute the various classes of soldiers among different places according to their respective fitness. He has to train up the infantry (*Patti*) in fighting under different conditions, viz., (1) low and marshy land, (2) in high and dry land, (3) in broad day-light (*prakāśa*), (4) by strategy (*kūṭayuddha*), (5) in trenches (*khanakayuddhaṁ bhūmiṁ khātvā tatra sthitvā kriyamāṇam yuddham*), (6) from high ramparts (*ākāśayuddhaṁ prākārādikaṁ āruhya kriyamāṇaṁ yuddham*), (7) in day and (8) in night [*Ib*].

We may consider here some details on the subject in V. 3 indicating gradation of officers by their salaries. The highest Army Officer was *Senāpati*, Commander-in-Chief, one of the highest officers of the realm, equal in status to the Queen, Crown Prince and Prime Minister and receiving the same salary of 48,000 *paṇas*. Below him was the *Nāyaka* drawing 12,000. Then came the *Mukhyas* drawing 8,000 and *Adhyakshas* 4,000. Perhaps the *Mukhyas* and *Adhyakshas* in charge of the different forces, Infantry, Cavalry, Elephant and Chariot, were administration officers and not field officers as mentioned above.

Equipment : Greek account. Details regarding the equipment of the infantry may be derived from a variety of sources. According to Arrian, 'the foot soldiers carry a bow of equal length with the man who bears it. This they rest upon the ground and pressing against it with their left foot, thus discharge the arrow, having drawn the string far backwards ; for the shaft they use is little short of being three yards long and there is nothing which can resist an Indian archer's shot—neither shield nor breastplate nor any stronger defence, if such there be. In their left hand they carry bucklers of undressed ox-hide, which are not so broad as those who carry them but are about as long. Some are equipped with javelins instead of bows, but all wear a sword which is broad in the blade, but not longer than three cubits, and this, when they engage in a close fight (which they do with reluctance), they wield with both hands to fetch down a lustier blow."

Account of Kautilya. Kauṭilya, however, gives a complete account of weapons and military engines then in use. These he classifies according to their uses whether in battles, in the construction or defence of forts or in the destruction of cities or strongholds of enemies. There were some machines which were immovable ((*sthita-yantrāṇi*) ; others that were movable (*chalayantrāṇi*) like *Chakra*, *Triśūla*, *Mudgara*, *Gadā* etc. ; there were also weapons with piercing sharp edges (*halamukhāni*) such as *Śakti*, *Prāsa*, *Kunta*, etc. There were varieties of bows according to their make whether of bamboo, wood, or horn, as also of bow strings and of arrows tipped with iron, bone or wood so as to cut, rend or pierce. Three kinds of swords are mentioned, with a crooked point or with curved blade, sharp and long ; their handles were made of the horns of the rhinoceros, buffalo, or of the tusks of elephants or of wood etc. There are also razor-like weapons such as *paraśu*, *kuṭhāra* etc. Some machines are for hurling stones. There were also varieties of armour or coat of mail for the whole body such as *loha-jāla* (complete armour and helmet), *loha-jālikā* (armour without helmet), *loha-paṭṭa* (armour without arms), *loha-kavacha* (coat of mail with breast-plate and back cover), *sūtra kaṅkaṭa* (dress of woven threads), and different armours of skins of rhinoceros, elephant, alligator etc ; and shields for various parts of the body such as helmets (*śirastrāṇa*), collars (*kaṇṭhatrāṇa*), arm-guards (*kūrpāsa*), head-covers (*hastikarṇa*), belts (*peṭī*), all manufactured by skilled artisans [II. 18].

Soldier in Sculpture. The literary evidence, Greek or Indian, as to the arms and weapons of Ancient India is confirmed by the available evidence of old Indian art. A nearly life-size figure of an infantry soldier armed as described by Megasthenes appears among the sculptures of Bharhut which are generally taken to date from the age of Asoka. The most accurate description, however, of the early Indian arms may be obtained from the sculptures of Sanchi and other topes of the first century A.D. described by Cunningham and Fergusson. "In one of them," says Cunningham, "there is the representation of a siege...the soldiers wear a tight-fitting dress and kilt; the arms are a sword and bows and arrows. The swords are short and broad and tally exactly with the description of Megasthenes," given above. The bas-reliefs represent nearly all the foot-soldiers as archers, which is in accord also with the statement of Megasthenes. Some of them, Megasthenes states, use darts instead of arrows. This is also confirmed by one of the bas-reliefs showing a soldier covered by a shield and holding a dart horizontally, ready to launch it forward. The same dart is placed in one of the porter's hands at the western gate. The most usual shield represented in the bas-reliefs is also long and narrow and rounded at the top, as described by Megasthenes. The shields of the cavalry were, according to Megasthenes, smaller than those of the infantry. This is also the case throughout the bas-reliefs in which the horse-men's shield is always about 2 ft. in length.

The arms represented on the Bhilsa topes are bows and arrows, dagger, sword, spear with triangular head, axe, battle-axe, trident, infantry and cavalry shields.

On another of the bas-reliefs at Sanchi is represented a legend of Prince Siddhārtha shooting an arrow which pierced an iron target. In the foreground of the picture are three warriors armed with Parthian bow and short straight sword of Roman shape, carried over the right shoulder; they also wear cross-straps for carrying their quivers. Drums and pipes accompany them.

Indian Soldiers fighting in Europe. It may be noted that the valour of the Indian Army was known beyond the bounds of India in very early times. As early as 480 B. C. the army of Xerxes which invaded Greece comprised an Indian contingent clad in cotton garments (probably *sūtra-kaṅkaṭa* referred to by Kauṭilya, as mentioned above) and armed with cane bows and iron-tipped cane arrows.

Parade. The infantry had to take a regular drilling and training. The king himself was to hold a review of troops every day at sunrise and witness their military manoeuvres (*Śilpadarśanaṁ kuryāt, Śilpayogyāḥ kuryuḥ*) [V. 3.].

Strong points. One point of the infantry's superiority to the other arms of the military is stated by Kauṭilya to be that the infantry is capable of taking up arms (*śastravahanam*) and of military exercises (*vyāyāma*) on all kinds of soil or ground (*sarvadeśa*) and in all weathers, dry or wet (*sarva-kāla*). The horses, elephants, and chariots cannot operate in all weathers or on swampy soil [X. 4].

Address to Soldiers. By way of encouraging the army in the field of battle, Kauṭilya suggests the delivery of the following inspiring speeches to them. The king should address his soldiers as follows : "I am a paid servant like yourselves; this country is to be enjoyed (by me) together with you ; you have to strike the enemy specified by me (*Tulyavetanosmi*; *bhavadbhisśaha bhogyamidaṁ rājyaṁ*; *mayābhihitaḥ parobhihantavyaḥ*) [X. 3].

His Minister and Priest should encourage the army by saying thus: "It is declared in the Vedas that the destiny which is attained by sacrificers properly performing their sacrifices is the very destiny which lies in store for the brave" (*Vedeshvapyanuśrūyate*—'*samāptadakshiṇānāṁ yajñānāmavabhṛitheshu sā te gatir yā śūrāṇām iti*' [*Ib.*]

Again: 'Beyond those places which Brāhmaṇas desirous of getting into heaven attain by their sacrifices and practice of penance are the places which brave men, losing their lives in righteous battles, are destined immediately to attain" (*yān yajñasaṅghais tapasā cha viprāḥ, svargaishiṇaḥ pātrachayaiśchā yānti* |

Kshaṇena tānapyatiyānti śūrāḥ, prāṇān suyuddheshu parityajantaḥ | |).

"A soldier on the other hand is destined to go to hell and shall not receive the privilege of proper funeral rites being performed at his death if he does not fight in return for the subsistenee he owes to his master (*Navaṁ śarāvaṁ salilasya pūrṇaṁ, susaṁskṛitaṁ darbhakṛitottarīyam* |
tat tasya mā bhūnnarakaṁ cha gachchhed, yo bhartṛipiṇḍasya kṛite na yuddhyet | |)

Astrologers and other followers of the king should infuse spirit into his army by pointing out the impregnable nature of its array and phalanx and they should also frighten the enemy (*Vyūhasampadā kārtāntikādiśchāsya vargaḥ śarvajñadaivasaṁyogākhyāpanābhyāṁ svapakshāṁ uddharshayet parapakshaṁ chodvejayet*).

Soothsayers and court-bards should describe heaven as the destination of the brave and hell for the timid. They should also extol the caste, corporation, family, deeds and character of the soldiers (*sūtamāgadhāḥ śūrāṇāṁ svargamasvargaṁ bhīrūṇāṁ jātisaṁghakula-karmavṛittastavaṁ cha yodhānām varṇayeyūḥ*).

Spies, carpenters, and astrologers should proclaim promptly the success of their own operations and the failure of those of the enemy (*Satrikavardhaki mauhūrtikāḥ svakarmasiddhimasiddhiṁ pareshām*).

Rewards. Lastly, the Commander-in-chief used to declare the rewards and honours graded according to the value of the feats performed or the triumphs achieved. These were 100,000 (*paṇas*) for slaying the hostile king, 50,000 for slaying his Commander-in-chief and heir-apparent, 10,000 for the chief of the brave, 5000 for the commander of an elephant or a chariot-division, 1000 for the commandant of a cavalry division, 100 for the leader of the infantry (*patti-mukhya*), 20 for bringing a head and twice the pay in addition to whatever is seized [X. 3]."

Cavalry. The special work of cavalry in a battle is stated by Kauṭilya to be the supervision of the discipline of the army, lengthening its line, protection of its sides, first attack, turning the movement of the army, pursuit and the like [X. 4].

Superintendent of Horses (*Aśvādhyaksha*). Horses were so necessary and important for Chandragupta's army that there was a department of Government to look after their recruitment and proper training. The Superintendent of horses had to keep a register of horses ; classify them according to their breed, age, colour, and size etc ; to provide for their stabling, fix their diets, arrange for their breaking and training and the treatment of their diseases by veterinary surgeons.

Recruitment. The horses of Chandragupta's cavalry, considering its numerical strength, had to be recruited from various places which are thus named by Kauṭilya [II. 30] : Kamboja [Afghanistan, the Kaofu of Hiuen-Tsang], Sindhu (Sind), Āraṭṭa (Punjab), Vanāyu (Arabia), Balhīka [Balkh], Sauvīra (Sind or Indus delta), Pāpeya, and Tāitala (unknown). 'Western horses' in general are highly prized in the *Mahābhārata*, but those of Sindhu and Kamboja are most mentioned [*Mbh.* III. 71, 12]. Equally famous were the steeds from Balhi [*Mbh.* I, 221, 51 ; v. 86, 6., etc.].

Stabling. The mettle of horses was tested by certain measurements of parts of its body as stated by Kauṭilya. Stables were built in conformity to the rules of hygiene and health. There were also strict regulations governing the horse's diet under different conditions.

Training. War horses received special and regular training in the various movements required on the battle field.

Veterinary Surgeons. The Superintendent had to report the diseases of horses. The Veterinary Surgeons had not only to treat those diseases but also to see that the physical growth of the animal was harmonious. Errors in treatment were punished [II. 30].

Greek Account of Equipment. The equipment of the cavalry has been thus described by Arrian [*Indica*, Chap. XIV]: "The Indians do not put saddles on their horses nor do they curb them with their bits, but they fit on, round the extremity of the horses' mouth, a circular piece of stitched raw ox-hide studded with pricks of iron or brass pointing inwards but not very sharp. Within the horse's mouth is a piece of iron like dart to which the reins are fastened." This, however, contradicts the statement of Megasthenes [McCrindle, Frag. XXXX] who says that "it is the practice of Indians to control their horses with bit and bridle and to make them move at a measured pace, and in a straight course. They neither, however, gall their tongue by use of spiked muzzles nor torture the roof of their mouth." Megasthenes is also supported by the Sanchi sculptures which show how perfect was the headgear of the horses at the time.

The War-chariots. These were important factors of the army. Their functions in war are thus described by Kauṭilya [X. 4]. "Proection of the army; repelling the attack made by all the four constituents of the enemy's army ; seizing and abandoning (positions) during the time of battle; restoring a broken array or phalanx, breaking the compact array of the enemy's army, frightening, inspiring awe by magnificence and sound" (*Svabalarakshā chaturaṅgabalapratishedhaḥ saṅgrāme grahaṇaṁ mokshaṇaṁ bhinnasandhānam abhinnabhedanāṁ trāsanam audāryam bhīmaghoshaśchetṭi rathakarmāṇi*).

Superintendent of Chariots : (*Rathādhyaksha*). As pointed out by Megasthenes, there was a separate Department of the War Office charged with the duty of maintaining the efficiency of the chariot as an element of the army. The Head of the Department was called the Superintendent of Chariots (*Rathādhyaksha*) whose functions have been detailed by Kauṭilya [II. 33]. He had primarily to attend to the construction of the chariots according to standard sizes corresponding to seven different kinds of chariots then in use. The war-chariots (*sāṁgrāmika* or *parapurābhiyānika*) were ten *purushas* (probably=7½ ft.) in height and 6 *hastas* or 9 ft. in width. The chariot manufacturers had to be adequately paid. The next important duty of the Superintendent was to maintain the efficiency of the training of the chariotmen in shooting arrows, hurling missiles and darts, charioteering, controlling the steeds, and generally fighting from the chariot [*Ib.*].

Defeat of Poros. Poros depended largely upon his chariots in his resistance of Alexander and the following description of his chariots by Curtius [VIII. 14] is very interesting reading: "Each chariot was drawn by four horses and carried six men, of whom two were shield-bearers, two archers posted on each side of the chariot, and the other two charioteers as well as men at arms; for when the fighting was at close quarters they dropped their reins and hurled dart after dart against the enemy."

Kauṭilya [II. 33] also requires the chariot warriors to be skilled in the art of shooting arrows (*ishu*) and hurling clubs and cudgels (*astraprahараṇa*).

But, "on this particular day," continues Curtius, "the chariots proved to be scarcely of any service, for the rain had made the ground slippery and unfit for horses to ride over, while the chariots kept sticking in the muddy sloughs and proved almost immovable from their great weight."

Thus the cause of the defeat of Poros was the unsuitability of the ground for the chariots which, according to Kauṭilya, would work best on the land which is free from mounds and wet lands and which affords space for turning (*Toyāśayāśrayavatī nirutkhātinī kedārahinā vyāvartanasamartheti rathānāmatiśayaḥ* [X. 4]. The time also was unsuitable, for chariots work best in the dry season (*alpavarshapaṅkaṁ varshati maruprāyam*) [IX. 1]. The space and time suitable for chariots are also indicated in the *Mahābhārta* (*apaṅka-garta-rahitā rathabhūmiḥ praśaśyate* [*Śānti* P. XXIV].

A Vyuha of Chariots. It may be noted that a Vyūha of chariots or a regiment of charioteers which may be taken to be the unit of this branch of the army is stated by Kauṭilya [X. 5] to comprise 45 chariots, each of which was drawn by five horses. Thus, besides the chariots, this section of the army is calculated to consist of 225 horses, 675 warriors, and another 675 servants (*pādagopa*).

It is also calculated that there should be three men or foot soldiers to oppose a horse (*pratiyuddha*) and 15 soldiers to oppose one chariot. Five horses are again to be pitted against one elephant while there will be required 15 servants for attending the horse, chariot, and elephant [*Ib.*].

The chariot in Sculpture. The representations of old Indian chariots appear on the Sanchi bas-reliefs which shows the car on two wheels, with sixteen spokes to each wheel, with a cubicle body open behind and drawn by two horses. There is also one long pole in the middle, curving upward near the neck of the horses with two short shafts on the sides reaching only as far as the flanks but there is no yoke. There is barely accomodation in the car for two persons to stand or sit side by side. The car in the sculpture, however, is used for religious purposes. The whip is also delineated at Sanchi and is shown as a stiff leather, though attached to a short handle.

The Elephant-of-war. The elephant force was of great importance for on that depended the victory of kings and the destruction of the enemy's army as stated by Kauṭilya (*hastipradhāno vijayo rājñām* [II. 2]; *hastipradhāno hi parānīkavadha iti*) [VII. II]. This is also echoed by Megasthenes in his reference to elephants 'turning the scale of victory.'

Strong Points. The special work of the elephants in war has been thus stated by Kauṭilya : "Marching in the front (*Puroyānam*) ; marching where there are no roads (*akṛitamārga*), places of shelter or landing places along rivers ; protecting the flanks ; crossing the tivers ; penetrating into places rendered inaccessible by bushes and shrubs ; breaking through the phalanx of the enemy's army (*sambādha*) ; setting fire to the enemy's camp and quenching it in one's own ; capable of achieving victory by itself without the help of other limbs of the army (*ekāṅgavijaya*) ; restoring the broken phalanx and breaking through that of the enemy forces (*bhinnasandhānām abhinnabhedanam*) ; protection against danger (*vyasane trāṇam*) ; trampling down the enemy forces (*abhighāta*); terrorising the army (*vibhīshikā*) ; inspiring terror (*trāsanam*) ; giving an imposing appearance to the army (*audāryam=sainyamahattvam*) ; capturing (*grahaṇam*) the enemy's soldiers and releasing (*mokshaṇam*) one's own ; destruction of ramparts (*sāla*), gates (*dvāra*), towers (*aṭṭālaka*) and the rooms over them ; and carrying treasure'. [X. 4.] In another passage [II. 2], Kauṭilya points out that elephants being of stupendous bodies (*atipramāṇaśarīrāḥ*) are capable of breaking through the enemy's phalanx (*parānīkavyūhapramardanam*), destroying his fortifications (*Durga*) and his military camp (*Skandhāvāra*), besides other destructive feats.

Time of operation. The time suitable for the operation of elephants was all seasons of the year except the hot season when "elephants profusely perspire causing injury to their skin and leprosy (*kushṭhino*). When they cannot have bath in water and cannot profusely drink water, they are consumed by an inner heat (*antaravakshārāḥ*) and become blind (*andhībhavanti*) [IX. I]. Therefore, the elephants should be employed on expeditions in a well-watered country (*prabhūtodake deśe*) and when it rains (*varshati*).

Place. As to the place suitable for the operation of elephants, Kauṭilya [X. 4] prescribes as follows : "Accessible hills (*gamyaśaila*), low-lying swamps (*nimnavishamā*) and uneven ground with trees which can be pulled down, with plants that can be uprooted, and which is not boggy and broken into holes and pits (*paṅkabhaṅgura-daraṇa-hīnā*) ; also that which is full of dust (*pāṁsu*), mud (*kardama*), swamps, grass and weeds, and free from the obstruction of the branches of big trees [X. 4].

Superintendent of Elephants (*Hastyadhyaksha*) [II. 31, 32]. The training and efficiency of elephants as a fighting force were looked after by a special branch of the War Office, as pointed out by Megasthenes. The Department was presided over by an official called the Superintendent of Elephants (*Hastyadhyaksha*) assisted by a regular staff of subordinate officers who attended to the manifold duties and operations necessary for the rearing up of an adequate elephant force for the State.

Acquisition. Firstly, there was the work of securing the elephants from various places and keeping the wild animals in specially appointed forests or preserves. Elephants came from the following places : (1) Kaliṅga, (2) Aṅga, (3) Prāchya (eastern India), (4) Chedi, (5) Karūśa, (6) Daśārṇa, (7) Aparānta (western India), (8) Surāshṭra and (9) Pañchanada (Punjab).

Superintendent of Elephant forests (*Nāgavanādhyaksha*) [II. 2]. The elephant-forests or preserves were under the control of the superintendent called the *Nāgavanādhyaksha* with staff of assistants called the *Nāgavanapālas* who controlled the approaches to and from the forests.

Elephant-Trainers. Secondly, there was the work of the capture and training of wild elephants requiring another set of officers having special knowledge and experience of that difficult work. These were drivers or grooms of elephants (*Hastipaka*), boundary-guards (*Saimika*), foresters (*Vana-charka*), those who slip nooses round the legs of the elephant (*Pāda-pāśika*), and the elephant-trainers (*Anīkastha*) [II. 2]. The trainers had to perform the important initial function of discriminating between elephants which were worthy of capture and those which were not so for disease or other defects such as extreme youth (*vikka*), disease (*vyādhita*), pregnancy or having young ones to suckle (*garbhiṇī* and *dhenukā*) and the smallness (*mūḍha*) or absence of tusks(*matkuṅa*) [II. 31].

Capture of Elephants : Khedda. Female elephants were used in the capture of elephants (*Hastibandhakī*) which were pursued by the traces of their dung and urine, their foot marks the places of rest or the damage caused by them in their course (*kūlapātoddeśena*). The mode of capture has been described by Megasthenes: it was to place a few female elephants in an enclosure with a surrounding deep trench into which the wild animals found their way by a bridge to be subsequently withdrawn.

Stabling Staff. Thirdly, there were the stabling arrangements requiring a special stabling staff which included among others the physician (*Chikitsaka*), the trainer (*Anīkastha*), the mahout, ordinary (*Ārohaka*) or expert (*Ādhoraṇa*), the groom (*Hastipaka*), the attendant (*Aupachārika*), the cook (*Vidhāpāchaka*), the grass-supplier (*Yāvasika*), the guard (*Kuṭīrakshaka*) and those who look after the animal at night (*Aupaśāyika*) [II. 32]. These regulated the diet and the daily necessities (such as bathing exercise, training and rest) of the animals.

Military Training. Fourthly, there was the important work of giving the State elephants, especially those meant for war (*sānnāhya*), a proper training for which regular expert assistance was needed. They had to be trained in all the movements necessary in war (*sāṁgrāmika*) such as rising, bending or jumping (*upasthāna*), turning (*saṁvartana*), killing or capturing (*vadhāvadha*), fighting with other elephants (*hastiyuddha*) and even assailing forts and cities (*nāgarāyaṇam*) [II. 31; 32].

Riders. Acccording to Megasthenes [Frag. XXXV], the war-elephant, "either in what is called the tower, or on his bare back, in sooth, carries three fighting men of whom two shoot from the side while one shoots from behind. There is also a fourth man who carries in his hand the goad wherewith he guides the animal much in the same way as the pilot and captain of a ship direct its course with the helm."

Thus quite a variety of officers co-operated for the rearing up of a good breed of elephants to serve in war. The contribution of the elephants to the fighting force of the empire under Chandragupta was not inconsiderable.

Eastern India home of Elephants. From a comparison of the contemporary armies of India which we have referred to above, it is evident that the army under Chandragupta was an advance upon them in respect of elephants, in the securing and training of which the east, i. e. Magadha, had the pre-eminence, according to the unanimous testimony of the Indian records (Rhys Davids, *Buddhist India*, p. 266]. We may recall in this connection the mention by Kauṭilya of *Prāchya* (the east) as the region which supplied the best elephants, and also a passage of the *Mahābhārata* [XII. 101] which in comparing the military skill attained by different peoples, points out the pre-eminence of the *Prāchyas* at elephant-fighting. With this we may also compare the statement ascribed to Megasthenes [*Ancient India*, p. 118] that the largest elephants in all the land were those called the *Praisian* i.e , of the land of the Prasii or eastern people, the Māgadhas.

Admiralty : Superintendent of Shipping (*Nāvadhyaksha*). We have now dealt with the main divisions of the army and shall close our account by a reference to the Board of Admiralty which, according to Megasthenes, was a department of the War-Office of Chandragupta. The evidence on the Mauryan Navy is rather scanty. According to Kauṭilya, the Admiralty was the portfolio of an officer called the Superintendent of ships and boats who had to deal with all matters relating to war, The use of vessels in war first shows itself in the campaigns of Alexander who effected his passage across the Indus [V. A. Smith, *Early History of India*, p. 55] and the Hydaspes [*Ib.*] by means of his flotilla of boats. Arrian notes (my *History of Indian Shipping*, p. 102] the construction of dock yards and the contribution of galleys of 30 oars and of transport vessels by the tribe called Xathroi. The construction of ships was the monopoly of the State but the ships were let out on hire (Strabo, XV. 46]. This is confirmed by Kauṭilya [II. 28]. It was the duty of the Admiralty to pursue and destroy piratical boats and ships (*hiṁsrikāḥ*) as well as those from an enemy's country (*amitravishayātigāḥ*). The Admiralty in fact policed the rivers and sea-shore. They had also to collect all tolls levied at ferries, harbour dues, and customs, but they were bound to offer free passage to "men who were engaged to carry things (provisions and orders) to the army" [*Ib.*]. Thus boats were needed not so much for actual fighting as for purposes of transport of arms and provisions for the army along water-ways.

Policy. The vast military resources of the empire were to be applied with reference to a policy aiming at two objectives called (1) *Śama*, enjoyment in security of results achieved by (2) *Vyāyāma* or effort [VI. 2].

These two aims, again, depended upon the six-fold Policy called *Shāḍguṇyam* comprising (1) *Sandhi* or *Paṇabandha*. agreement between States with pledges or guarantees; (2) *Vigraha* or *Apakāra*, war; (3) *Āsana* or *Upekshaṇa*, neutrality; (4) *Yāna* or *Abhyuchchaya*. expedition based on a collection of materials of war preparation; (5) *Saṁśraya* or *Parārpaṇam*, seeking a shelter of a more powerful king by surrendering money or hostages; (6) *Dvaidhībhāva*, making peace with one and war with another [VII. 1].

The results to follow from this six-fold policy are the three conditions for the State: *Kshayaḥ* or decline, *Sthānam*, stationary state; and *Vṛīddhi*, expansion.

The condition of the State will depend upon its policy, good (*naya*) or bad (*apanaya*), and also upon luck (*daiva*), good (*aya*) or bad (*anaya*).

The ideal king must aim at *Vṛiddhi*, expansion of his territory, which he must achieve as a conqueror (*Vijigīshu*).

His successs (*Siddhi*) will depend upon his strength (*Śakti*).

Śakti is of three kinds: that of (1) Wisdom (*jñānabalam*) and counsel (*mantraśakti*), (2) Resources, material and military (*kośadaṇḍa-balaṁ prabhu-śakti*) and (3) Determination (*vikramabalaṁ utsāha-śaktiḥ* [VI. 1].

The sphere of application of the sixth-fold policy is what is called the Circle of States with which the king cultivates relations, friendly, or unfriendly (*Shāḍguṇyasya prakṛiti-maṇḍalaṁ yoniḥ*) [VI. 2]

These foreign relations are thus differentiated:

The neighbouring king is to be treated as the enemy. His neighbour is the friend. Other Powers will be the enemy's ally, and the allies of the king, or the conqueror's allies, and the allies of the enemy's allies.

There is also the *Madhyama* king between the conqueror and his enemy, who may help either.

And, lastly, there is the neutral (*udāsīna*) king.

The programme of conquest laid down is, first, to seize the enemy's territory and then that of the *Madhyama* and of *Udāsīna* [XIII. 4].

This is the first way of conquest (*eshaḥ prathamo mārgaḥ prithivīṁ jetum*).

Where there is no *Madhyama* or *Udāsīna* State and the conqueror is left to deal with the enemy by himself, he is to attempt conquest by his own superior power being applied first to win over the enemy's Ministers and, later, his army, and then secure his treasury (*ariprakṛitīḥ amātyādīn sādhayet Tata uttarāḥ prakṛitīḥ kośadaṇḍādikāḥ*). This is the second way of conquest.

Where there is no Circle of States (*Maṇḍala*) to be conquered, he should conquer his friend by his enemy or his enemy by his friend by a war between them so as to weaken both and conquer both. This is the third way.

Or he may, with the help of his ally, subdue his enemy, and, with his power doubled, subdue the second, and with power trebled, the third king. This is the fourth way to conquest,

He must behave as a conqueror (*jitvā cha prithivīm*) by ruling by Dharma or Law [*Ib.*].

He is to 'cover the defects of the conquered king by his own virtues and by doubling his own virtues by good administration, by concessions (*anugraha*), remissions (*parihāra*), gift (*dāna*) and honours (*māna*), and thus contribute to the contentment and good of his new subjects (*prakritipriyahitāni anuvarteta*).' He is advised to adopt the manners and customs (*śīla*), dress (*vesha*), language (*bhāshā*), and laws (*āchāra*) of the conquered peoples. He should respect their religion, social institutions (*samāja*) and festivals (*utsava*). His spies (*Satriṇaḥ*) will report to the leaders of the people of different localities (*deśa*), villages (*grāma*), castes (*jāti*) and corporations (*saṅgha*) on the injuries inflicted on the country (*apachāra*) by the enemy, and on his own power, affection for them, and measures for their welfare. He is to honour their gods, and reward their men of letters (*Vidyāśūra*), orators (*Vākyaśūra*), and religious people (*Dharmaśūra*) by gifts of land, goods. and remissions of taxes. He should celebrate his conquest by a general gaol-delivery (*sarvabandhanamokshaṇam*) and sanction the maintenance of the destitute, the helpless and the diseased. He is to prohibit the slaughter of animals for half a month during the period of *Chāturmāsya* (July to September), for four nights at the time of full moon, and for a night on the day of the *nakshatra* marking the king's birth and his conquest of the country (*rājanakshatra*, and *deśa-nakshatra*, as explained by the commentator). He should, finally, adopt all measures necessary to ensure his safety and conquest in a new country by dealing effectively with all sources of mischief and discontent [XII. 5].

No better maxims and principles can be thought of for empire-building for an emperor like Chandragupta Maurya who had to deal with so many communities of different social systems and religions making up his vast empire comprising the foreigners or *Yonas* at its north-western end and, in the rest of the empire, within India proper, peoples in different stages of social evolution from the aboriginal peoples, forest-tribes (the *Āṭavikas*) and nomads, up to the cultured classes (the *Āryas*) brought up under the *Varṇāśrama-dharma* system at the top of the social structure. It was only a wide principle of synthesis and comprehension, as enunciated by Kauṭilya for the *Digvijayī* emperor, which could accommodate within its extensive range so many differences and such a large amount of social and cultural diversity so as to reconcile them in a composite whole and weld them together as parts of a common political system or empire. Kauṭilya and Chandragupta thus rank as India's first empire-builders by virtue of their sound imperial theory and practice. They founded their empire on the stable and broad basis of complete cultural freedom for all its communities, respect for their differences in language, custom, and creed, and protection of all their rights, social, religious, and linguistic, which make up communal integrity.

CHAPTER XI

SOCIAL CONDITIONS

Social System: Castes. Society was based on the orthodox Brahminical system which divided it among four principal castes (*varṇas*) as already described, together with many lower castes (*avara-varṇa*) [VI. 1 ; VII. II].

Mixed Castes. There was also in the country any number of mixed castes (*antarāla*) as the outcome of marriages between persons of different castes. The fruits of such inter-marriage between them are thus mentioned by Kauṭilya [III. 7.] : (1) Offspring of *anuloma* marriage : Ambashṭha, Nishāda or Pāraśava (of Brahmin father) : Ugra (of Kshatriya father) ; Śūdra (of Vaiśya father) ; (2) offspring of *pratiloma* marriage : Āyogava, Kshatta, and Chaṇḍāla (of Śūdra father) ; Māgadha and Vaidehaka (of Vaiśya father) ; and Sūta (of Kshatriya father).

Offspring of further mixtures are thus stated : The son of an Ugra by a Nishāda woman is called *Kukkuṭaka* ; of a Nishāda by an Ugra woman *Pukkasa* ; of an Ambashṭha by a Vaidehaka woman, *Vaiṇa* ; of a Vaidehaka by an Ambashṭha woman, *Kuśīlava* ; of an Ugra by a Kshatta woman, *Śvapāka.*

Ascendancy of Brahminism. It is to be recalled that "the Mauryan empire", as F. W. Thomas puts it [*Cambridge History*, I. 484], "began with a Brāhman, as well as a national reaction, and, under Kauṭilya's leadership, regulated society by the rules of *Varṇāśramadharma* as explained above. The apex of this society was the Brāhmaṇa who, as *Purohita*, and the king's preceptor, influenced politics and administration to a very large extent, and also legislation as a member of the *Parishad.* His social position of pre-eminence was recognised by laws exempting him from taxation and confiscation, from corporal punishment and the death penalty, branding and banishment being in his case the *ultima ratio* [IV. 8]. But all this social honour was due to the fact that he hardly belonged to the society as such : he was in the world but not of it. His true office was study and teaching, and his proper abode was the forest hermitage where he maintained the sacred fires and lived for another world" [*Cambridge History*, [*Ib.*].

But such a social order was now threatened by the growth of heterodox and proselytising sects like Jainism, Buddhism, and many others mentioned in the literature of the times [See writer's *Hindu Civilization*, pp. 222-26], which were threatening its foundations by organising brotherhoods of ascetics (*pravrajia*), Accordingly, we can well understand why Kauṭilya, as the champion of the Brahminical system, does not at all look with favour upon premature renunciation of the world and of the obligations of domestic life without the formal sanction of legal authorities (cf. *āprichchhya dharmasthān* in II. 1) and without provision for son and wife (*putradāraṁ apratividhāya*) [*Ib.*]. He even forbids giving any quarter in the villages to such unlicensed ascetics for fear of disturbance to rural society (*na janapadaṁ upaniviśeta* [*Ib.*]

"Accordingly, we see in the Mauryan age the beginning of a stage of concentration, in which only a few great sects could maintain themselves by the side of a settled Brāhmaṇa orthodoxy. And this was a natural corollary of a great empire" [*Cambridge History*, *Ib.*].

Greek accounts of Hindu Society: Confusion between Caste and Craft. It is not at all a matter of surprise that the Greek notices of Hindu Society do not show a complete comprehension of a system which is rather singular and strange to foreigners. Megasthenes, and the Greek writers after him, describe the seven "classes of India by a confusion between castes proper and the crafts associated with them. "But his seven classes may truly reflect", as Bevan well points out [*Ib.* 409], "the various activities which a Greek resident at Pāṭaliputra could see going on round about him in the fourth century B. C."

The Brahmin as seen by Megasthenes. It is, howover, possible to separate the Greek accounts of caste from those of the occupations followed by the different classes of people with which they are mixed up, or the different occupations followed by the same caste.

Megasthenes has recorded the following observations on Brahmins as a caste:

He calls the Brahmins "philosophers who are first in rank but form the smallest class in point of number" [Frag. XXXIII].

But we owe to Strabo [XX. i, 58-60] a fuller account of what Megasthenes has recorded on the subject:

'Brachmanes'. "The philosophers are of two kinds: (1) *Brachmanes* and (2) *Sarmanes*. The Brachmanes are the best esteemed,, for they have a more consistent dogmatic system."

Studentship. (As students) they "have their abode in a grove in front of the city within a moderate-sized enclosure. They live in a simple style, and lie on beds of rushes or (deer) skins. They abstain from animal food and sexual pleasures, and spend their time in listening to serious discourse."

Householder's State. "After living in this manner for seven-and-thirty years, each individual retires to his own property, where he lives for the rest of the days in ease and security.

"They then array themselves in fine muslin, and wear a few trinkets of gold on their fingers and in their ears. They eat flesh, but not that of animals employed in labour. They abstain from hot and highly seasoned food."

This is a description of the first *Āśrama* of life, that of the Brahmachārī, followed by that of the householder. Only there is a mistake in taking the period of studentship at 37 years, which is exceptional and is the limit contemplated by Manu [III. 1.] Here Megasthenes also shows his ignorance of the Hindu division of life into four *āśramas.*

Megasthenes also indicates the occupations followed by the Brahmins of the day.

Occupations. They serve as priests "private persons who wish to offer sacrifices or perform other sacred rites."

They also "are employed publicly by kings at what is called the Great Synod where, at the beginning of the new year, all the philosophers are gathered together, and any philosopher who may have committed any useful suggestion to writing, or observed any means for improving the crops and the cattle, or for promoting the public interest, declares it publicly."

Diodorus, in his epitome of Megasthenes, puts the matter a little differently.

He says that "in requital of their services (as priests), they receive valuable gifts and privileges."

"To the people of India at large they also render great benefits when. gathered together at the beginning of the year, they forewarn the assembled multitude about droughts and wet weather, and also about propitious winds and diseases,, and other topics capable of profiting the hearers. Thus the people and the sovereign, learning beforehand what is to happen, always make provision against a coming deficiency, and never fail to prepare beforehand what will help in time of need.

Arrian also observes as follows on the same subject : "The sophists are not so numerous as the others, but hold the supreme place of dignity and honour ; for they are under no necessity of doing any bodily labour at all or of contributing from the produce of their labour anything to the common stock, nor indeed, is any duty absolutely binding on them, except to per form the sacrifice offered to the gods on behalf of the State."

Sarmanes (*Śramaṇas*). To return now to the other class of philosophers called *Sarmanes* by Megasthenes : Strabo says : "As to the *Sarmanes*, the most highly honoured are called *Hylobioi*, 'forest-dwellers' (*vānaprasthas* or *vanavāsins*). They live in the forest on leaves of trees and wild fruits, and wear garments made from the bark of trees. They also abstain from sexual intercourse and from wine." According to Clemens, " they neither live in cities nor even in houses. They wear barks of trees and live on acorns. They neither marry nor beget children." This description corresponds to Brahmachārīs who preferred to remain as such throughout life, and were called *Naishṭhika-Brahmachārīs.*

The term *Sarmanes* stands for Sanskrit *Śramaṇas* which was then a general term for ascetics whether Buddhist or non-Buddhist, though by the time of Asoka the term was used exclusively for Buddhist monks or Bhikshus.

As Bevan points out : "It has been thought that we have in the *Sarmanes* of Magasthenes the first mention of Buddhists by Western writers. In the description, however, there is nothing distinctively Buddhist and the term *Sramaṇa* is used in Indian literature of non-Buddhist sects. If, therefore, the people to whom Magasthenes heard the term applied were Buddhists, he must have known so little about them that he could only describe them by features which were equally found in various sorts of Hindu holy men. His description applies to Brahmin ascetics rather than to Buddhist" [*Cambridge History*, I. 420].

It will appear from the description of these *Śramaṇas* that they were Brahmins of the third and fourth *Āśramas* of life and known as *Parivrājakas* and *Saṁnyāsīs.*

Gautama, in his *Dharma-sūtra*, calls a man of the third *āśrama* a *Bhikshu* who is described as (1) *Anichaya*, devoid of store of articles and (2) *Ūrdhvaretā*, devoid of desire for sexual intercourse (as stated also by Megasthenes); and a man of the fourth *āsrama*, a *Vaikhānasa* who should (as Megasthenes also says), live in the forest (*vane*), subsist on roots and fruits, and wear only bark and skin (*chīrājina*) [III and X].

Baudhāyana and Āpastamba use the term *Parivrājaka* for the fourth *āsrama* and also the term *Saṁnyāsī.*

Their occupations. The Greek writers tell of the activities of these ascetics or *Śramaṇas.*

" They communicate with the kings who consult them by messengers regarding the causes of things, and who, through them, worship and supplicate the deity.

" Some of them are physicians engaged in the study of the nature of man. They effect cures rather by regulating diets than by the use of medicines. Of medicines, they attach greater value to those applied externally than to drugs. The remedies most esteemed are ointments and plasters. All others they consider to be in a great measure pernicious in their nature.

" They, too, like Brāhmans, train themselves to endurance, both by undergoing active toil, and by the endurance of pain, so that they remain for a whole day motionless in one fixed attitude."

As Elphinstone points out: " The habits of these physicians seem to correspond with those of Brāhmans of the fourth stage."

And McCrindle also rightly remarks: " It is indeed a remarkable circumstance that the religion of Buddha should never have been expressly noticed by the Greek authors, though it had existed for two centuries before Alexander. The only explanation is that the appearance and manners of its followers were not so peculiar as to enable a foreigner to distinguish them from the mass of the people."

Strabo further says about their habits that " they do not live in the open air. They live on rice and meal, which they can always get for the mere asking, or receive from those who entertain them as guests in their houses."

They are also stated to cultivate " a knowledge of Pharmacy."

Some of these *Sarmanes* again are stated to be " diviners, sorcerers, and adepts in the rites and customs relating to the dead, who go about begging both in villages and towns."

Some of these again " are of superior culture and refinement and inculcate superstitions which they consider favourable to piety and holiness of life."

Women. " Women pursue philosophy with some of them, but abstain from sexual intercourse." We may instance the case of the Upanishadic Ṛishi, Yājñavalkya, whose wife Maitreyī followed her husband from home into the forest in the pursuit of highest philosophy.

Pramnai (*Prāmāṇikas*). Strabo [VI. 22] mentions a third class of Philosophers whom he calls the *Pramnai.* " They are philosophers opposed to the Bracmanes and are contentious and proud of argument. They ridicule the Brachmanes who study physiology and astronomy as fools and impostors. Some of them are called the

Pramnai of the mountains, others the *Gymnetai*, and others again the *Pramnai* of the city or the *Pramnai* of the country.

"Those of the mountains wear deer-skins and carry wallets filled with roots and drugs, professing to cure diseases by means of incantations. charms, and amulets.

"The Gymnetai, in accordance with their name, are naked, and live generally in the open air, practising endurance, as I have already mentioned, for seven-and-thirty years.

"Women live in their society without sexual commerce.

"The Pramnai of the city live in towns, and wear muslin robes, while those of the country clothe themselves with skins of fawns or antelopes."

Sophists. Arrian [*Indika*, XI. XII] who calls the philosophers *Sophists* also states the following particulars.

"To them the knowledge of divination among the Indians is exclusively restricted, and none but a *Sophist* is allowed to practise that art. But the private fortunes of individuals they do not care to predict.

"These sages go naked, living during winter in the open air, to enjoy the sunshine, and, during the summer, when the heat is too powerful, in meadows and low grounds under large trees.

"They live upon the fruits which each season produces, and on the bark of trees—the bark being no less sweet and nutritious than the fruit of the date-palm."

Arrian [XII] also mentions the singular fact that "the Sophists could be *from any caste*, for the life of the Sophist is not an easy one, but the hardest of all." This shows that the life of a *Saṁnyāsī* was open to persons of all castes, because the *Saṁnyāsī*, in renouncing the world, and all social ties, was beyond the rules of caste. This also points to the liberality of Hinduism which makes no distinctions of caste in the life spiritual.

Buddhists. Lastly, we owe to Clemens of Alexandria the following statement:

"Among the Indians are those philosophers also who follow the precepts of Boutta whom they honour as a god on account of his extraordinary sanctity." As Colebrooke has pointed out, "here the followers of the Buddha are clearly distinguished from the *Brachmanes* and the *Sramanes*" (cited by McCrindle).

These various descriptions of the highest intellectual and cultured classes of India whom the Greeks severally call Philosophers, Sophists, Brachmanes, the Pramnai, the Gymnetai, and followers of the Boutta (Buddha) may be taken to be descriptions of the various classes of ascetics, Brahminical and non-Brahminical, Buddhist, Jain and the like.

Pre-Buddhist Ascetics. India, in the fourth century B.C. and, indeed, since the rise of Jainism and Buddhism in the fifth century B.C. had been noted for the multiplicity of its schools and sects of ascetics. Their forerunners were the wandering ascetics of the Vedic days, the *Charakas,* and later, the *Parivrājakas,* followed by pre-Buddhistic sects like the *Ājīvikas* (who went about naked), the *Nirgranthas* (of scanty clothing), the *Jaṭilakas,* and the like. In the *Dialogues of the Buddha* [II. 165], the ascetics of different orders are described under the general name, *Samaṇa-Brāhmaṇa,* 'leaders in religious iife (*gaṇino*)', a name occuring very often in the Edicts of Asoka. The *Aṅguttara* [IV. 35] mentions two classes of ascetics whom it calls *Parivrājakas*: (1) *Brāhmaṇa* and (2) *Aññatitthiya,* i.e., other non-Buddhists ascetics. The *Brāhmaṇa Parivrājakas* are characterised as *Vādaśīla,* disputatious [*Sutta Nipāta,* 382], *Vitaṇḍas* and *Lokāyatas,* Sophists, casuists and materialists [*Chullavagga,* V. 3, 2], and the like. The situation is well summed up in the *Udāna* [pp. 66-7, ed. Pali Text Society]: "*Sambahulā nānātitthiyā Samaṇa- Brāhmaṇā Paribbājakā nānā-diṭṭhikā nānā-diṭṭhi-nissayanissitā*: there were very many, and various, sectaries of *Śramaṇas* and *Brāhmaṇas,* all *Parivrājakas,* followers of different *Diṭṭhis, Darśanas* or systems, and organisations."

Prāmāṇikas. Regarding the class of philosophers described by Strabo under the name of *Pramnai* "on the basis of some other source than Megasthenes," Bevan rightly points out that "the people intended are undoubtedly the *Prāmāṇikas,* the followers of the various philosophical systems, each of which has its own view as to what constitutes *Pramāṇa,* a 'means of right knowledge.' These philosophers are, as a rule, orthodox Brāhmans, but they view with contempt these Brāhmans who put their trust in Vedic ceremonies" [*Cambridge History,* I. 421].

General view: Living and Clothing. Taking all the Greek versions together, we find that the Brahmans are described as living (1) on the mountains, (2) in the woods, (3) in the plains, (4) in the cities and (5) in the country. Some go naked, some, those of the mountains, wear deer-skins. Those of the country side also wear 'skins of fawns or antelopes.' Those of the towns are dressed in fine muslin, wear finger-rings and ear-rings of gold, "with skins of deer or of gazelles hung from their shoulders, growing beards and long hair which is twisted up and covered by a turban" [*Cambridge History,* I. 422], Those of the woods wear garments of barks of trees. As students, they lie on beds of rushes and skins which they also wear.

Food. Students abstain from animal food.

The ascetics of the woods live on leaves and fruits and also eat nutritious barks of trees.

Householder-Brāhmans eat meat, but not that of animals employed in labour, such as cattle. They avoid hot and over-spiced food. They eat rice and barley meal.

Occupations : Priesthood. Some beg their food.

They do not serve on pay.

They work as priests and get presents in return as sources of livelihood.

Meditation. Their chief occupation is meditation which they continue unmoved in a fixed position for a whole day.

Divination. They acquire powers of divination and are utilised by the State to give forecasts of weather, drought, and storms, and even epidemics.

But they do not divine for private individuals.

Their advice is sought by kings.

Philosophical Congress. There were annual Philosophical Congresses assembled by the kings. At these they announced their own discoveries as to religion and philosophy. The Greeks say that they gave their suggestions as to agriculture and cattle and also advised on politics and general affairs of the country. The Upanishads speak of such learned Conferences of which they were themselves the products. The most famous of these was the Congress of Philosophers convened by king Janaka of Videha with Ṛishi Yājñavalkya as its most prominent figure.

Practice of Medicine. Lastly, the Greeks noticed how some of these had specialised in Medicine and practised as Physicians, but preferring to cure diseases by diet rather than drugs. They invented valuable ointments and plasters. They also cured diseases by Mantras and amulets. They specialised in Physiology, Pharmacy, and Astronomy.

They abstained from wine and women.

Women Ascetics. We are also told : "The Brāhmans do not admit their wives to their philosophy : if the wives are wanton, they might divulge mysteries to the profane ; if they are good, they might leave their husbands, since no one who has learnt to look with contempt upon pleasure and pain, upon life and death, will care to be under another's control."

This, however, applies to the life of the householder. For we are told that "in the case of some *Śramaṇas* (those who are forest-dwellers), women also are permitted to share in the philosophic life, on the condition of observing sexual continence like the men," as we have already seen.

Brahman's Spirituality. Megasthenes makes a true observation typical of Brāhmans as a class when he states : "The chief subject on which the Brahmans talk is death ; for this present life, they hold, is like the season passed in the womb, and death for those who have cultivated philosophy is the birth into the real, the happy, life. For this reason they follow an extensive discipline to make them ready for death."

This is a correct appreciation of the Brāhmanical way of life and ideals. The 'extensive discipline' referred to is the discipline extended over the four *Āśramas* of life which are a direct preparation for death.

Ascetics seen by the Greeks in the Panjab. At the time of Alexander's invasion, the Greeks first saw the Indian ascetics at Takshaśilā. As they won't care to come to see Alexander, Alexander sent to them Onesicritus who reports that he saw 15 ascetics about 10 miles from the city, given to meditation in the sun, sitting naked. On being told that the Yavana king wanted to learn their wisdom, one of them bluntly answered that, "no one coming in the bravery of European clothes—cavalry cloak and broad-brimmed hat and top-boots, such as the Macedonians wore—could learn their wisdom. To do that, he must strip naked and learn to sit on the hot stones besides them" [*Cambridge History*, I, 358].

Aristobulus in his book states that he saw at Takshaśilā two of these ascetics, one with a shaven head, and the other with long hair, while both had their group of disciples. When they went to the market place, crowds flocked to them for counsels [*Ib.* 42].

The leader or Guru of these ascetics is named by the Greeks Dandamis (or Mandanis), an unbending idealist, who did not care to see Alexander even on pain of death and sent his reply in noble words like the following : "God alone is the object of my homage. Alexander is not God since he must taste of death. I have no fear or favour to ask. What Alexander can offer is utterly useless. The things that I prize are these leaves which are my house, these blooming plants which supply me dainty food. Having nothing which requires guarding, I have tranquil slumber, whereas had I gold to guard, that would banish sleep. The Brahmins neither love gold nor fear death. Death means that one will be delivered from his ill-assorted companion, the body" [Frags. LIV and LV].

These words truly represent the philosophy of life followed by the ascetics of India in all ages up to this day, believing in *chittavṛtti-nirodha*, 'withdrawal of mind from the objective world of matter', as the foundation of religious life and spirituality for man.

Kshatriyas. These correspond to the fifth class of Megasthenes in India's population. In the words of Arrian : "It consists of the warriors who are second in point of numbers to the husbandmen but lead a life of supreme freedom and enjoyment. They have only military duties to perform. Others make their arms and others supply them with horses, and they have others to attend on them in the camp, who take care of their horses, clean their arms, drive their elephants, prepare their chariots and act as their charioteers. As long as they are required to fight, they fight, and, when peace returns, they abandon themselves to enjoyment—the pay which they receive from the State being so liberal that they can with ease maintain themselves and others besides.'

Vaisyas and Sudras. These come under the second, third, and fourth castes mentioned by Megasthenes. "The second caste consists of the husbandmen who form the bulk of the population and in disposition most mild and gentle. They are exempted from military service, and cultivate the lands undisturbed by fear. They never go to town, either to take part in its tumults or for any other purpose, but live in the country with their wives and children. The work of these tillers of the soil consists of ploughing or gathering in their crop, pruning the trees or reaping the harvest."

Next, there are "the traders who vend wares, and artisans who are employed in bodily labour. Of these, some are armourers, who fabricate the weapons of war. Some are ship-builders, some are sailors employed in the navigation of rivers. They receive wages and victuals from the king for whom alone they work. They also make the implements which husbandmen and others find useful in their different callings."

Then there are "the hunters and herdsmen who neither settle in towns nor in villages but live in tents and lead a wandering life. They alone are allowed to hunt and to keep cattle and to sell draught animals and lend them to hire. By hunting and trapping, they clear the country of wild beasts and fowls, and of the pests with which it abounds, those wild beasts and birds which devour the seeds sown in the fields by the husbandmen. In return for their services they receive an allowance of grain from the king."

Occupations. The sixth and the seventh castes noticed by Megasthenes are misnomers. He confounds caste with craft or occupation. Those two castes are really made up of government servants of different grades.

Informers. The sixth caste is made up of what are called the 'Overseers' whose duties have been already described.

Councillors. The seventh caste is made up of what are called the Councillors and Assessors who "deliberate on public affairs, to whom belong the highest posts of Government; the Tribunals of justice, the Advisers of the king, the Treasurers of the State, the Generals of the Army, the Chief Magistrates."

According to Arrian, "the seventh caste consists of the Councillors of State who advise the king or the self-governed cities in the management of public affairs, and enjoys the prerogative of choosing Governors, Chiefs of Provinces, Deputy Governors, Superintendents of the Treasury, Generals of the Army, Admirals of the Navy, Controllers, and Commissioners, who superintend Agriculture."

It may be noted that the herdsmen and hunters of Megasthenes are called *Gopālakas*, *Lubdhakas*, and *Āṭavikas* and other workers employed under the Superintendents of Agriculture, Cattle and Pastures in the *Arthaśāstra*, as described above.

The 'armourers' are mentioned as belonging to the Department of *Āyudhāgārādhyaksha* and 'ship-builders' as serving under *Nāvadhyaksha.*

The Artisans plying other crafts are mentioned by Kauṭilya under different Departments.

We have already pointed out the correspondence of the Officers called Overseers and Councillors by Megasthenes to the *Gūḍhapurushas* and the *Amātyas* and the various other *Adhyakshas* of Kauṭilya.

Caste and Occupation. When Megasthenes states that "a soldier cannot become a husbandman, or an artisan a philosopher," or that "no one is allowed to marry out of his own caste, or to exercise any calling or art except his own," or "to exchange one profession or trade for another," or "to follow more than one business", he is evidently making a confusion between Caste and Occupation. An 'artisan' who was a Śūdra by caste could not become a 'philosopher' or a Brahmin, nor could a soldier, a Kshatriya by caste, become a husbandman who was a Vaiśya. Megasthenes further states [Frag. XXXIII]: "An exception is made in favour of the philosopher who for his virtue is allowed this privilege."

This points to the Hindu law premitting a Brahmin to follow an occupation belonging to the lower castes, by way of an *āpad-dharma*, for the sake of livelihood as a necessity which knows no law, in an emergency.

Manners and Customs: Dress. Megasthenes observed at Pāṭaliputra, that in dress the Indians, for all their general simplicity, showed a partiality for richness and bright colours, liberally using ornaments of gold and gems and flowered muslins, with attendants carrying umbrellas after them.

Nearchus describes the dress of the Indus people as being of shining cotton and comprising "a tunic down to the middle of their shins, and two other pieces of stuff, one thrown over their shoulders and one twisted round their heads. They wear ear-rings of ivory and shoes of white leather, very elaborately worked, and high-heeled so as to make the wearer seem taller."

Diet. The Greeks were struck by the absence of wine from the Indians' diet. "Their staple food was pulpy rice. Each man took his food by himself. There was neither a common meal nor a fixed time for it. At the time of supper, it was served on a table in a gold dish in which was first put rice fully boiled, and, on it, seasoned meats."

Marriage. According to Megasthenes, Indians were known to be polygamous. He refers to brides being purchased for a yoke of oxen. This must be understood to refer to the *Ārsha* form of marriage prescribed by Manu, in which the bride's father was entitled to receive a pair of oxen or cows (*gomithuna*) as a customary charge (*dharmataḥ*) [Manu III, 29]. According to Nearchus, among certain Indian peoples, girls were secured as prizes of victory in physical feats. Perhaps it was the *Svayaṁvara* Institution.

Suttee. *Suttee* was seen by the Greeks. Onesicritus saw it among the Kathaioi or the Kaṭhas. Diodorus also states that among the Kathaians prevailed the custom that widows should be burnt along with their husbands [p. 279 in McCrindles' *Invasion of India by Alexander*]. Aristobulus relates that in 316 B. C. an Indian military leader who had gone to Iran to fight under Eumenes, accompanied by his two wives, was unfortunately killed in the battle, whereupon the two wives vied with each other to be the *Satī*. The elder being with child, the other one proceeded to the pyre and "lay down beside her husband. As the fire seized her, no sound of weeping escaped her lips."

Funeral. The Greeks were struck by the absence among Indians of funeral pomp or imposing monuments. The Indians thought that the virtues of the dead were more enduring than brass, as also the songs which were sung over them [*Cambridge History*, I. 412-16].

Slavery. Megasthenes is the source of the statement of Arrian that "all Indians are free, and not one of them is a slave." In fact, the supposed slavery prevailing in India was of such a mild character and limited extent as compared with the slavery known to the Hellenic world that Megasthenes could not notice its existence. We have besides the injunctions of the *Arthaśāstra* that an *Ārya* was not to be kept in the condition of slavery [III 13].

Kauṭilya calls the Śūdra an *Ārya* by birth (*Āryaprāṇa*). He contemplates the possibility of a man selling himself into slavery (*Sakṛidātmādhātā*), children being provided for in that way in times of distress, and also captives of war. But in all such cases it is open to the so-called slave under Hindu Law to buy back his freedom by means of earnings which he is permitted to make, irrespective of his earnings in his master's service. Over and above this, there was a provision that his kinsmen could and should redeem him from bondage by payment of ransom A slave was also entitled to the inheritance of his father. The slave woman who has been taken to her master's bed acquires freedom thereby, as also do her children (*Svāminaḥ svasyāṁ dāsyāṁ jātaṁ samātṛikaṁ adāsaṁ vidyāt*) (*Ib*].

Religion. The *Arthaśāstra* mentions the following deities popularly worshipped in those days : (1) Aparājitā (Durgā), (2) Apratihata (Vishṇu), (3) Jayanta (Subrahmaṇya), (4) Vaijayanta (Indra), (5) Śiva, (6) Vaiśravaṇa, (7) Aśvi, (8) Śrī, (9) Madirā [II. 4], (10) Aditi, (11) Anumati, (12) Sarasvati, (13) Savitā, (14) Agni, (15) Soma [XIV. 1], (16) Krishṇa, and (17) Paulomī [XIV. 3].

Spells and exorcisms formed part of the popular religion of the times. Evil was sought to be warded off by utterance of secret *Mantras* or spells (*aupanishadakam*), so that Brahminical Society might be protected against the attacks of the irreligious (*chāturvarṇya-rakshārtham*). There are mentioned incantations for terrorising the enemy by producing wonders (*adbhūtotpātaiḥ*). It is also stated that "the king should protect his own people and injure that of his enemy by the application of *Mantras*, drugs and spells." For these incantations, the inferior deities were invoked such as Bali-Vairochana, Śambara, Devala, Nārada, Manu, Pramilā and the like [XIV. *Ib.*]

The Brāhmaṇas practised the Vedic religion of sacrifice for which special sylvan retreats were provided [II. 1]. In the royal palace was provided a separate place for the performance of sacrifice (*ijyā-sthānam*). Ascetics of various types were abroad. They are described as *Siddhatāpasapravrajita*, while there was Tapovan a for the *Tapasvī* [IV. 4; II. 1].

Among the heretical sects are mentioned the *Śākyas* and *Ājīvikas* [III. 20]. Their entertainment was banned.

It will thus appear that Kauṭilya knows more of Vedic religion, sacrifice, deities, and the Atharvavedic rites and spells than of later classical Hindu deities and religious practices.

CHAPTER XII

ECONOMIC CONDITIONS

Economic Life : State Control. A good deal of the economic life of the country, as has been already apparent, was controlled by the State. The State was the largest employer of labour. It controlled and organised the agriculture, industry and the trade of the country

Agriculture. As we have already seen, the State had a large part of the agriculture of the country directly in its own hands in its vast crown estates. No doubt, it did not interfere in the actual work of cultivation, provided its established share of the produce was paid in as the land revenue demand, but it was specially the State's business to organise and extend the agricultural productivity of the country by schemes of colonisation, encouraging the surplus population to settle new or abandoned tracts, and also by assisting the emigration of foreigners to settle in the country (*bhūtapūrvaṁ abhūtapūrvaṁ vā janapadaṁ paradeśāpavāhanena svadeśābhishyanda-vamanena vā niveśayet*).

The village. Each village, besides its area under houses (*vāstu*), had its full apparatus of agricultural life in its (1) *Kedāra* or fields sown with crops, (2) *Pushpa-Vāṭa*, horticultural gardens (2) *Phala-vāṭa*, orchards (4) *Shaṇḍa*, plantations of bananas, sugarcane and the like ; and (5) *Mūla-vāpa*, fields for growing roots like ginger, turmeric and the like (*ārdrakaharidrādi*). Thus grains, flowers, fruits, vegetables, spices, sugar-cane and bananas were all grown in the village [II. 6].

The recorded and registered (*nibandha*) area of the village, after deducting from it the area covered by boundaries (*sīmāva-rodhena*), was made up of the following parts : (1) cultivated (*kṛishṭa*) area (2) uncultivated (*akṛishṭa*) wastes, (3) high and dry ground (*Sthala*), (4) *Kedāra*, (5) *Ārāma* (grove, *upavana*), (6) *Shaṇḍa* (*kadalyādi kshetram*, plantations of fruits like plantains), (7) *Vāṭa* (*ikshvādibhūmiḥ*, sugarcane plantations), (8) *Vana* (as source of firewood for the village and other requisites), (9) *Vāstu* (area under houses), (10) *Chaitya* (sacred trees), (11) *Devagriha* (temples) (12) *Setubandha* (embankments), (13) *Śmaśāna* (cremation grounds), (14) *Sattra* (almshouse), (15) *Prapā* (store-house of drinking water),

(16) *Puṇyasthāna* (holy places), (17) *Vivīta* (grazing ground for village cattle), and (18) *Pathi* (area covered by roads) [II. 35].

The Pāli texts of the times also throw light on village planning on similar lines. First was the arable land of the village, beyond which lay its common grazing grounds or pastures [*Jātaka*, I. 388] for its herds of cattle [III 149; IV. 326] or goats [III 401], whether belonging to the king [I. 240] or the commoner [I. 194, 388]. The villages employed a common neat-herd whose duty was to pen the flocks at night or to return them to their owners by counting heads [I. 388; III 149]. He was called *Gopālaka*, the protector of the flocks [V. 350]. The pasturage was changed from day to day [*Aṅguttara Nikāya*, I. 20].

Beyond the pastures lay the groves at the outskirts, like the Veluvana at Rājagṛiha, the Añjanavana at Sāketa, or the Jetavana at Śrāvastī.

Lastly came the uncleared jungles upon which the village could draw for its supply of fire-wood and litter [*Jātaka* I. 317; V. 10]. Examples of such forests were the Andhavana of Kośala, Sītāvana of Magadha, or the Prāchīna Vaṁsadāya of Śākya country, which are described as the haunts of wild beasts and brigands preying on caravan traffic passing through them [I. 99] [my *Hindu Civilization*, pp. 297-298].

Villages are also described from the fiscal point of view as (1) *Parihāraka*, rendered revenue-free by royal favour as a gift, (2) *Āyudhīya*, paying revenue in the form of military service (3) *Dhānya-pratikara*, paying land revenue in the form of grain, (4) *Paśupratikara*, (5) *Hiraṇyapratikara*, (6) *Kupyapratikara* and (7) *Vishṭi-pratikara*, paying revenue in cattle (e.g., cows for milk, bullocks for carrying load, sheep and goats for their wool); in gold, silver or copper; in forest produce and in labour, respectively [II. 35].

Among the crops grown in the villages are mentioned rice of different varieties; coarse grain (*kodrava*), sesamum (*tila*), pepper and saffron (*priyaṅgu*); pulses like *mudga*, *māsha*, *masūra*, *kuluttha*, *yava*, *godhūma* (wheat), *kalāya*, *atasī* (linseed), *sarshapa* (mustard); vegetables called *Śāka*, *Mūla*; fruits like plantains, pumpkins, gourds, grapes (*mṛidvīkā*); sugar-cane [II. 24].

Government Agricultural Farms. These model farms were of great use for the improvement of agriculture in the country. Seeds of various crops to be grown were collected here. Government had its own flower-, fruit-, and vegetable-gardens and undertook cultivation of commercial crops like cotton (*kārpāsa*) and jute (*kshauma*) [*Ib.*].

Agricultural Labour. There were landless agricultural labourers (*vishṭi*) who worked as domestic servants on the basis of free food and a little of wages in cash. There were also ordinary labourers (*Karmakara*) who worked for wages, and those who sold themselves into slavery (*Dāsas*). There were, lastly, agriculturists proper, or peasant proprietors, who worked on the basis of sharing of produce with the State, the State charging a sixth of the produce as its share or land-revenue demand.

It may be noted that the Buddhist literature of the times holds up the ideal of the landlord cultivating his own land from which he should not divorce himself. It attaches a social stigma to the agricultural labourer or hireling who is ranked below the slave [*Dīgha Nikāya*, I, 51; *Aṅguttara Nikāya*, I, 145, 206; *Milinda Pañha*, 147, 331]. The *Jātakas* [e g., I, 339] deplore as a sign of social decadence the distressing sight of sturdy peasants leaving at home their own empty barns, and swelling the ranks of landless agricultural labourers to toil as hirelings on the estates of royal capitalists.

Cattle. The village cattle comprised cows, buffaloes, goats, sheep, asses, camels, pigs and dogs (*Śunakāḥ* in XIV. 3) [V. 2].

The State maintained cattle-farms, stud-farms, and dairy farms, and employed the necessary staff comprising the *Gopālaka* (cowherd), *Piṇḍāraka* (for buffaloes), *Dohaka* (milker), *Manthaka* (churner), together with the hunters (*Lubdhakas*) and keepers of hunting hounds [*Śvagaṇinaḥ* (II. 29, II. 34)] to keep the pasture grounds clear of wild animals.

The cattle-farms reared calves, steers, draught oxen, stud-bulls, and buffaloes. It also undertook the taming of wild cattle.

There was also poultry-farming [V. 2].

Irrigation. Irrigation was the concern of the State as an important source of revenue derived from the water-rates levied in accordance with the means of irrigation employed. It controlled the distribution of water by sluice-gates. It was also responsible for constructing new sources of water supply by excavating tanks and canals.

The Pali texts of the times (specially the *Jātakas*) refer to the arable land of the village divided into individual holdings which are separated from one another by channels dug for co-operative irrigation [I, 336; IV. 167; V. 412 (Fausboll ed.)]. The cultivated fields of Magadha, which were thus divided by ditches, rectangular and curvilinear, are described by the Buddha as resembling his monks' uniform, a patch-work of torn pieces of cast-off clothing [*Vinaya Texts*, II, 207-9].

Village Public Works. A village had its full complement of public works of utility and social institutions. It had its *ārāmas* (rest-houses), *prapā* (tanks), *sattras* (alms-houses), *puṇyasthānas* (holy spots), *chaityas* (trees for worship), *deva-gṛihas* (temples), and its halls of public amusements such as music, dancing, theatrical performances (*prekshā*) and also for public dinners [*pravahaṇa*, III. 10]. There were also some structures for decoration of the village (*grāma-śobhāḥ*). These public works, as we have seen, were carried on by the joint enterprise and collective agreement (*samaya*) of co-operation among the villagers (*sambhūya*) [II. 1; III. 10]. Any one not making his contribution to such agreed communal undertakings would be fined [*Ib.*].

Village Service. There were paid workmen in the service of the village. These were called *Grāmbhṛitakas* and included workers like the carpenter (*Kuṭṭaka*), the blacksmith (*Karmāra*, *Ayaskāra*), the potter, the inevitable barber (*Nāpita*) [II. 1; V. 2], and the washerman [V. 3]. A village had also its diggers (*Medaka*) and rope-makers (*Rajjuvartaka*). Grants of land without right of alienation were made to the following rural officers: (1) *Adhyaksha* (such as *Suvarṇādhyaksha* (2) *Saṅkhyāyaka* (the village accountant), (3) *Gopa*, (4) *Sthānika*, (5) *Anīkastha* (trainer of elephants), (6) *Chikitsaka* (physician proper), (7) *Aśvadamaka* (trainer of horses), (8) *Jaṅghā-karika* (courier [II. 1].

Village Amusements. There were others workers to minister to the public amusements of the day, both in towns and villages. These were artists of various classes enumerated as follows: (1) *Naṭa* (actor) (2) *Nartaka* (dancer), (3) *Gāyaka* (musician), (4) *Vādaka* (instrumentalist), playing on instruments like *vīṇā*, *veṇu*, and *mṛidaṅga* (5) *Vāgjīvana* (rhapsodist), (6) *Kuśīlava* (dancing expert), (7) *Plavaka* (gymnast), (8) *Saubhika* (magician), (9) *Chāraṇa* (bard), (10) *Pāṭhaka* (reciter), (11) *Gandha-saṁyūhaka* (prefumer), (12) *Mālya-sampādaka* (garland-maker), (13) *Saṁvāhaka* (shampooer), (14) *Chitra-kara* (painter), (15) *Vaiśika* (teacher of erotic) and (16) *Parachitta-jñānavid* (thought-reader) [II, 27]. All these were in the pay of the Government.

Rural Well-being. The duties of the State towards the village and its welfare are summed up to include (1) demarcation of properties (*Setu*), (2) opening up of inaccessible tracts by roads (*pathisaṁkramāt*), (3) works of rural development (*grāma-śobhāḥ*) and protection (*rakshā*) [III. 10]. The protection of the village was in the hands of the rural police recruited from the classes called (1) *Vāgurikas* (trappers), (2) *Śabaras* (Bhils), (3) Pulindas (*Kirāta*), (4) *Chaṇḍālas* and (5) *Araṇyacharas* (foresters) [II. 1]. There was also a provision for the protection of a village by constructing a palisade (*upasālam*) of pillars built of stone or wood round it [III. 10].

The Jātakas also tell of the village being enclosed by a wall or stockade with gateś (*grāmadvāra*) [I. 239; II. 76, 135, III. 9].

The arable land of the village (*grāmakshetra*) was protected from pests, beasts and birds by fences [I. 215], snares [I. 143, 154], and field-watchmen [II. 110; IV. 277] about whom Kauṭilya gives full details.

Thus village life was built up on the basis of private property, security of life and property, communications and public works.

Uncultivated Wastes : Forestry. While cultivated lands were thus disposed of, the vast stretches of waste lands lying beyond the village (*akṛishyā bhūmiḥ*) were utilised fully by the plantation of pastures (*vivīta*) for the grazing of the village cattle and of forests of different kinds. First came these grazing grounds, and then the woodland retreats for Brāhmaṇas for their study of the Veda and performance of Soma sacrifices (*Brahma-Somāraṇya*) and for hermits for doing penance in their *tapovana*.

Beyond these lay the belt of forests. The first was the forest reserved for the king's hunt (*vihāra*) followed by the ordinary forests.

These were of various kinds and were distinguished by their products such as *Dāru* (timber), *Veṇu* (bamboo), *Vallī* (cane), *Valka* (bark), *Rajju* (fibres for robe-works) ; *Patra* (material for writing such as palm-leaves or bark of birch, *tāla-bhūrja-patra*) ; *Pushpa* (flowers for dyeing like *Kiṁśuka*, *Kusumbha* or *Kuṅkuma*) ; *Aushadha* (medicinal herbs), *Visha* (poisons) [II. 17], firewood, and fodder (*Kāsṭha-yavasa*). Specially favoured were the forests of elephants so necessary for war and of timber as building materials for towns and fortifications. Elephant forests were in the keeping of the Conservator called *Nāgavanādhyaksha* [II. 2].

The forest also yielded various animal products of economic value such as hides, skins, sinews, bones, teeth, horns, hoofs, and tails of creatures like leopard, tiger, lion, elephant, buffalo, yak, crocodile, tortoise, snake, and birds.

Forest Staff. The forests were under the Conservator called *Vanapāla*. There were also in the Forest Service persons known for their special knowledge of the properties of trees and the economic value of each of their parts (*vṛiksha-marmajña*) [II. 17].

Then there were also the artisans who would work up the various forest products into their finished forms in the village factories (*dravyavana-karmāntāḥ*). They manufactured such necessary articles as plough, pestle, mortar, implements, weapons, and carts.

Industry : State Control. The State had a monopoly in many industries which depended on pioneering and costly enterprise.

Mining industry was nationalised for its supreme importance to the State as primary source of its wealth (*ākara-prabhavaḥ kośaḥ*).

The mines worked by government are mentioned as those of gold, silver, diamond, gems, precious stones and of other inferior metals like copper, lead (*sīsa*), tin (*trapu*), iron (*tīkshṇa* or *ayas*) and bitumen (*śilājatu*).

The State also explored the ocean mines in search of *muktā* (pearls), *śukti* (mother of pearl), *śaṅkha* (conch-shell) and *pravāla* (coral).

The State also worked the oilfields (yielding *rasa* like mercury).

Minerals were also extracted from the earth.

The manufacture of salt was also a government monopoly worked under a system of licences granted to private lessees of salt-fields.

There was a special officer called *Khanyādhyaksha* to look after the government business in pearl, conch-shells, corals, diamonds and precious stones.

There was another special officer called *Sauvarṇika* in charge of gold and silver turned out in the State workshop called *Akshaśālā* [II. 13].

The State also had its cotton, oil, sugar, and dairy industries [II. 6].

The State reserved to itself the manufacture of wines and liquors and their sale.

It also had a monopoly in armament industry and the building of boats and ships.

The right of coining belonged to the State whose officers received from the public bullion to be shaped into coins on the basis of seignorage charges. The Mint Master was called *Lakshaṇādhyaksha.*

The prisons had factories which employed penal labour. The State Spinning House was both a Spinning and Weaving Mill which manufactured yarns of cotton, silk, and jute ; clothing ; mail armour (*varma*) ; ropes ; blankets (*āstaraṇa*) ; and curtains (*prāvaraṇa*). It employed the labour of women who were helpless and even supplied purdah women with orders for spinning yarn through its women-employees.

Otherwise labour was employed on contract at the State factories. It was penal to hold back wages.

Thus the State had to run its own factories and workshops for the utilization of the products of its own agricultural lands, forests, and mines, which were received and accumulated in the State warehouses (*Koshṭhāgāra*). These accumulations were due to the system by which the dues of the State, its revenue demands, were paid not in cash (*hiraṇya*) but in kind, and called for a network of warehouses distributed throughout the country to receive these goods. Thus the Factory came in the wake of the Warehouse.

Private Industrial Enterprise. The entire Industry of the country was, however, not in the hands of the State. A large field was occupied by individual private industry.

While Kauṭilya naturally pays more attention to the former, other texts throw light on the part played by private enterprise in industry. The most important of these texts are the *Jātakas* on which craftsmen drew so largely for their themes treated in the early sculptures of Bharhut or Sanchi in the third and second century B.C. The *Jātakas* are documents of older history, as pointed out by Rhys Davids. They speak of eighteen chief handicrafts of the times, such as those of wood-workers, smiths, leather-dressers, painters, workers in stone, ivory-workers, weavers, confectioners, jewellers, workers in precious metals, potters, makers of bow and arrow. These handicrafts were also organised in guilds or craft-guilds called *Śreṇīs*, each under its President or Foreman called *Pamukha*, and the Alderman called *Jeṭṭhaka*. We are also told of federations of guilds under a common Head called *Bhāṇḍāgārika*. Like Industry, Trade also was organised in Merchant-Guilds whose chief was called *Seṭṭhi*. Anāthapiṇḍika of Sāvatthī was a *Mahāseṭṭhi*, chief of a commercial federation controlling 500 *Seṭṭhis*, the heads of its constituent guilds. Caravan-traffic for its risks was carried on as a co-operative enterprise in which different traders with their carts, goods, and men formed themselves into a Company under a captain called *Sātthavāha* to give directions as to halts, watering, routes, fords, and danger-spots, and also other common officers or land-pilots called *Thalaniyyāmaka* who acted as guides and escorts against the dangers to travel from "drought, famine, wild beasts, robbers and demons." We are similarly told of sea-going merchants chartering a common vessel, or of concerted action in freights between dealers, and of partnership concerns in business such as export of birds to Babylon, or of import of horses from the 'north' to Benares. There was also localisation in Industry. We read of villages of potters, of wood-wrights, ironsmiths, or even trappers; while within the town were ivory-workers' street (*vīthī*), dyers' street, Vessas' streets or the weavers' quarter (*ṭhāna*). There were also the *hīna-sippas* or despised callings which were segregated; those of hunters and trappers, fishermen, butchers, tanners; or snake-charmers, actors, dancers, musicians, rush-weavers and chariot-makers who were mostly the aboriginal folks [*Hindu Civilisation*, pp. 301, 307, 308].

Trade. The State had a special responsibility in the matter of Trade. Its revenue depended upon a profitable disposal of the vast quantities of various goods which were constantly accumulating in its hands in its factories and workshops under circumstances described. The State thus became the biggest trader in the country, and had to control its entire trade to safe-guard its own interests.

The control of trade was based on the State control of Prices. The system of control was based on certain inevitable provisions.

Goods could not be sold at the place of their origin, field or factory. They were to be carried to the appointed markets (*paṇya-śālā*) where the dealer had to declare particulars as to the quantity, quality and the prices of his goods which were examined and registered in the books.

Every trader had to get a licence for sale. A trader from outside had to obtain a passport in addition.

The Superintendent of Commerce (*Paṇyādhyaksha*) fixed the whole-sale prices of goods as they were entered in the Customs House. He allowed a margin of profit to fix the retail prices.

Smuggling and adulteration of goods were severely punished.

Speculation and cornering to influence prices were not allowed.

Strikes of workmen to raise wages were declared illegal.

The State had to undertake a heavy and irksome responsibility in protecting the public, customers and consumers, against unauthorised prices and fraudulent transactions. It had to post an army of spies or market inspectors on the trade-routes to detect false declarations as to goods and apprize merchants of same [II. 21].

Apart from the State control of prices was the State control of weights and Measures. The official standard was made a little lower than the public so as to provide a convenient source of revenue in the difference which amounted to a *vyājī* of 5 per cent. It was like the seignorage charge on the minting of coins.

Trade was taxed all along its way by export and import duties, octroi and excise. Its progress through the country was punctuated by halts enforced for payment of taxes at different stages. The foreign merchants were mulcted of their profits on the frontiers, by road taxes (*vartanī*) and tolls, and by octroi at the gates of cities, which were carefully guarded by officers in charge of the Customs Houses provided even with a *dounane* and a place for detention for merchants evading the law.

But if Trade was thus taxed, it received compensation in the protection assured to it in those olden days when life and property were not secure everywhere. The transit of goods was guarded all along its way. Any loss suffered in their transit was to be made good by the Government officer in charge of locality through which the goods passed. In the village, the responsibility was that of its head-man (*Grāma-svāmī* or *Grāma-mukhya*); beyond the village the *Vivītādhyaksha*; beyond his jurisdiction the responsibility was that of the government Police, the *Chora-rajjuka*; and beyond him was *Sīmā-svāmī*, the chief of the frontier.

Trade had to be protected in those days against the gangs of dacoits who were abroad (*chora-gaṇas*), the turbulent Mlechchha tribes (like the *Kirātas*) and the wild people of the forests (*Āṭavikas*) who were all out for plunder [VII. 10].

We have already referred to the rural police. But every village was directly guarded against thieves (*taskara*) by the hunters and keepers of dogs (*lubdhaka-śvagaṇinaḥ*) already mentioned, whose method of dealing with them was to collect people by sounding alarm by conch shell or drum from a height, hill, or tree, unperceived, or by running fast to give information to the village [II. 34].

Trade-routes. Trade depended upon its routes, which presented a problem for a continent like India.

Grand Trunk Road. The Greeks tell of the Royal Road leading from the North West Frontier to Pāṭaliputra, the Grand Trunk Road of those days, with a length of 10,000 stadia=about 13,00 miles. [Strabo XV. 1, 11]. We have also seen how Megasthenes refers to Government officers in charge of roads and how signboards were set up at intervals to indicate turnings and distances.

It may be noted that Megasthenes refers to the Royal Road from the North West to Pāṭaliputra as the road existing in earlier times.

As he entered India, Megasthenes was struck by this Royal Road leading from the Frontier to Pāṭaliputra down which he must himself have travalled in prosecution of his mission. It is stated to have been constructed in eight stages, the distances between which were measured up to the Hyphasis (Beas) by Alexander's survey officers named Baeto and Diognetus, while the distances from the Hyphasis to the Ganges are supposed to have been measured for Seleukos Nikator by Megasthenes and other Greek visitors. These stages are thus described:

1. From Peukelaotis (Sans. Pushkalāvatī, the capital of Gandhāra, modern Charsadda) to Taxila. 2. From Taxila across the Indus to the Hydaspes (Jhelum). 3. Thence to the Hyphasis (Beas) near the spot where Alexander erected his altars. 4. From the Beas to the Hesidrus (Satlej). 5. From Satlej to the Iomanes (Jumna). 6. From the Jumna via Hastināpura to the Ganges 7. From the Ganges up to a town called Rhodopha (said to be Dabhai near Anupshahar). 8. From Rhodopha to Kalinapaxa (probably Kanyākubja or Kanauj). 9. From Kanauj to Prayāga at the junction of the Ganges and the Jumna. 10. From Prayāga to Pāṭaliputra. 11. From Pāṭaliputra to the mouth of the Ganges probably at Tāmralipti. Every mile of the road was marked by a stone indicating the by-roads and the distances. The road was in charge of the officers of the P. W. D. who were responsible for its up-keep, repairs and for erection of mile-stones and sign-posts at every ten stadia (Pliny, *Natural History*, VI, 21).

Buddhist Texts on Roads. The Buddhist literature of earlier times throws much light on the roads of traffic.

Inland Roads. The inland trade was carried on by carts and caravans. We read of Anāthapiṇḍika's caravans travelling south-east from Sāvatthī to Rājagaha and back (about 300 miles) [Jāt., I. 92. 348], and also to the "borders", probably towards Gandhāra [*Ib.*, i, 377 f]. To ensure easy fording of rivers, this route must have passed along the foot of the mountains up to Kusinārā between which and Rājagaha, lay halts at twelve intermediate stations (*gāmas* or *nagaras*) including Vesāli, with a single crossing of Ganges at Patna according to the recorded itinerary of the Buddha's last ministering journey [*Dīgha*, II, *Suttanta*, XXXI. 81. ff.].

Another important route led south-west from Sāvatthī to Patiṭṭhāna (Paithan) with six intermediate halts [*Sutta-Nipāta*, 1011-13] and frequent crossing of rivers. We read of boats going up the Ganges to Sahajāti [*Vinaya Texts*, iii, 401] and up the Yamunā to Kosambī [*Ib.* p. 382]. There were no bridges in those days but only fording-places and ferries for crossing rivers [*Jāt.*, iii, 288]. Manu speaks of car-ferries [viii. 404 f.]. *Setu* was not a bridge but only an embankment.

A third route led west-wards to Sind, the home of horses and asses [*Jāt.* ii, 124, 178, 181, ; ii, 31, 287] and to Sovīra [*Vimāna Vatthu* (Comm.), 336] and its ports, with its capital called Roruva [*Jāt.*, iii, 470], or Roruka [*Dīgha*, ii, 235 ; *Divyāvadāna*, 544]. We read of overland caravans going "east and west" [*Jāt.* I, 98, f], and across deserts requiring days to cross (the deserts of Rājputana), steering in the coolness of nights by the stars, under the land-pilot, *Thalaniyyāmaka* Ib. 1, 107].

Beyond the western ports, merchants went "out of sight of land" into the ocean and traded with Bāveru (Babylon).

Lastly, there was the great north-west over-land trade-route linking India with the Central and Western Asia by way of Taxila and cites of the Gangetic Valley like Sāketa, Sāvatthī, Benares, or Rājagaha [*Vin.* Texts, ii, 174, ff. ; *Mahāvagga,* viii, I, 6 ff.]. As a very frequented road, it was free from dangers. We read of students travelling in numbers to Takkasilā, unattended and unarmed [*Jāt.* ii, 277], for education.

Sea-borne Trade. There is some evidence as to the sea-borne foreign trade of those days, though it is scanty. We read of Prince Mahājanaka sailing from Champā for Suvaṇṇabhūmi [*Ib.* vi, 34 f], of Mahinda from Pāṭaliputra to Tāmalitti and thence to Ceylon [*Vin.* iii, 388 (*Samantapāsādika*)]. A whole village of defaulting woodwrights is described as escaping at night down the Ganges in a "mighty ship" from Benares out to the sea [*Jāt.* IV, 159]. An accomplished helmsman brings safe by ships "passengers for India from off the sea to Benares by river" [*Ib.* ii, 112]. We read of traders coasting round India from Bhārukachha to Suvaṇṇabhūmi [*Ib.* iii, 188], touching at a port of Ceylon on the way [*Ib.* ii, 127 ff.]. The cargo of a newly-arrived ship attracts a hundred merchants to buy it up [*Ib.*, i, 122]. The ships of the times were large enough to accommodate "hundreds" of passengers. We read of 500 traders on board ill-fated ships [*Ib.* 128; v, 75], and of 700 under the safe pilotage of Suppāraka [*Ib.*, iv,138, ff] [*Hindu Civilization*, pp. 302-304].

Sanskrit Texts. The testimony of the Pāli Texts to the existence of an overland trade-route is confirmed by Pāṇini's mention of *Uttarapatha* [V. 1, 77]. He speaks of travellers going by *Uttarapatha* (*Uttarapathena gachchhati*) and of goods gathered by that route (*Uttarapathena āhṛitam*).

According to Strabo, the river Oxus in the time of Alexander was quite navigable so that goods from India were carried down the river to the Caspain Sea on their way to the west. As Warmington points out [*Commerce between Roman Empire and India*, p. 21] there were three natural approaches to India from the west; (1) where the mountains of Afghanistan become very narrow just north of the head of the Kabul river where only the Hindukush separates the basins of the Oxus, and the Indus; (2) 500 miles to the west and south-west, where the Afghan mountains end and open up an easy way over 400 miles of plateau from Herat to Kandahar and to Kabul, along the Helmund valley, and another way from south-east of Kandahar into the Indus lowlands through the Bolan or the Mūla Pass; (3) by way of the deserts of Makran or along the coast of Baluchistan.

The *Uttarapatha* of Pāṇini must have been the first or the second of above routes. It may be noted that Chandragupta Maurya's conquest of these regions by which the boundaries of his empire were practically extended up to Persia must have resulted in an increase of India's trade with the west along these routes. Within India, this overland trade-route (*Uttarapatha*) must have passed through and linked up her chief cities mentioned by Pāṇini and Patañjali, such as Bālhīka, Kāpiśī, Pushkalāvatī Maśakāvatī, Takshaśilā, Śākala, Hastināpura, Kauśāmbī, Kāśī and Pāṭaliputra.

Patañjali (commenting on Pāṇini II. 2, 18 and III. 3, 136) mentions the formations, *Nish-Kauśāmbiḥ* and *Nir-Vārāṇasiḥ* in respect of travellers who have passed beyond Kauśāmbī and Vārānasī, thereby indicating the Grand Trunk Road of those days connecting the two cities of Kauśāmbī and Vārāṇasī. In connection with Pāṇini's rule, III, 3, 136, Patañjali instances the cities of Śāketā and Pāṭaliputra as lying on the same road so as to enable us to construct the length of a Grand Trunk Road that connected the two cities of Sāketa and Kauśāmbi, Vārāṇasī and Pāṭaliputrā. Curiously, the *Kāśikā* mentions Kauśāmbī as the starting-point of a journey instead of Sāketa mentioned by Patañjali, though both retain Pāṭaliputra as the other end of the journey. "There may be a personal and psychological reason involved in this difference between the two grammarians. Each was perhaps thinking of his own native city forming the centre of his geographical horizon" [My Note in *Indian Culture*, II, 2].

The *Ārthaśāstra* **on Roads.** The *Arthaśāstra* follows in the wake of all this earlier evidence.

According to Kauṭilya [VII. 12], Trade-routes (*Vaṇikpatha*) are to be established as ways of profit.

Water-ways. One view is that, of trade-routes by land, and by water, the water-route is preferable as yielding more profit on the ground that transport of goods by water costs less money and less labour (*alpavyaya-vyāyāmaḥ prabhūtapaṇyodayaścha*).

Kauṭilya does not agree to this view. In his opinion, water-route does not admit of any way to help in danger (*saṁruddhagati vipadi sarvato-niruddhagamanaḥ*). It cannot be used in all weathers (*asarvakālikaḥ*) ('such as rains'), is more exposed to risks, without remedies against them.

Kauṭilya classifies waterways into (1) ways along the coast (*Kūla-patha*), (2) ways through mid-ocean (to foreign countries) (*Saṁyāna-patha*). Of these, again, he prefers the former as a source of greater profit for its access to many port-towns (*Paṇya-paṭṭana-bāhulyāt*).

The river is a third water-way. This also has some points in its favour. It is without break and not exposed to serious risks.

Roads of Traffic. As to land-routes, their broad division is into (1) *Haimavata*, or *Uttarāpatha*, the road which leads to the northern snows ; (2) *Dakshiṇāpatha*.

Uttarāpatha. One view holds the Haimavata route better, as it gives access to more profitable things (*sāravattarāḥ*), such as elephants, horses, the rare article *kastūrī* or musk (*gandhaḥ kastūrī*), ivory, skins, silver and gold.

Dakshiṇāpatha. But Kauṭilya, though a Northerner, stands up for the South. He says that 'if the southern route does not lead to countries from which come blankets (*kambala*), skins, or animals like horses, it brings in far more valuable products like conch-shells, diamonds, gems, pearls and gold. The southern road, moreover, leads through many mines (*bahu-khaniḥ*) and lands yielding valuable commodities (*sārapaṇyaḥ*), and does not mean risky or difficult travelling (*prasiddhagatiḥ alpavyāyāmaḥ*).

On the same ground of profit, Kauṭilya wants the State to provide the country with roads for cart-traffic (*chakra-patha*) by which much merchandise can be always carried (*vipulāraṁbhatvāt*). He also recommends the tracks for beasts of burden like asses and camels [*Ib.*].

Different Classes of Roads. Kauṭilya [II. 4] speaks of various classes of roads in the country such as :

(1) *Rāja-mārga*, or the king's way, highway ;

(2) the provincial roads leading to different administrative head-quarters such as *Sthānīya-patha* ;

(3) *Droṇamukha-patha* ;

(4) *Rāshṭra-patha*, leading to the rural areas ; or

(5) *Vivīta-patha* leading to the pasture lands on the country side ; and other classes of roads called

(6) *Saṁyānīya-patha* leading to market towns (*Saṁyānīyaṁ kraya-vikraya-vyavahāra-pradhānaṁ paṭṭanam tatpathaḥ*) ;

(7) *Vyūhapatha*, the path for the army ;

(8) *Setupatha* leading to irrigated fields ;

(9) *Vanapatha*, the path to the forests ;

(10) *Hastipatha*, the path for elephants ;

(11) *Kshetrapatha*, leading to cultivated fields ;

(12) *Rathapatha*, the road for chariots ;

(13) *Paśupatha*, the track for cattle ;

(14) *Kshudrapaśupatha*, the track for smaller animals like sheep etc. and lastly ;

(15) *Manushyapatha*, the path for men.

Merchandise. All these various roads brought to markets commodities of different kinds from all parts of the country from which they were derived, from out-of-the-way places like mines and forests.

Pearls. Their different varieties were named after the places of their origin. These were (1) *Tāmraparṇika* derived from a place in the Pāṇḍya country, where the river Tāmraparṇī falls into the sea (*Samudra saṅgama pradeśa samutpannam*) ; (2) *Pāṇḍyakavāṭaka* derived from Malayakoṭi hill in the Pāṇḍya country ; (3) *Pāśikya* derived from the bed of the river Pāśikā near Pāṭaliputra ; (4) *Kauleya* derived from the bed of the river Kulā of village named *Mayūra* in the island of Siṁhala (Ceylon) ; (5) *Charṇeya* derived from the bed of the river Chūrṇī of the town (Paṭṭana) called Murachi in Kerala country ; (6) *Māhendra* derived from the mountain Mahendra ; (7) *Kārdamika* derived from the bed of the river Kardamā of Pārasīka or Persia ; (8) *Srautasīya* derived from the bed of the river Srāutasī on the coast of Barbara ; (9) *Hrādīya* derived from the bed of a lake named Śrīghaṇṭa in Barbara on the sea ; and (10) *Haimavata* derived from Himālaya.

Gems. Gems (*Maṇi*) were gathered in from the mountains known as Koṭi and Mālā and from the hill called Rohaṇa in Ceylon (*Pāra-samudrakaḥ pārasamudraḥ Siṁhaladvīpastho Rohaṇādriḥ tajjaḥ*).

Diamonds. Diamonds came from Sabhārāshṭra, the name of the Vidarbha country ; Madhyama-rāshṭra which is the Kosala country ; Kāstīra-rāshṭra : the hill called Śrīkaṭana ; Maṇimantaka, a hill in the *Uttarāpatha*; and Indravānaka, a hill in the Kalinga country.

Corals. Corals were obtained from the place called Alakanda, a sea-port in the lands of the Barbaras ; Vivarṇa, a place on the beach in the island of the Yavanas.

Fragrant Woods. There was trade in fragrant woods like sandal (*chandana*), aloe (*agaru*) or *kāleyaka*. Most of these were the products of Kāmarūpa or Assam.

Skins. There was a large trade in skins of different kinds derived from places like Kāntanāva and Preya which are the regions of the Himalayas (*Uttaraparvata*). Skins of varieties called Bisī and Mahābisī came from twelve noted Himalayan villages inhabited by Mlechchhas (*Dvādaśagrāmīye*). Various kinds of skin came from another Himalayan region known as Āroha.

Another country on the Himalayas named Bāhlava was the source of other varieties of skins.

Lastly, there was trade in the skins of aquatic animals.

Blankets. There was considerable trade in blankets of wool. Nepal is mentioned as a source of good blankets ; of rain-proof (*varshāvāraṇam*) blankets made up of eight pieces joined together and of black colour, known as Bhingisi ; as well as blankets known as *Apasāraka.*

Silk. The *dukūla* (white silk garments) came from Vaṅga ; Puṇḍra in northern Bengal supplied the stuff called *Pauṇḍraka,* while the place called Suvarṇakuḍḍa in Assam was also known for its silk.

Linen. *Kshauma* or Linen came from the country called Kāśi, and from Puṇḍra.

Fibrous garments (*Patrorṇāḥ*) were the products of Magadha, Puṇḍra, and Suvarṇalukuḍḍa.

Of the same kind are the garments known as *Kauśeya* (produced in the country called *Kośakāra*) and *Chīnapaṭṭ* (*Chīnabhūmijaḥ*). V. R. R: Dikshitar proposes to identify *Chīna* with *Shina,* a Gilgit tribe known for its manufacture of silk [*Mauryan Polity,* p. 7].

Textiles. Cotton fabrics (*Kārpāsikam*) of the best quality were produced at the following places : Madhurā, the capital of Pāṇḍya country; Aparānta (Koṅkaṇa); Kaliṅga; Kāśī; Vaṅga; Vatsya; Māhishmatī, the capital of Kuntala country.

Urban Life. Urban life had its own amenities like life in a village. These were offered by a number of institutions of different kinds. Every city had its rest-houses for travellers (*Dharmāvasathas*), its factories where worked its artists (*Śilpī*) and craftsmen, its shops, its vintners (*Śauṇḍikāḥ*), its restaurants offering meals of cooked meat(*pakkvamāṁsa*), rice (*odana*), and cake (*āpūpa*), and its taverns (*pānaśālā*). It had many public amusements like theatrical performances (*prekshā*), music, vocal, and instrumental, exhibition of acting, dancing, jugglery (*chakra-chara*), sorcery (*kuhaka*), story-telling, rhapsody, gymnastics, painting and the like, which were all given by its various classes of artists trained in its Schools of Art maintaned by the State [II. 36; II. 27 ; IV, 4].

The city's learning and culture were represented by persons noted for their knowledge, their oratorical gifts, their spirituality, who were all given the highest honours and allowances for their maintenance (*Vidyā-Vākya-Dharma-Śūra* [XIII, 5]. We have already seen how religion and learning were endowed by grants of land made tax-free and in perpetuity (*adaṇḍa- karāṇi abhirūpadāyakāni*) by the State to their votaries named (1) Ṛitvik, (2) *Āchārya,* (3) *Purohita* and (4)

Śrotriya [II. 1]. The State also bestowed stipends of honour (*pūjā-vetanāni*) upon the teachers of music (*Āchāryāḥ Gandharvāchāryāḥ*) and the men of learning (*vidyāvantaḥ*) in the city whose services were always at the disposal of the public (*sarvopasthāyinaḥ*). The stipends were granted in accordance with merit (*yathārhaṁ*) [V. 3].

Coins. The Maurya empire was based upon a money-economy.

The literary references to the use of coins are older than their actual finds.

The Vedic term for a coin is taken to be *Nishka* [*Rv.* I. 126, 2].

The *Bṛihadāraṇyaka Upanishad* speaks of a gift made to Yājñavalkya in the form of five *pādas* of gold with which the horns of 1000 cows were hung, a total gift of 10,000 *pādas*. Weight of gold and probably a gold currency are indicated in such terms as *Ashṭāprud* [*Kāṭhaka Samhitā*, Chapter XI, 1,] or *Śatamāna* defined as "a weight of 100 *krishṇalas*' [*Śatapatha Brāhmaṇa*, V. 5, 5, 16]. The *Śatapatha* [XII. 2, 3. 2] also refers to payment of sacrificial fee in terms of gold (*hiraṇya*), whether *Suvarṇa* or *Śatamāna*.

We also read of gold (*hiraṇya*) being obtained from the beds of rivers like the Indus [*Rv.* X. 75, 8], or extracted from the earth [*Av.* XII, 1, 6, 26, 44] or from ore by smelting [*Śata Br.* VI, 1, 3, 5] or from washings [*Ib.* II, 1, 1, 5].

Pāṇini (*c.* 500 B. C.) in his Grammar testifies to the continued use of some of these Vedic terms for coins. He knows of the gold coins *Nishka*, *Śatamāna* and *Suvarṇa*. Things valued in terms of *Nishka* are called *Naishika*, *Dvinaishkika*, and so forth [V. 1, 20; 30]. A man of 100 *Nishkas* was called a *Naishka-Śātika*, a man of thousand a *Naishka-Sāhasrika* [V. 2, 119].

An article bought for 1 *Śatamāna* is called a *Śātamānam* [V.1,27].

It is interesting to note that Mr. Durga Prasad of Benares (whose recent death is a great loss to Indian Numismatics), who had specialised in the study of punchmarked silver coins and handled thousands of them so far discovered, ascertained that 39 silver coins which were found in the earliest layers at Taxila weighed 100 *rattis* each=180 grains. These coins cannot be taken to be the double Persian *sigloi* mentioned below, for the Persian *sigloi* weighed not more than 36.45 grains and a double weighed 72.9 grains. They, therefore, are to be taken as indigenous coins called aptly *Śatamāna* coins in our texts. It may be further assumed that weights of these coins followed a decimal system. The *Śatamānas* had their *Pādas* which may also be identified with certain broad pieces punched with 4 symbols and weighing 25 *rattis* or 1/4 *oj* *Śatamānas*.

Pāṇini also refers to objects valued in terms of *Suvarṇa* taken as a coin [IV. 3, 153 ; VI. 2, 55].

He also knows of a gold coin *Sāṇa* [V. 1, 35].

In the *Charaka-Saṁhitā* (Kalpa-Sthāna, XII. 89), 1 *sāna*=4 *māshas*.

Kauṭilya, as we have seen [II. 14], takes 1 *Suvarṇa*=16 *Māshas* and a *pāda* of *Suvarṇa*=4 *māshas*, the equivalent of a *Sāṇa*.

The *Kārshāpaṇa*, the established coin of ancient India, is fully known to Pāṇini who refers to transactions made in terms of money taken to be the *Kārshāpaṇa* [V. 1, 21 ; 27 ; 29 ; 34[.

He also knows of 1/2 (*ardha*)) and 1/4 (*pāda*) as denominations of *Kārshāpaṇa* [V. 1, 48 ; 34].

Kārshāpaṇa, as the standard coin, was in silver. Kauṭilya uses the form *paṇa*.

Pāṇini again knows of the small coin called *Māsha* [V. 2, 34). Kauṭilya takes *Māsha* as 1/16 of *Kārshāpaṇa*, and as a copper coin [II. 19] It would be too small in size in silver, though even some specimens of the silver *Māsha* have been found at some places like Taxila. Therefore, as a copper coin, it admitted of smaller denominations known as 1/2 *Māshaka*, 1 *Kākaṇi*=1/4 *Māsha* and 1/2 *Kākaṇi*=1/8 *Māsha*. *Kākaṇi* and *Ardhakākaṇi* are known to Kātyāyana [*Vārttika* on V. 1, 33] and also to Patañjali.

Pāṇini also uses the term *Vṛiṁśatika* in terms of *Kārshāpaṇa* of twenty parts. This coin was in circulation in the country in some parts, along with the *Kārshāpaṇa* of 16 parts, as known to *Kauṭilya*.

It appears that Mr. Durga Prasad found coins weighing 40 and 60 *rattis* corresponding to 20 and 30 *Māshas*, 1 *Māsha* being=2 *rattis* of silver. These coins may thus be taken as examples of coins called aptly by Pāṇini *Viṁśatika* and *Triṁsatika* coins as known in his day.

It may be noted that the *Vinayapiṭaka* [*Aṭṭhakathā* II *Parājika*] furnishes the information that "at that time (of Bimbisāra or Ajātasattu) at Rājagaha, there was in circulation the *Kārshāpaṇa* of twenty *Māshakas* (*Viṁsatimāsako Kahāpaṇo*), whence the *Pāda* was five *Māshakas*. Buddhaghosha in his *Samantapāsādikā* dubs this coin as *Nīlakāhāpaṇa* and further states that the coin in circulation in the capital of the empire became the current coin in all its provinces (*Sabbajanapadeshu*). It is also stated that the coin was fashioned in accordance with the specifications of the old technical numismatic *Śāstra* (*Purāṇa-Śāstra*) [C. D. Chatterji in *Buddhistic Studies*, pp. 384-386].

Patañjali [on Pāṇini 1. 2. 64] refers to the *Kārshāpaṇa* of 16 *Māshas* as being older (*purākalpa*) than the one of 20 *Māshas* with which he was apparently more familiar Kauṭilya knows of this older *Kārshāpaṇa* as the standard of his days but refers to another silver coin called *Dharaṇa* of 20 parts. Both varieties of *Kārshāpaṇa* seem to have been in circulation in different local areas in the country. It may be noted that the Buddhist tradition cited above regards the coin of 20 *Māshas* as being older than that of 16 *Māshas*.

Thousands of actual examples of the silver *Kārshāpaṇa* have been found in different parts of India and designated now as punch-marked coins. Their average weight is 32 *Raktikās*=56 grains. This agrees with the standard mentioned by Kauṭilya, Manu [VIII. 136] or Yājñavalkya I. 364] and also in *Sāratthadīpanī* where the weight of a '*Rudradāmaka*' coin=42 grains is stated to be 3/4 of a *purāṇa* (old) *Kārshāpaṇa* [*Buddhistic Studies, Ib.*].

Pāṇini uses the term *rūpa* [V. 2, 120] and explains the formation *rūpya* as 'beautiful' or 'stamped' (*āhata*). The latter sense applies to a coin. The *Arthaśāstra* takes the term *rūpa* in the sense of a coin alone and mentions an officer known as *Rūpadarśaka*, 'the examiner of coins,' as we have already seen. It is interesting to note that Patañjali in commenting on *Vārttika* on Pāṇini's sūtra, I, 4, 52, refers to a *Rūpaṭarka* 'who examines (*darśayati*) the *kārshāpaṇas*'. It may be also recalled that Kauṭilya uses the terms *Rūpyarūpa* and *Tāmrarūpa* for silver and copper coins.

We shall now turn to the actual specimens of ancient Indian coins discovered so far.

The oldest variety has been found in the parts of India in the northwest which belonged to the Achaemenian Persian empire in the sixth and fifth century B.C. Some of these coins were found in an early layer at Taxila along with a gold coin of Diodotus (250 B. C.), and, in another stratum, with the coins of Alexander the Great, looking "fresh from the mint," and one Achaemenid *siglos* of the 4th Century B. C. These weigh, as we have seen, 100 *ratis*=180 grains on an average. The *sigloi* weighs 86.45 grains, while the Attic standard=67.5 grains.

These coins are "thick, slightly bent bars of silver, stamped with wheel or sunlike designs resembling the 6 armed symbol to be seen on the later punch-marked silver coins, while they form only a single type" [Allan, *Catalogue of the Coins of Ancient India*, xv. xvi].

It was probably these pieces in which Āmbhi, the king of Taxila, had paid to Alexander his present of what the Greek writers describe as "80 talents of coined silver" [Curtius, VIII. 12, 42].

According to Durga Prasad [*JRASB*, Numismatic Supplement, XLVII, p. 76], these older pre-Maurya coins are struck on a standard of 100 *rattis* as against the later Maurya coins of standard 32 *rattis* weight. This confirms the truth of the *Vinayapiṭaka* that the older *Kārshāpaṇa* of 20 *Māshakas* was of lesser weight.

Next, a hoard of coins was found at a deep stratum in Golakhpur at the site of ancient Pāṭaliputra. These are taken to be the earliest known punch-marked silver coins and to be pre-Maurya, perhaps, Nanda, coins. They bear a pre-Maurya symbol, 'the hare and dog on hill', which may be taken as the Nanda symbol. It may be noticed that many of these were punched by the Mauryas with their own symbol to make them 'legal tender', or *kośa-praveśya*, as Kauṭilya calls them, as contrasted with the coinage current among the public for purposes of business transactions and aptly called by Kauṭilya *vyāvahārikī paṇya-yātrā*, as we have already seen. We may recall that the *Kāśikā* mentions a tradition about Nandas inaugurating a royal measure (*Nandopakramāṇi mānāni*) [II. 4. 21 ; VI. 2, 14], while their proverbial wealth as mentioned in literature may be due to their new coinage and currency system.

Following the Golakhpur find in the chronological order is a vast body of silver punch-marked coins found in thousands in different parts of India, from Punjab to Malwa, and from M. P. to Deccan and up to Madras and Mysore. These may be grouped under six classes in accordance with the variations in their symbols and marks. Yet they are all struck on a common standard, 32 *rattis*=56 grains like the *paṇa* or *dharaṇa*. Another common feature they present is that "they have regularly on one side a group of five punches found in a great variety of combinations, and on the reverse have one or more punches, normally different from those found on the obverse" [*Ib.* xiii].

The five punches on the obverse show figures of (1) Sun, (2) Circle with six arms, 3 arrow-heads, and 3 taurine symbols, (3) mountain, (4) Peacock, dog (or rabbit), or tree on a hill, (5) Animals, such as elephant, bull, dog seizing a rabbit, rhino, and even fishes and frogs, and, in some cases sacred tree within a railing (perhaps a mark of Buddhist influence which was so widespread in the time of Asoka Maurya) [*Ib.* XX f.]

The symbols on the reverse of these coins are only the marks of punching made by authorities and shroffs in checking them. It may be assumed that the larger the number of these punch-marks, the older must be the coins. This may supply a clue to the dating of these coins.

It may be noted that Kauṭilya's Mint-Master called *Lakshaṇādhyaksha* was in charge of the *Lākshaṇas* to be imprinted on the imperial coins. Coins in circulation had also to be checked from time to time and this was done by the *Rupadarśaka* who punched his test marks each time on them. This means increase in the number of these test marks on the reverse, of which the maximum has been found to be 14 so far. Coins bearing larger number of marks appear to be older and more worn out.

It is difficult to comprehend fully the meaning of these symbols and punch-marks. That they have a meaning is indicated by Buddhaghosha who mentions in the *Samantapāsādika* the ancient numismatic treatise known as *Rūpasutta* as stating how a moneyer (*Heraññako*) could spot the village, the *nigama* or the *nagara*, and even the mint where a coin was manufactured, in the light of its marks, and whether it was 'on a hill or on the bank of a river' (*nadītīre vā*) [*Buddhistic Studies*, p. 432]. These puzzling punch-marks Buddhaghosa describes as *chitta-vichitta*, "of various designs and forms" [*Ib.*]. The mother of the boy Upāli was full of fears that his eyes would be spoilt, if he chose the profession of a shroff [*Mahāvagga*, SBE, xiii. 201, f]. Indeed, all eyes would suffer to this day if applied to find out the meaning of the bewildering punch-marks borne by these ancient Indian coins to which the key is lost in the absence of the old *Rūpasutta* !

Of the six Classes into which these coins are grouped, it is to be noted that Classes 2 and 6 are more closely connected and taken to be Maurya on grounds explained below. Indeed, a careful examination of the various symbols and marks borne by these numerous punch-marked silver coins found in so many parts of India, together with the evidence that they were in circulation in the country in the fourth, third, and second centuries B.C., suggests the conclusion that they were "the coins of the Maurya Empire." "That these coins were issued by a government authority and not by private individuals, there is not the slightest doubt. Only a central authority could have carried out such an apparently complicated, but no doubt—if we had the clue—simple, system of stamping the coins in regular series.

"The regular recurrence of five symbols on the obverse naturally suggests a Board of Five, such as Megasthenes says was at the head of most departments of Mauryan administration. It can hardly be that the symbols are those of the five officials actually concerned in the issue of each piece, as some symbols like the sun and the six-armed symbol occur over a wide range of coins. The punches, though not struck with one disc, were struck at one time. They may represent a series of officials of diminishing area of jurisdiction. The last and most frequently changing symbol would represent the actual issuer of the coin. The constant symbol, the sun, would represent the highest official, perhaps the king himself, and the next commonest, the various forms of six armed symbol, the highest officials next under him" [Allan, *Ib.*, lxx, lxxi].

The Maurya connection of these coins is perhaps further attested by the figure of the *peacock* on a hill common on the coins of Group II under Class 2 and also on Group IV of the same Class, where it appears both on obverse and reverse. The peacock, as has been pointed out above, was the dynastic symbol of the Mauryas. We may also note that of all the animals portrayed on the coins, the elephant is the most prominent as the principal factor in Mauryan military strength.

Durga Prasad considers that the figure of 'Hill-with-crescent-on-top' was a specific Maurya symbol, apart from the peacock. This symbol, he points out, appears on most silver coins found all over the country, and also on known Mauryan Monuments (as mentioned above). It also appears on the base of the Maurya pillar recently excavated at Kumrahar in Patna. It is seen on the Sohagaura copper-plate of *c.* 320-300 B.C. bearing an inscription which states that at famines, grain was distributed from public granaries, a provision also mentioned by Kauṭilya, as we have seen Lastly, the symbol appears on a seal on three terracotta plates recently discovered at Bulandibagh at Mauryan level at the site of old Pāṭaliputra, along with three other symbols. Jayaswal agreed with Durga Prasad in taking the seal to be the Maurya imperial seal, the *Narendrāṅka* by which, according to Kauṭilya, royal properties like weapons [V. 3] or cattle [II. 29] were marked [Jayaswal's Presidential Address to the Oriental Conference at Baroda, 1933].

Durga Prasad also makes the ingenious suggestion that where a coin bears on the *reverse* this Maurya symbol of a Hill-with-crescent-on-top or a peacock, it is to be taken as a pre-Maurya coin which was restruck by the Maurya kings [*Ib. Num. Sup.* p. 67 f].

As has been already stated, of the six Classes into which the above type of coins may be grouped, Classes 2 and 6 are taken to be Maurya. "Their composition is almost everywhere the same," though they are very different in style and fabric, Class 2 consisting of small thick pieces and Class 6 of large thin pieces. Yet the constant association of these two Classes is surprising. It has been found that these two Classes of coins "circulated together from Peshawar to the mouth of the Godāvarī, and from Palanpur in the west to Midnapore in the east." The distinction between them is not one of place. The same authority must have issued them as current coins in all the localities under its control. "The authority that issued these coins must have ruled the Ganges valley, the upper Indus valley, thrust its way up the tributaries of Jumna to the west, and come along the east coast through Orissa and penetrated far into the Deccan. This is what the find-spots suggest" [Allan, *Ib.* lv, lvi]. The find-spots also agree with the distribution of Asoka's inscriptions and thus point unmistakably to the Maurya empire as the authority that issued the coins of these two Classes which are found to be so closely connected.

Foreign Coins Since a part of the Punjab came under the dominion of the Achaemenian (Hakhāmani) Emperors of ancient Persia, it was natural that their money must have come into India in the wake of their conquest. But it is not easy to prove it by actual finds of Persian coins in India.

The standard gold coin of ancient Persia was the *Daric*, weighing about 130 grains, probably first minted by Darius who first annexed to his empire the valley of the Indus. This coin is marked by the portrait on its obverse of the great king, armed with bow and spear, in the act of marching through his dominions.

The gold coin of Persia could not, however, obtain wide circulation in India for an important economic reason. India was known for its abundance of gold, so much so that its value relatively to silver was very low, as low as 1 : 8 as compared with the ratio of 1 : 13.3 maintained by the Imperial Persian Mint. Therefore, the *Darics* that would find their way into India appeared to be an artificially inflated currency and would find no place in the Indian currency system, and would be exported at once. There was no profit in holding such *Darics* in India when they could be exchanged for more silver elsewhere. Therefore, Persian gold coinage has not been found in any appreciable quantity in India.

As regards the corresponding Persian silver coinage, it consisted of what were called *Sigloi* or *Shekels* of which twenty were equivalent to a *Daric*. They weighed about 86.45 grains. Such silver coins would find their way into India where they had more value and would buy more gold. Many *sigloi* coins have been found in India with peculiar counter marks closely resembling those found on the square pieces of silver constituting India's oldest native punch-marked coinage.

The Persian *sigloi*, however, did not long survive the overthrow of Darius III by Alexander.

The Persian conquest of the Punjab was followed by the so-called Greek conquest, which was short-lived. The effect of Alexander's campaigns in the Panjab was only to unify the country all the more. Smaller principalities were brought together in the larger kingdom which was Alexander's gift to his whilom adversary, Poros. Another consequence of the pressure of the foreign invasion was the formation of the confederacies of free peoples already described. These unities, as we have seen, paved the way of Chandragupta Maurya in building up his great Empire.

It is not easy to ascertain how far the currency of India was at all affected by this Greek contact. The disappearance of the Persian *Sigloi* from the field after Darius IV no doubt opened the way to Greek influence. But it was slow to show itself.

Imitation Athenian 'owl' coins first appeared in the period of Macedonian ascendancy, but the specimens at the British Museum from Rawalpindi were not of Indian but central Asian origin.

Nor is the Indian provenance established for the Greek coins found in India, whether *tetradrachms* or *didrachms* or *drachms*. The proper Greek *drachm* minted on the Attic standard weighs 67·5 grains, whereas the *drachm* found in India weighs not more than 58 grains. Further, in these smaller denominations of coins, whether *drachms* or *diobols*, the Athenian owl is replaced by eagle. A find of a series of silver *drachms* of Attic weight made in the Punjab by Cunningham perhaps proves that the smaller Athenian imitations were known in the north of India Their obverse shows the head of a warrior, wearing a close-fitting helmet, wreathed with olive, while the reverse shows a cock and a caduceus symbol. These coins give an impression that they were designed after an Athenian prototype. These are supposed to have been the issues of king Sophytes or Saubhūti, and, if so, these coins form a memorial of Alexander's invasion of India.

It is doubtful whether Alexander as conqueror had issued any money of his own in India. Some coins bearing the name of Alexander have been classed as Indian, of which the best example is a bronze piece. But it is doubtful whether their provenance is India. Even a number of silver *tetradrachms* showing Zeus and eagle and the significant satrapal tiara which were found at Rawalpindi were of Central Asian origin. The later issues of these coins were those of Antiochus I who had no connection with India after the defeat of his predecessor, Seleukos. by Chandragupta Maurya.

It is to be noted that these pieces do not bear the king's title. But both title and name appear on an extraordinary silver *decadrachm* of Attic weight now in the British Museum. Its obverse shows a horse-man, with lance at rest, charging down upon a retreating elephant carrying on its back two men who are turning round to face their pursuer. Its reverse shows a tall figure, wearing cuirass, cloak and cap, with a sword hanging by his side and holding a thunderbolt and spear. The figure is supposed by Head to be the figure of Alexander himself. Head interprets the obverse to represent the retreat of Poros, one of whose companions on the elephant, the rear-most one, wields the lance aimed at the pursuing horseman. It is Paurava mounted on the State elephant at the Battle of the Hydaspes and aiming his javelin at Āmbhi, the traitor king of Taxila, galloping after him on horse. The story is thus told by Arrian (Chap. XVIII): "Taxiles, who was on horseback, approached as near the elephant, which carried Poros, as seemed safe, and entreated him, since it was no longer possible for him to flee, to stop his elephant and to listen to the message he brought from Alexander. But Poros, on finding that the speaker was his old enemy, Taxiles, turned round and prepared to smite him with his javelin, and he would have probably killed him, had not Taxiles instantly put his horse to the gallop and got beyond the reach of Poros".

Town Planning, Architecture, and Art. According to the Greek writers, the Panjab in those days was full of towns which were no doubt the centres of industry and economic prosperity. Many of these figure as forts or centres of defence, such as the famous Massaga (Maśakāvatī) or Aornos (Varaṇā) in the country of the Aśvakas already referred to. The free clan called the Glaussai had as many as 37 towns in their territory, while there were as many as 5,000 towns in the territories of the other peoples, the Malloi, Oxydrakai, and others. "The smallest of these towns contained not less than 5,000 inhabitants, while many contained upwards of 10,000. Some of the villages were not less populous than towns" [McCrindle's *Invasion of India by Alexander*, p. 112]. According to Strabo [*Ib.*], in the territories of 9 nations between the Jhelum and the Beas there were as many as :oo cities.

Taxila was "a great and flourishing city, the greatest, indeed, of all the cities which lay between the Indus and the Hydaspes" [*Ib.*, p. 92[.

Some of the cities were remarkable for the design shown in town-planning and architecture and for the strength of their fortifications.

Massaga, for instance, was built up as a fort commanding great natural advantages on an eminence inaccessible on all sides against steep rock, treacherous morass, deep stream, and a rampart guarded by a deep moat to boot. The rampart was "35 *stadia* (=about four miles) in circumference, with a basis of *stone-work* supporting a superstructure of unburnt, sun-dried bricks. The brickwork was bound into a solid fabric by means of stones" [*Ib.* p. 195 (Curtius)].

The fortress of Aornos was similarly constructed on a high hill with its water-supply arranged by tapping a local spring, and food grown with the labour of a thousand men in an adjoining field to render the fort self-sufficient against a siege.

It is stated that these forts were possessed of fortifications and battlements which were so strong that Alexander had "to bring up military engines to batter down their walls" [*Ib.* p. 67]

The Kathaians had a strongly fortified city called Sangala with its walls made of brick [*Ib.* p. 119].

The Malloi had also many walled cities with citadels on commanding heights and difficult of access. Alexander had to apply scaling ladders on all its sides and to undermine its walls. The walls had towers at intervals. In scaling the walls, Alexander was assailed from every side from the adjacent towers. Bars closed the gates of the wall between the towers [*Ib.* pp. 145-149 (Arrian)].

Megasthenes makes the following general statement or the cities of Maurya India : "Of their cities, it is said that the number is so great that it cannot be stated with precision, but that such cities as are situated on the banks of rivers or on the sea-coast are built of wood, for where they are built of brick they would not last long—so destructive are the rains, and also the rivers when they overflow their banks and inundate the plains. Those cities, however, which stand on commanding situations and lofty eminences are built of brick and mud" [McCrindle's *Megasthenes and Arrian,* p. 209].

The description of the above cities and also of Pāṭaliputra bears out the truth of these remarks.

Further light is thrown on Town-planning by the Pali texts of the times. An older city of Magadha was old Rājagriha known as Girivraja which was the capital of emperor Bimbisāra (c 603-515 B.C) The *Mahābhārata* refers to Girivraja as the capital of the much older king Jarāsandha of Magadha, and describes it as being protected by five hills which are still traced, the hills called Vaibhāra, Varāha, Vṛishabha, Ṛishigiri, and Chaityaka. The famous Sattapaṇṇi cave where was held the first Buddhist Council in c. 543 B. C. was situated on the Vebhāra hill. Ajātaśatru helped in the meeting of this Council (*Dhammasaṅgīti*) by building with expedition a large Hall at the entrance to the Cave, 2 platforms for the President and the speakers, and spreading costly mats on the floor for the seating of members [*Mahāvaṁsa*, Ch. III]. Later, Bimbisāra changed the capital to Rājagṛiha also known as Bimbisārapurī The town-planning engineer and the palace architect is called Mahāgovinda. The gate of the city was closed in the evening to all, including the king [*Vinaya*, IV. 116f] The walls and fortifications of old Rājagṛiha are still visible, showing how they were built of rude and rough cyclopean masonry which made the structures so durable to this day.

The inscriptions of Chandragupta Maurya's grandson, Asoka, make mention of the following chief cities of the Maurya empire, viz., Pāṭaliputra, Bodh-Gayā, Kosāmbī, Ujjenī, Takkhasilā, Suvarṇagiri, Isila, Tosalī, and Samāpā. These cities were the capitals of the provinces, the headquarters of the local administrations or centres of pilgrimage. Other towns which were populous and selected for that reason for the location of his inscriptions by Asoka were Shahbazgarhi and Mansehra, Kālsi, Sopārā, Girnar, Jaugaḍa, Dhauli, Chitaldroog, Rupnath, Sahasram, Bairat (Bhabru), Maski, Govimath and Pālkiguṇḍu in Kopbal District and Gooty in Kurnool district. The names of these places are not Maurya but modern names and most of these are now out of the way and deserted places, and not the centres of population and civilisation as they were in Maurya India. The course of civilisation changes through the ages.

The structures known as *Stūpas* formed an important part of the architectural inheritance and achievement of Mauryan India. The *stūpa* literally means 'something raised', a mound. It came to be used as a Buddhist architectural term for a mound containing relics of the Buddha, his ashes, bones, or tooth or relics of famous Buddhist saints or teachers.

The oldest *Stūpa* so far discovered is that found in ruins at Piprahwa on the Nepal border. It was built in brick round an urn bearing the following inscription : "This shrine for relics of the Buddha, the August One, is the pious foundation (*sukṛiti*) of the Śākyas, His brethren, in association with their sisters, their children, and their wives". The *Stūpa* was built as a solid cupola or domed mass of brickwork round and on a massive stone coffer. The bricks were huge slabs measuring up to 16×11×3 inches. Vincent Smith thus describes the *Stūpa* : "The masonry of the *Stūpa* is excellent of its kind, well and truly laid; the great sandstone coffer could not be better made; and the ornaments of gold, silver, coral, crystal, and precious stones which were deposited in honour of the holy relics display a high degree of skill in the arts of the lapidary and goldsmith" [*Imperial Gazetteer*, II. 102-3].

As the inscription on the *Stūpa* describes the Śākyas as its builders, it may be taken to be one of the original *Stūpas* in which, according to the *Mahāparinibbāna-suttanta*, were enshrined relics of the sacred body of the Buddha, after its cremation at Kusinārā, by eight contending claimants among whom figured the Śākyas of Kapilavastu.

We have also the testimony of Asoka himself to the existence of *Stūpas* before his time. For in his inscription on the pillar at Nigālī Sāgar he himself states that he had enlarged to twice its original size the *Stūpa* consecrated to the sacred memory of a previous Buddha, the Buddha Koṇāgamana (Kanakamuni).

As to *Art*, it is seen at its best in the examples executed by Asoka. These are examples of different types of architectural activity for which Asoka is known to this day. He was the builder of cities, *stūpas*, *vihāras* or monasteries excavated in hard rocks, rock-cut caves, palaces and pillars of stone. The pillars are the master-pieces of Mauryan Art in the shining polish imparted to them which is supposed to be the despair of modern masons, and in the degree of perfection in which they were shaped, dressed, and decorated in accordance with the Emperor's design. They carried to a high standard the art of the delineation of natural forms of animals and plants in stone. They are also notable as feats of engineering when it is considered that all these pillars weighing on an average 50 tons, and measuring a height of 50 feet, are all monolithic productions, showing how large masses of rocks were shaped into these pillars, and also how these great weights were handled for the purposes of their transport over distances of several hundreds of miles to their appointed sites at which they were to be located in accordance with the imperial scheme of public welfare which they were intended to serve. For instance, a chain of pillars was called for to indicate the Pilgrims' Progress towards the holy lands of Buddhism from Pāṭaliputra to the place of the Buddha's nativity.

Just as the *Stūpa* was pre-Asokan, so also was the Pillar. Aśoka himself refers to the existence of pillars before his time, and his utilising them for purposes of his Inscriptions [Minor Rock Edict, Rupnath Text, and Pillar Edict VII ; see my *Asoka*, p. 87].

But if Mauryan Art is admitted to have achieved so much progress in the days of Asoka, such progress could not have been achieved in a day. It must have been preceded by a long course of evolution from its origins and crude beginnings in earlier times. Fortunately, these beginnings of Indian Art are traceable in certain examples still extant. There is a class of colossal statues of stone which are admittedly pre-Asokan, and perhaps pre-Mauryan. These statues represent the folk-art of the times inspired by the popular worship of certain minor deities. The religion of the masses centred round the worship of the minor gods and goddesses known as Yakshas and Yakshīs, Nāgas or Nāgīs, Gandharvas, Apsaras and even tree-and water-spirits. Up to now eleven examples of these oversized figures of deities have been discovered, namely, (1) Parkham (Mathura) Yaksha ; (2) Baroda (Mathura) Yaksha ; (3) Yakshī in another village at Mathura, worshipped as Mansā Devī ; (4) another Mathura Yaksha newly discovered (*U.P.H.S.J.*, May 1933, p. 95) ; (5) Patna Yaksha, now in the Indian Museum ; (6) another Patna Yaksha statue in the Indian Museum ; (7) female *chauri*-bearer from Didarganj, Patna ; (8) inscribed Maṇibhadra Yaksha from Pawaya (Gwalior) ; (9) Besnagar female statue ; (10) a second Besnagar female statue ; (11) fragments of a Yaksha statue found at Kosam. Some of these statues bear inscriptions naming the deities they represent. Thus Nos. (1) and (8) represent Maṇibhadra, the Yaksha general of Kubera ; No. (3) represents Yakshī Lāyāvā. One of the Patna statues is that of *Bhagavān Akshata-nīvika* (Kubera), while the other is Yaksha *Sarvatra Nandi*. Nos. (1) and (3) are also stated to be works of a School of Sculptors represented by Kuṇika, his pupil, Nāka, and his grand-pupil Gomitaka.

That this Art of statuary or portraiture in stone is very old is also demonstrated by the fact that it continued up to later times and also in imitations. While these statues stand by themselves as independent objects of worship, they figure as parts of a whole in the scheme of Bharhut sculptures of second century B. C. The Bharhut sculptures are full of images of these secondary deities figuring in the religion and worship of the masses.

The later examples of this type of Folk-Art are seen in the Bodhisattva images which are supposed to be the works of the Mathurā School of Art. The colossal Bodhisattva image found at Sarnath bears an inscription which assigns it to the year 3 of Kanishka and describes it as a gift of Bhikshu Bala of Mathurā. Thus the Bodhisattva images were the continuations of the Yaksha images in a different religious reference.

According to Dr. A. K. Coomaraswamy, even this supposed primitive or folk-art is not without its own artistic merits. It is no doubt primitive and crude as compared with the finished art of the time of Asoka, the art of the cultured classes, the official or Court-Art, as it may be called, which was meant to cater for the religious requirements of Hīnayāna Buddhism of those days. Coomaraswamy considers these colossal statues to be "informed by an astounding physical energy not obscured by their archaic stiffness, and expressive of an immense material force in terms of sheer volume," representing "an art of mortal essence almost brutal in its affirmation, not yet spiritualised, and without any suggestion of introspection, subjectivity or spiritual aspiration". "Stylistically, the type is massive and voluminous and altogether plastically conceived, not bounded by outlines."

As regards the distinction between the primitive, rural, and the refined urban art, we have some evidence in the grammar of Pāṇini (*c.* 500 B. C.). Pāṇini [V. 4, 95] makes a distinction between the *Grāmaśilpī* and the *Rājaśilpī*. The former represented the artists in the employ of the village community, while the latter refers to the court-artists catering for the cultured classes and the aristocracy. It may also be noted that all these statues are marked in common by an ornament like the necklace or the torque for which Pāṇini has the significant formation *Graiveyaka* [IV, 2, 96].

It may, therefore, be assumed that Asokan art had its earlier beginnings in the time of his predecessors in these statues representative of rural worship and folk-art of the times.

PLATE I

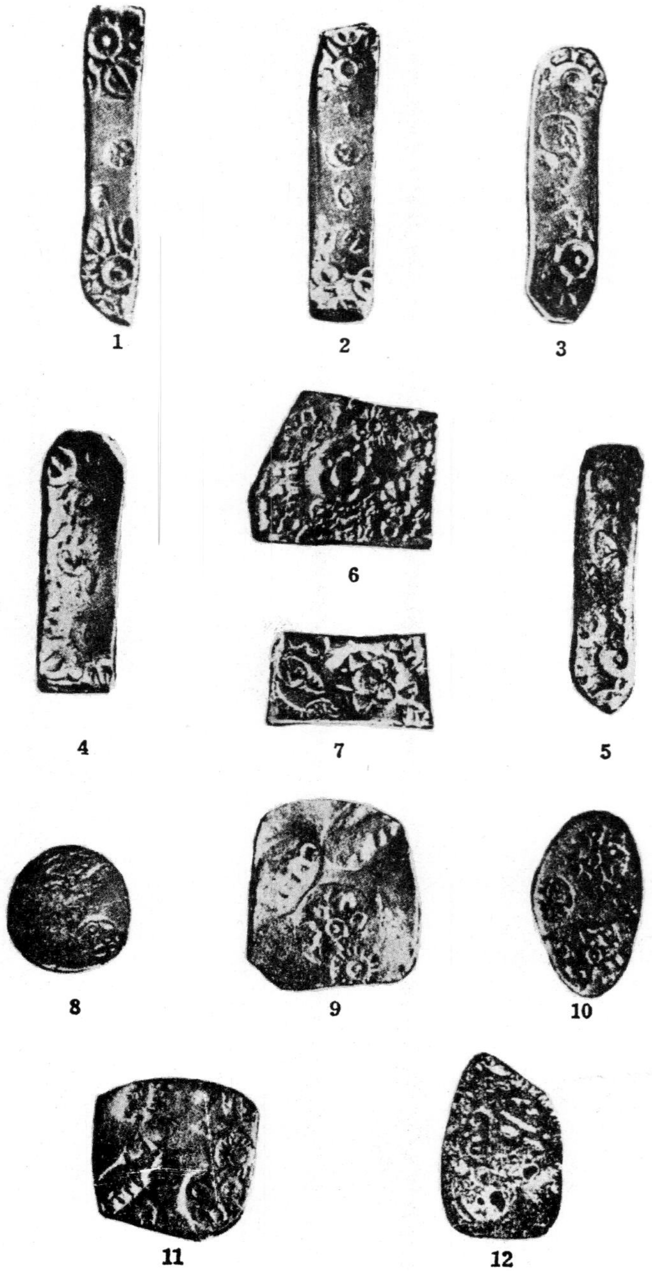

KEY TO PLATES SHOWING TYPICAL MAURYA PUNCH-MARKED COINS.

PLATE I.

Figs. 1-5.

Bent bar silver punch-marked coins from Taxila. Wt. 175 to 178 grs. These represent the ancient *Śatamāna* Coins of 100 *Ratti* wt. referred to in the *Śatapatha Brāhmaṇa* (XIII. 2, 3, 2), *Kātyāyana-Śrautasūtra* (XXVI 2, 17), and by Pāṇini (V. 1. 27).

Fig. 6

Silver punch-marked coin. From Lucknow. Wt. 105·7. grs.=57.7 Rattis. Identified as the *Trimśatka* coin of Pāṇini. 14 symbols on one side only. Very rare.

Fig. 7.

Silver punch-marked coin known as *Trimśatka*. From Partabgarh Ancient Kosala Currency. Wt. 58·06 Rts.=104·4 grs. 1 obverse and 5 reverse symbols punched on the same side.

Fig. 8.

Silver punch-marked coin. From Madhuri, Dist. Shahabad, Bihar. Wt. 40 Rts. Two prominent symbols on one side only. Specimen of a *Vimśatika* coins.

Fig. 9.

Silver punch-marked *Vimśatika* coin. From Bhabhua, Bihar. Wt. 40·2 Rts. Obverse symbols, Sun, Six-armed symbol with Oval and Arrow, Bull and Lion.

Fig. 10.

Vimśatika coin of alloyed silver. From Madhuri. Wt. 38 Rts.=68·4 grs. Four obverse symbols of which two are identical.

Fig. 11.

Silver punch-marked coin from Patna. Wt. 25 Rts.=45 grs. Size. 8″ × 8″. A regular group of five symbols on obverse including a rhinoceros. Identified as *Pāda* or one quarter of *Śatamāna* coin.

Fig. 12.

Silver punch-marked coin. From Partabgarh Wt. 44.98 Rts. =80·95 grs. Two obverse symbols and one small symbol on one side. Identified as *Adhyardhapaṇa*.

PLATE II.

Figs. 13-20.

Silver punch-marked coins or *Kārshāpaṇas* belonging to the weight standard of 32 Rts., although the actual weight is more often a little less. They bear on the obverse a regular group of five symbols of which the first symbol is the Sun which remains constant on all the coins of the series. The second symbol is often designated by Numismatists as a *Shadchakra*, i.e., a six-armed symbol. It also occurs on all Kārshāpaṇa coins conforming to the wt. standard of 16 *māshas* or 32 Rts. This symbol varies in the form of its spokes, on some, consisting of three ovals and three arrows, and on others, of three taurines and three arrows, with a great variety in between. The coins having the six-armed symbol with an oval as its component part (see Figs. 13, 14, 15, 18) are considered earlier than those on which it is absent. Coins bearing arrows and taurines are considered later and may be assigned to the Maurya Period (No. 20). The coin shown as fig. 17 is specially remarkable, as in it the solar and six-armed symbols are replaced by a group of three human figures. This specimen comes from Charsadda in the Peshawar district.

Fig. 21.

Fig. No. 21 shows a punch-marked coin of copper with traces of very thin silver plating over it. These seem to represent the debased coinage introduced by the Mauryan administration to replenish their exchequer or meet some unusual drain on their currency.

Fig. 22.

It is a Half-*Kārshāpaṇa*, 14·6 Rts. in weight, known as *Ardha* both in the *Ashṭādhyāyī* of Pāṇini and the *Arthaśāstra* of Kauṭilya.

Fig. 23.

A tiny silver punchmarked coin named *Māshaka* of which the official weight was 2 Rts. although actual specimens weigh a little less. In point of numbers, the smaller submultiples of the *Kārshāpaṇa* currency are much fewer than the standard *Kārshāpaṇas* of 32 Rts. weight.[1]

1 The numismatic and other data contained in Pāṇini's *Ashṭādhyāyī* I owe largely to dissertation prepared by Dr. V. S. Agrawala, under my supervision and approved for the Degree of Ph. D. of the Lucknow University.

PLATE II

13

14

15

16

17

18

19

20

21

22

23

APPENDIX I

Chāṇakya and Chandragupta Traditions

(From Buddhist Sources).

Abridged references to these traditions are given in the body of the work but they may be given in greater detail in an Appendix. An easy access to these is furnished by Turnour in his translation of the *Mahāwanso* (1837) with an Introductory Essay upon which this Appendix is mainly based. Turnour's chief source is *Mahāvaṁsaṭīkā* composed by "Mahanāmo Thero." The *Tīkā* throws new light on the history of the Nandas. The Nandas were brothers numbering nine. The eldest brother is described as "a provincial person" who became a "confederate" of a band of bandits, finding their "mode of life" to be excellent. They did not believe in the "toils of tillage or cattle tending" but gave themselves to the more profitable pursuit of "pillaging towns and villages, and laying up stores of riches and grain, and providing themselves with fish and flesh, toddy and other beverage, passing their life thus jovially in feasting and drinking." The romance of this adventurous life made the eldest Nanda seek admission to this brotherhood of bandits. They elected him as their leader in place of the one slain in an unsuccessful attack upon a town. He "proclaimed himself to be Nanda" and "wandered about, pillaging the country", inducing his brothers also to join the gang. Very soon he thought that the career of marauders was not a fit one for valiant men but fit only for "base wretches", and so decided : "Let us aim at supreme sovereignty." Then, "attended by his troops, and equipped for war, he attacked a provincial town, calling upon its inhabitants either to acknowledge him sovereign, or to give him battle." By this means, "reducing under his authority the people of Jambudīpo in great numbers, he finally attacked Pātiliputta, and usurping the sovereignty, died there a short time afterwards, while governing the empire. His brothers next succeeded to the empire in the order of their seniority. Their ninth youngest brother was called Dhana-Nando, from his being addicted to hoarding treasure."

As regards "Chānakko," the *Ṭīkā* tells us that he lived with his father at Ṭaxila and was known for his devotion to his mother for whose sake he had his teeth destroyed, because she saw in them signs of his sovereignty which would make him neglect her. He was known for his proficiency in the three Vedas, in the Mantras, skill in stratagems, dexterity in intrigue and policy, but also for his physical ugliness, disgusting complexion, deformity of legs and other limbs, for which he is dubbed *Kauṭilya* in Hindu works.

The *Ṭīkā* also tells how Dhana-Nando, "abandoning his passion for hoarding, became imbued with the desire of giving alms, and built for the purpose a Hall of Alms-Offerings in his palace." One day, the king entered the Hall in state, "decked in regal attire, attended by thousands of state palanquins glittering with ornaments, escorted by a suite of a hundred royal personages, with their martial array of the four hosts of cavalry, elephants, chariots, and infantry, bearing the white parasol of dominion, having a golden staff and golden tassels," and found that Chānakko, 'who came to Pupphapura in his quest of disputation,' had appropriated the seat which was reserved for the chief of the Brahmans. The king at once had him ejected from the seat. Chāṇakya, leaving, cursed the king and escaped arrest by stripping himself naked as an Ājīvika and running into the centre of the palace where, in an unfrequented place, he concealed himself. At night, he entered secretly into a league with the Crown Prince named Pabbato who showed him the way out, on his promising him sovereignty. He "fled into the wilderness of Winjjha where, with the view of raising resources, he converted (by recoining) each *Kahāpaṇa* into eight, and amassed 80 *Koṭis* of *Kahāpaṇas*. He next searched for a person who was entitled by birth to be raised to sovereign power and lighted upon Chandagutta of Moriyan dynasty."

The circumstances leading to the meeting of Chāṇakya and Chandragupta have been briefly related in the text. But the *Ṭīkā* gives some interesting details relating to the birth and early life of Chandragupta. At the conquest of Moriya-nagara, its king was slain, and his queen, then pregnant, fled from the city with her elder brothers and lived at Pupphapura in disguise. There she was duly delivered of a child who became known as Chandragupta. The mother for its safety placed the child in a vase and deposited it at the door of a cattle-pen where it was watched over by a bull named Chanda. There he was reared by a herdsman who put him to tend his cattle till he was taken away by a huntsman. As he was growing up, he was tending cattle with other village boys whom he profitably employed in a 'game of royalty' which he improvised by a natural instinct: "He himself was named *Rājā*; to others he gave the offices of sub-king, etc. Some being appointed Judges were placed in a Judgment Hall; some he made officers of the king's household; and others, outlaws or robbers Having thus constituted a Court of Justice, he sat in judgment. On culprits being brought up, regularly impeaching and trying them, on their guilt being clearly proved to his satisfaction, according to the sentence awarded by his judicial ministers, he pronounced the punishment.

"Chāṇakko, happening to come to that spot, was amazed at the proceeding he beheld." He at once bought of the huntsman the boy for 1000 *Kahāpaṇas* and decorated the boy with a golden necklace "worth a lac." He also decorated the other boy, Prince Pabbato, with a similar necklace.

Next, Chāṇakya educated him "for six or seven years", and "rendered him highly accomplished and profoundly learned."

When he found Chandragupta "capable of forming and controlling an army," he brought out his hidden wealth, by spending which he "enlisted forces from all quarters and formed a powerful army which he entrusted to him." "From that time, throwing off all disguise, and invading the inhabited parts of the country, he commenced his campaign by attacking towns and villages. In the course of their warfare, the population rose *en masse*, and surrounding them, and hewing their army with their weapons, vanquished them." Thus defeated, both retired into wilderness where they decided: "Relinquishing military operations, let us acquire a knowledge of the sentiments of the people." In disguise, they travelled about the country and mixed with the people. It was while thus travelling that they heard the dialogue between a mother and her son who ate a cake wrongly by throwing away its edges and eating only its centre, thus imitating Chandragupta who, "without subduing the frontiers, before he attacked the towns, invaded the heart of the country, and laid towns waste. On that account, both the inhabitants of the towns and others, rising, closed in upon him, from the frontiers to the centre, and destroyed his army."

Taking their lessons from this conversation, they changed their strategy. "On resuming their attack, by again raising an army, on the provinces and towns, commencing from the frontiers, reducing towns, and stationing troops in the intervals, they proceeded to their invasion. After a respite, adopting the same system, and marshalling a great army, and in regular course reducing each kingdom and province, then assailing Pātiliputta and putting Dhana-Nanda to death, they seized that sovereignty."

The Author of the *Ṭīkā* remarks: "The discovery of Chanda gutta is thus stated (in the former works): He discovered this prince descended from the Moriyan line."

He further states: "All the particulars connected with Chandagutta, both before his installation and after, are recorded in the *Atthakathā* of the Uttarawihāro priests. Let that work be referred to by those who are desirous of more detailed information. We compile this work in an abridged from, without prejudice however to its perspicuity."

The *Ṭīkā* brings to light two interesting facts in the life of Chandragupta. It appears that the commencement of his administration was marked by an outbreak of lawlessness in the country. To suppress the disorder, Chandragupta "sent for a former acquaintance of his, a Jaṭilian (i.e., a Jaṭila Brāhmaṇa ascetic), named Maniyatappo (=*Maunītupasvī*), and conferred a commission on him. "My friend, (said he), do thou restore order into the country, suppressing the lawless proceedings that prevail." He replying '*sadhu*', and accepting the commission, by his judicious measures, reduced the country to order. Chandragupta thus "conferred the blessings of peace on the country by extirpating marauders who were like unto thorns in a cultivated land."

The other fact which the *Ṭīkā* tells about his life concerns his marriage. It seems that he married "the daughter of the eldest of the maternal uncles who accompanied his mother to Pupphapura. Chandragupta wedding the daughter of his maternal uncle raised her to the dignity of Queen Consort."

APPENDIX II

Chāṇakya and Chandragupta Traditions

(From Jaina Sources)

The chief source of the Jaina traditions regarding Chāṇakya and Chandragupta is the work known as *Sthavirāvalī-charita* or *Pariśishṭaparvan* written by Hemachandra as an Appendix to the larger work of the same author known as *Ṭrishashṭi-Śalākāpurushacharita* dealing with the lives of 63 great personages, divine or human, who, as believed by the Jainas, have controlled the history of the world. These compromise the 24 *Tīrthakaras* or *Prophets*, 12 *Chakravartins* or universal emperors, 9 *Vāsudevas*, 9 *Baladevas*, and 9 *Prativāsudevas*. The work has been edited by Jacobi with a summary of its contents.

Jaina sacred literature had its origin in the doctrines and sermons preached by the religious leaders who used to illustrate them by apologues and legends. These, when reduced to writing, gave rise to what is known as *Kathānaka*-Literature. This Literature is marked by four stages or layers in its development : (1) *Sūtras* embodying the aphorisms of religious leaders as the nucleus ; (2) *Niryuktis*, which give fuller expositions of the subjects of the Sūtras to which they belong ; (3) *Chūrṇis*, which are the Prākrit commentaries on the *Sūtras* and *Niryuktis* ; and (4) *Ṭīkās*, which are more elaborate commentaries on the connected *Niryuktis* and *Chūrṇis*. These four divisions of literature are not, however, very rigid : Nos (2) and (3) reveal some amount of overlapping and mixture.

Hemachandra's source of the *Chāṇakya-Chandragupta-Kathā* embodied in verses 194-376 of Canto VIII of *Pariśishṭaparvan* is the *Chūrṇi* and *Ṭīkā* on *Āvaśyaka-Niryukti*. The *Ṭīkā* was that written by Haribhadra.

Jain tradition represents Chāṇakya as the son of a Brāhman named Chaṇī, who lived in the village called Chaṇaka in the *Vishaya* or district known as Golla. His mother is called Chaneśvarī. Chaṇī is described as a devout Jain.

The Buddhist story of Chāṇakya's teeth is mentioned but with different details. Chāṇakya was born with all his teeth complete. This was taken as a promise of royalty which alarmed his too religious father as a source of sin leading to hell. So he had his son's teeth broken out. But still the monks foretold that he would rule by proxy.

The Jain story regarding Chāṇakya's plan to amass wealth is different. It was due to the insult to which his poor Brahman wife was treated by her rich relations meeting at her father's place at the wedding of her brother. The first step that he takes for the purpose is to go to Pāṭaliputra and have a share of the gifts which king Nanda was bestowing on renowned Brahmans. The story of Chāṇakya's ejection by Nanda is the same as the Buddhist, with small differences of trivial detail.

The Jain story makes Chandragupta the son of the daughter of a village chief, the chief of the village of the rearers of royal peacocks (*mayūraposhakas*).

Chāṇakya continues his quest of wealth and devotes himself to the study of Metallurgy (*dhātuvāda*) evidently for manufacturing coins, as the Buddhist story relates.

He came to the native village of Chandragupta and found him behaving like a king among his playmates upon whom he used to mount as his elephants and horses. Chāṇakya, to test his mettle as king, asked him for a present. The boy, in the royal manner, pointing to a herd of cows, said he could take them, without caring for their owners, as nobody would dare gainsay him. He also made the significant remark: "The earth is for enjoyment by heroes" (*vīrabhogyā vasundharā*). Chāṇakya at once chose him for his mission.

With the wealth which Chāṇakya had acquired by his knowledge of Metallurgy, he levied troops and laid seige to Pāṭaliputra, surrounding it on its four sides (*chaturdiśamaveshṭayat*). But his army was defeated by the more numerous army of King Nanda, so that he and Chandragupta had to escape by flight. Nanda, however, sent swift horsemen to overtake them. When one of them nearly came up to them, Chāṇakya, then resting on the bank of a lake, in the guise of an ascetic, ordered Chandragupta to plunge into it. Asked by the rider about the runaway youth, Chāṇakya pointed to the lake, into which he plunged, doffing his armour. Chāṇakya instantly seized the sword with which he severed the soldier's head. A second horseman also came up to them in pursuit but was disposed of by Chāṇakya by a similar trick. This time he made a washerman run away by saying that the king had a grudge against his whole guild (*tachchhreṇirushito rājā*) and then took over his work. Chandragupta's implicit faith in his master endeared the master to him, as he told him that he plunged into the lake without caring for his life out of blind devotion to his master.

Next, the Jain story repeats the Buddhist regarding the village boy being rebuked by his mother for eating a cake by a mistaken method, like that of Chāṇakya It was that Chāṇakya had not secured the surrounding country before attacking the enemy's stronghold. Then Chāṇakya proceeds to the country called Himavatkūṭa and entered into an alliance with its king Parvataka. Here the Buddhist version is different. The Allies then opened their campaign by reducing the outlying parts (*bahiḥ*) of Nanda's kingdom. They, however, failed to conquer one town. Chāṇakya took recourse to a stratagem. He entered the town in the guise of a beggar, as a Tridaṇḍin monk, and saw a temple of the Seven Mothers, the tutelary goddesses (*pāhidevatā*) of the town. Its citizens, tired of the protracted siege, asked the ascetic when it would be raised. He answered: "Not till the goddesses were in the temple and protected the town." The credulous citizens at once removed the idols from the temple. At this, Chāṇakya hinted to Chandragupta and Parvataka that they should retire with their army to some distance from the town. Thus the citizens were thrown off their guard and were rejoicing over their restored liberty, when they returned and took the town by surprise. They devastated the country, laid siege to Pāṭaliputra, and compelled king Nanda to capitulate, with his decreased resources (*kshīṇakośaḥ*), strength (*bala*), wits (*dhīḥ*), prowess (*vikrama*) and spiritual merit (*puṇya*). He at last threw himself on the mercy of Chāṇakya who spared his life and permitted him to leave his kingdom, carrying with him all that he could in one chariot. He carried with him his two wives and a daughter and as much treasure as could be accommodated in the vehicle. Thus king Nanda (*Nandarāṭ*) made his exit from his kingdom. While thus proceeding (*samāyāntam*), the Princess saw Chandragupta and fell in love with him at first sight. Then the father said to her that she might select him as her husband by the rite of *svayaṁvara*, because "very often the daughters of Kshatriyas have recourse to this practice." Thus Nanda is here taken as a Kshatriya The Buddhist version of Chandragupta's marriage is different from Jain

The Jain version, like the Buddhist, refers to outbreak of lawlessness at the commencement of Chandragupta's rule. It mentions Nanda's followers as the culprits instigating it. It also mentions a different remedy taken to suppress the disorder. Chāṇakya, observing a weaver (*Kolika*) killing bugs by setting fire to those places in his house which contained their nests, chose him for his method, that of tearing away evil from its roots (*mūlādunmūlya*). The weaver was appointed as the chief of the city (*Nagarādhyaksha*). He succeeded in allaying the suspicions of Nanda's followers, who were the robbers, by his gifts, and then having them murdered.

The next interesting point in the Jain story is its mention of a twelve years' famine in the country. At that time, the Jain Āchārya Susthita lived in Chandragupta's capital. He sent his following (*Gaṇa*) to some other country to avoid the famine. It is, however, to be noted that this is Śvetāmabara tradition which is contradicted by Digambara tradition on the subject. Chandragupta was now showing Jain leanings and patronising heretical teachers (*Chandraguptaṁ tu mithyādṛikpāshaṇḍamatabhavitam*). Chāṇakya tried to wean him away from them by saying that they were morally corrupt. But Chandragupta wanted the charge to be proved. It was proved by Chāṇakya against some Jain ascetics one day, but it failed against others the next day. Chandragupta made them henceforth his spiritual guides (*gurūn mene*).

Another interesting fact furnished by the Jain story is that Chandragupta's Queen bore the name of Durdharā. She is also stated to be the mother of Bindusāra.

In the Jain story, Chandragupta's ally, Parvataka, died by some unfortunate coincidence, whereupon Chandragupta got possession of two kingdoms, those of Nanda and Parvataka [*dve api rājye tasya jāte* (*Āvaśyaka-Sūtra*, p. 435)].

Jain story is also very valuable for the light it throws on the date of Chandragupta's accession to sovereignty. This point has been discussed in his Introduction (pp. xx-xxi) by Jacobi. In his *Pariśishṭaparvan*, VIII. 339, Hemachandra states that "155 years after the *nirvāṇa* of Mahāvīra, Chandragupta became king (*nṛipa*)." This date is not accepted by Merutuṅga as being contradicted in his opinion by all other sources (*Vichāraśreṇī*, Memorial verses, 1-3). But it is not true. It is accepted by Bhadreśvara who, in his *Kahāvalī*, states: "And thus, on the extinction (*uchchhinna*) of the Nanda dynasty, and 155 years after the *nirvāṇa* of Mahāvīra, Chandragupta became King (*rāyā*)." Jacobi states: "The date 155 AV for Chandragupta's accession to the throne cannot be far wrong, since the Buddhists place that event in 162 AB. If we assume the earliest possible date, 322 B.C., as the beginning of Chandragupta's reign, the *corrected* date of Buddha's death comes out to be 484 B.C., and that of Mahāvīra 477 B C. This result is at variance with a notice in several Buddhist canonical works" to the effect that Mahāvīra had pre-deceased Buddha. In the *Saṁgīti-Suttanta*, Sāriputta reports: "The Nigaṇṭtha Nātaputta, friends, has *just* (*adhunā*) died at Pāvā." In the *Pāsādika-Suttanta*, it was Chuṇḍa who delivers the news of Mahāvīra's death to Ānanda at Sāmagāma in the Malla country. At this news, Ānanda exclaimed: "Friend Chuṇḍa, this is a worthy subject to bring before the Exalted One" [*Dialogues of the Buddha*, III. 203 f]. Jarl Charpentier holds [*IA*., 1914, p. 128] this statement in the Buddhist works to be founded on an error. From *Dīgha Nikāya* (III. 11 f.), it appears that the Buddhists thought that Pāvā where Mahāvīra died was the same Pāvā where the Buddha had stayed as the guest of Chuṇḍa the Smith on his way to Kusinārā where he died. But the place where Mahāvīra died was another Pāvā called Majjhimā Pāvā in the *Kalpasūtra*, now known as Pāvāpurī in Bihar Shariff in Patna district. In this view, there should be no objection to the revised dates for the Nirvāṇa of both Buddha and Mahāvīra at 484 and 477 B. C. respectively, especially as these lead to the acceptable date of 322 B.C. for Chandragupta Maurya's accession to sovereignty. For the other view, a reference may be made to my *Hindu Civilisation* (p. 230).

APPENDIX III

PARALLELISM BETWEEN ASOKA'S EDICTS AND KAUTILYA'S *ARTHAŚĀSTRA*

The purpose of this Appendix is to bring together the parallel passages in the *Arthaśāstra* of Kauṭilya and the Inscriptions of Asoka so as to show to what extent they throw light upon each othet, and may be considered as contemporary documents. The resemblance between the observations of Megasthenes and Kauṭilya has been worked out thoroughly to prove or to disprove that they were contemporaries, but the resemblance between Kautilya's work and Asoka's Inscriptions waits to be worked out for the same purpose. The resemblance extends both to words and ideas, to technical terms as well as to institutions peculiar to Mauryan polity. It may be set out as follows:

Asoka's Edicts.	*Kauṭilya's Arthaśāstra.*
1. *Mahāmātra*, a technical term for an officer of high rank occuring in many of the Edicts. They mention the *Mahāmātra* as being (*a*) in charge of cities like Isila, Samāpā [KRE. II] or Kosaṁbi [MPE]; (*b*) associated with the princely Viceroys, as at Tosalī [KRE. II], or at Suvarṇagiri [MRE. I, Brahm.]; (*c*) placed in charge of over thousands of lives [KRE II]; (*d*) deputed on quinquennial inspection of judicial administration, as on other duties [*Ib*]; (*e*) Heads of Departments as *Dharma-Mahamātras*, or *Strīadhyaksha-Mahāmātras* [RE. XII]; (*f*) Directors of different religious sects [RE. V; PE. VII; MPE]; and (*g*) Members of the *Mantriparishad* to whom the king confides urgent matters [RE VI].	1. In the *Arthaśāstra*, the *Mahāmātra* also figures as a minister [I. 10, 12,13] and as the chief executive officer of a city under the title *Nāgarika-Mahāmātra* [IV. 5]=*Mahāmātā-nagalaka* of KRE. I, Jaugada, while his status and influence will be evident from the fact that the seditious *Mahāmātra* is a cause of much concern to the king who has to send him out of the way [V.1].
2. *Devānaṁpiye evaṁ āha* (or *āṇapayati*) [occuring in so many edicts].	2. Both these formulae are also mentioned by Kauṭilya as appropriate for royal orders The former is mentioned as one of the set phrases prescribed for what is

Asoka's Edicts.	*Kauṭilya's Arthaśāstra*
	called by Kauṭilya a *prājñāpana-śasana* (writ of information), while *ājñā-lekha* (writ of command) is mentioned as a form of *rājaśāsana* (royal decree) [II.10].
3. *Nagala-viyohālaka* [KRE I]	3. Kauṭilya [I. 12] has the expression *Pauravyavahārika* for one of the eighteen chief officers of the State. He has also the expression *Puramukhya* [I. 16].
4. In KRE. I, there is a reference to judicial torture causing death and to Asoka's intention to check such abuses.	4. Kauṭilya also refers to the severity of judicial torture of which the arbitrary and excessive applications and abuses he makes penal [IV. 8; 9; 11].
5. *Nikhāmayisa hedisameva vagam* [KRE. I]--'depute a similar body of officers.'	5. The word Varga is also used in the same sense by Kauṭilya [I. 11] (*svaṁ svaṁ vargam*).
6. "*Te mahamātā nikhamisaṁti anusayānam*" [*Ib*]--'these Mahāmātras would thus set out on tour.'	6. Kauṭilya uses the word *niryāṇa* for the king's tour [I. 21] He also refers to transfer of government servants (*Yuktas*) from one post to another to prevent embezzlement [II. 9]. Some interpret the word *anusaṁyāna* in the sense of 'transfer.'
7. *Samāja* [RE. I] of both objectionable and commendable kinds.	7. Kauṭilya in one passage [II.25] refers to *utsava samāja* and *yātrā* where the drinking of wine was unrestricted for 4 days. This is the objectionable kind of *samāja* mentioned by Asoka. Kauṭilya also mentions the commendable kind of *samāja* which it is the duty of the king to encourage [XIII. 5].
8. Reference to import of medicinal herbs, roots, and fruits in RE. II.	8. Kauṭilya [II 21]. also encourages the import of seeds of useful and medicinal plants by exempting such import from tolls.
9. *Dbādasavasābhisitena* [RE. III]: the dates given in the Edicts are all counted from Asoka's coronation.	9. Kauṭilya [II. 6] also applies the term *rājavarsha* to the year counted from the king's coronation.
10. *Yuktas* [RE III and elsewhere] and *Purushas* [PE. I, IV and VII] indicative of Government servants.	10. Kauṭilya also uses the terms *yukta*, *upayukta* and *purusha* for Government servants [II. 5] and also the terms *yogapurusha*

Asoka's Edicts.	*Kauṭilya's Arthaśāstra*
	[I. 21]; V. 2] or *yugyapurusha* [VII. 4] in the sense of employees. [A commentator explains the term *upayukta* as an officer placed above the *yuktas* (*yuktānāṁ upari niyuktaḥ*)].
11. *Rājūke* [Girnar RE. III] or *Rajuke* (Mansehra).	11. Kauṭilya [II. 6] uses the expression *rajjū chorarajjūścha.* He also mentions [IV. 13] an officer called *chora-rajjuka=chora-grahaṇa-niyukta*, i.e., one whose duty was to apprehend thieves.
12. *Aparānta* [RE. V].	12. Kauṭilya also mentions *Aparānta* as the region known for its elephants [II. 2] and rainfall [II, 24].
13. Reference to the *Dharma-Mahāmātras* giving State help to the destitute and infirm by age (*anātheshu vṛiddheshu*) RE. V.	13. Kauṭilya also recognises the duty of the State to maintain the orphan, decrepit, diseased, afflicted and destitute [II. 1].
14. Reference to unjust imprisonment (*bandhana*), execution (*vadha*) and torture (*palibodha*) of prisoners and to Asoka's measures for checking such abuses in RE. X.	14. Kauṭilya also [IV. 9.] mentions such abuses as (*a*) confining persons without reason (*saṁruddhakamanākhyāya*), (*b*) putting them to unjust tortute (*karmakārayataḥ*), (*c*) molesting them (*parikleśayataḥ*) and (*d*) causing their deaths (*ghnataḥ*)
15. Reference in RE. VI to Asoka's readiness for public business at all hours, even when he is eating (*bhuṁjamānasa*), or in the harem (*orodhanaṁhi*), or inner apartments, or ranches (*vachaṁhi*), or parks (*uyānesu*).	15. The list of king's duties mentioned by Kauṭilya agrees with what is suggested heae. *E g.*, the *orodhana* of the Edict corresponds to *śayīta* of Kauṭilya; *bhuṁjāmanasa* to *snānabhojana*; *uyanesu* to *svairavihāra*; while as regards *vraja*, Kauṭilya refers to the king's duty of inspecting the horses, elephants, chariots and infantry as well as his livestock [I 19]. In II 6, Kauṭilya uses the term *vraja* of the Edict to include cows, buffaloes, goats, sheep, asses, camels, horses and mules. Lastly, as the Edict refers to the king going to his *udyāna* for pleasure, Kauṭilya [II. 2] provides for *mṛīgavana* for the king for the same pleasure.

Asoka's Edicts.	*Kauṭilya's Arthaśāstra*
16. *Prativedakas* are mentioned in RE.VI as officers who are to keep the king informed about the affairs of his people.	16. Kauṭilya also speaks of the Intelligence Department of the administration manned by officers called *Gūḍhapurushas* [I. 11-13].
17. *Mukhato āñapayāmi svayaṁ dāpakam* [RE. VI].	17. Kauṭilya also mentions [II. 7] an officer called *Dāpaka* who fixes and collects the amount of taxes to be paid by the *Dāyaka* (taxpayer).
18. Mention in RE. VI of the king referring an urgent matter [*āchāyike* (Girnar); *atiyāyike* (Kalsi, Dhauli and Jaugada)] to the *Mahāmātras* and the *Parishad.*	18. Kauṭilya also enjoins: "Summoning the Ministers and their Council (*Mantriparishadam*), the king shall speak to them on urgent matters (*ātyāyike kārye*) ... all urgent matters should the king attend to (*sarvamātyayikaṁ kāryaṁ śriṇuyāt* [I. 15, 19].
19. *'Nāsti hi me toso usṭānamhi atha saṁtīraṇāya va katavyamate hi me sarvalokahitaṁ*|	19. An echo of Kauṭilya [I. 19]; 'Rājño hi *vratamutthānaṁ* .. prajā sukhe sukhaṁ rājñaḥ *prajānāṁ cha hite hitaṁ...'*
'Tasa ca puna esa mūle usṭānaṁ cha atha-saṁtīraṇā-cha | *'Nasti hi kaṁmataraṁ sarvaloka-hitatpā . . . .'* [RE. VI].	"Tasmānnityotthito rājā kuryādarthānuśāsanam ! Arthasya *mūlamutthānam* .....
20. Devānāṁpriya Priyadarśī Rājā desires that in all places should reside people of diverse sects [RE. VII].	20. This is apparently against Kauṭilya's injunctions that "*Pāshaṇḍas* and *Chaṇḍālas* are to dwell near the cremation ground (beyond the city)" [II 4]. Elsewhere [II. 36], Kauṭilya also rules that no *Pāshaṇḍas* could be accommodated in a *Dharamśālā* without the permission of the city officer, *Gopa*, and their abodes should be searched for suspicious characters.
21. Reference to *vihārayātrā* and to *mrigayā* and similar diversions to which Asoka's predecessors were addicted [RE. VIII].	21. Kauṭilya gives us details about these. He provides for a reserved forest for the king's vihāra [II. 2] and discusses fully the merits of *mṛigayā* [VIII. 3]. While Piśuna condemns it as a *vyasana* or indulgence chiefly for its dangers to a king, Kauṭilya approves of it as a *vyāyāma* or healthy physical exercise which destroys the excess of phlegm, bile, fat, and perspiration and improves

Asoka's Edicts	*Kauṭilya's Arthaśāstra*
	one's marksmanship and knowledge of the temper of wild beasts. This opinion, is, indeed, worthy of the Minister of Chandragupta Maurya whom the Greek writers also refer to as a warm lover of hunting.
22. Reference to proper treatment of servants and dependents (*dāsa-bhaṭaka*) in several Edicts [RE. IX, XI, XIII, PE. VII]; also to relations [MRE. II, RE. IV, and XIII], friends, acquaintances and companions [RE. XIII] to whom Asoka also insists on liberality (*dānam*) [RE III and XI].	22. The details of such "proper treatment", the rights and obligations of *dāsas* and *bhṛitakas* (also called *karmakaras*) are fully discussed by Kauṭilya [III. 13 and 14] in two chapters. According to him, a man became a slave as a captive in war (*dhvajāhṛtah*) or for inability to pay off debts incurred to meet domestic troubles or government demand for fines and court decrees. But such slavery for an *Ārya* could always be redeemed. What Asoka means by 'proper' treatment' of these slaves and paid servants may, therefore, be taken to be the treatment to which they were entitled under law as expounded by Kauṭilya. The law made penal the following offences against *slaves, viz*, (a) defrauding a slave of his property and privileges (b) misemploying him (such as making him carry corpses or sweep) or hurting or abusing him As regards the *Karmakara*, the law secured to him his wages under the agreement between him and his master which should be known to thier neighbours (*karmakarasya karmasambandhamāsannā vidyuḥ*). The amount of the wages was to be determined by the nature of the work and the time taken in doing it. Non-payment of such wages was fined. The *bhṛitaka* was also entitled to his *vetana* or legal wages and to some concession if he was incapacitated for work (*aśaktaḥ*) or put to ugly work (*kutsita karma*) or was ill or in distress (*vyadhau vyasane*). It is thus clear that the full content of Asoka's repeated injunctions in his Edicts for 'proper treatment of

Asoka's Edicts.	*Kauṭilya's Arthaśāstra*
	slaves and dependents' can only be understood in the light of the details of such treatment as given by Kauṭilya. In another chapter [II. 1.], Kauṭilya lays down as the king's duty to correct (*vinayaṁ grāhayet*) those who neglect their duty towards slaves and relatives (*dāsāhitakabandhūnaśriṇvato*) and punishes with a fine the person of means not supporting his wife and children, father and mother, minor brothers or widowed sisters and daughters. Asoka is always insisting on the support of one's relations. Kauṭilya's *details* thus give a meaning to Asoka's seemingly general and pious exhortations, most of which were really of the nature of legal obligations which could not be disowned or violated with impunity.
23. '*Tadatvāye ayatiye chā*' in RE. X—'in the present time and in the future.'	23 Kauṭilya also uses the expression *tadātve cha āyatyāṁ cha in* V. 1 and 4.
24. The officer called *vacha* (*vracha*) *bhūmika* in RE. XII.	24. Some light is thrown on the meaning of this obscure and peculiar word by Kauṭilya. If *vracha* (also used in RE. VI.) is taken to be same as the word *vraja*, the expression *Vraja-bhūmīka* would mean the officer-in-charge of *Vraja*. Kauṭilya [II. 6] defines *Vraja* as a department of administration under the *Samāhartā* dealing with the live-stock of the country, comprising kine, buffaloes, goats, sheep, asses, camels, horses and mules But the Inscription refers to the *Vraja-bhūmīka* as an officer created by Asoka for the purpose of promoting toleration, and in that case, he must be some such officer as had to deal not with the dumb animals but rather with human beings for whom such moral teaching was suitable. The word *vraja* suggests that these might be the people of the rural parts, the pedestrians and pilgrims along the

Asoka's Edicts.	*Kauṭilya's Arthaśāstra*
	high roads, or in the rest-houses which Asoka was so liberal in providing for facilities of travelling. Now Kauṭilya in II. 1 lays down as the king's duty the protection of the highways of commerce (*vaṇik patham*) 'from molestation by courtiers, tax-collectors (*kārmika*), robbers and Wardens of the Marches (*Anta-pāla*), and from damage by herds of cattle, and of the live-stock of the country (*paśuvrajān*) from robbers, tigers, poisonous creatures and diseases.' Thus an officer like the *Vraja-bhūmika* might very well be needed for discharging this duty and obligation of the king in respect of the *paśuvraja* and *vaṇikpatha*, an officer in charge of cattle and communications including trade-routes by both land and sea (*sthala-patha vāri-pathaścha*) [Kauṭilya, II. 37]. The *Vivītādhyaksha* of Kauṭilya [II. 34] corresponds to such an officer. His duty was to establish wells and tanks, groves of flower- and fruit-trees in arid (*anudake*) tracts, to keep the roads in order, arrest thieves, see to the safety of caravans of merchants and to protect cattle.
25. The officers called *Strī-adhyaksha-Mahāmātras* in RE. XII.	25. Kauṭilya [I. 10] also refers to *Mahāmātras* who were attached to the royal harem. As they had to deal with women, the special qualification emphasised for them is sexual purity (*kāmo-padhāśuddhān*) and they are to be placed in charge of the places of pleasure both in the capital and outside [*bāhyābhyantara-vihāra-rakshāsu*]. In passing, it may be noted that the word *bāhya* of Kauṭilya occurs also in RE. V. in the expression "*Hida cha* (or *Paṭalipute cha*) *bāhilesu cha nagalesu.*" The *Strī-adhyaksha* of the Edict may be also compared with the *Gaṇikādhyaksha* of Kauṭilya [II. 27].

Asoka's Edicts.	*Kauṭilya's Arthaśāstra.*
26. Reference in RE. XIII to Asoka's conquest of forest-folks (*aṭavi or aṭaviyo*).	26. It is interesting to find that Kauṭilya [XIII. 5] mentions two kinds of conquest, viz., (1) the conquest of the *Aṭavyādi* or foresters and (2) the conquest of settled territory (*grāmādi*). He places the *aṭavyādi* under the administration of special officers called the *Aṭavipāla* [I. 16 etc.].
27. Reference in RE. XIII to *Dharma-vijaya*.	27. It is interesting to note that Kauṭilya [XII. I] distinguishes three classes of conquerors *viz.*, (*a*) the *Dharma-vijayī* who is satisfied with the mere obeisance of the conquered; (*b*) the *Lobha-vijayī* whose greed has to be satisfied by the surrender of territory and treasure; and (*c*) the *Asura-vijayī* who would demand the surrender of not merely territory and treasure, but also of the sons and wives of the conquered enemy, and even taking away his life.
28. Mention of officers called *Anta-Māhamātras* in PE V.	28. Kauṭilya [II. 4] mentions *Anta-pālas* among the eighteen *Tīrthas* or Heads of Departments in the administration.
29. List of protected creatures in PE. V.	29. It is interesting to note that Kauṭilya [II. 26] also gives a list of protected creatures (*pradis-ṭābhayānām*) among which are included in common with this Edict the following, *viz.*. Haṁsa, Chakravāk, Śuka, Śārika, and other auspicious creatures (*maṅ-galyāḥ*). It may be also noted that though Kauṭilya does not make his list of protected creatures as exhaustive as the Edict, he lays down the principle of such protection which is only applied in the Edict to individual cases mentioned. According to that principle, those creatures, beasts, birds and fishes, are to be protected which do not prey upon other living creatures (*apravṛitta-vadhā-nām*), as also those which are regarded as auspicious (*maṅ-galyāḥ*) like the cow. On this principle, Kauṭilya also generally

Asoka's Edicts.	*Kauṭilya's Arthaśāstra*
	forbids under penalty the killing of the calf, the bull and the milch-cow even among the animals that did not come under the usual protected class (*vatso vṛisho dhenuśchaishām avadhyāḥ*).
30. Reference to prohibition of slaughter of life on the three *Chaturmāsīs* and on the Tishya fullmoon day.	30. Kauṭilya [XIII. 5] has the following corresponding prohibition. "The king should prohibit the slaughter of animals for half a month during the period of *Chātur māsya*, for four nights on the full-moon days, and for one night to mark the date of his birth or celebrate the anniversary of his conquest."
31. '*Nāgavana*,' elephant forest as mentioned in PE. V.	31. Kauṭilya mentions *Nāgavana* and has a chapter on *Nāgavanādhyaksha*, Superintendent of elephant forests [II, 2 and 31].
32. Reference to 25 jail-deliveries in PE. V.	32. Kauṭilya [II. 36] refers to such jail-deliveries in celebration of the king's birthday. The prisoners to be thus occasionally liberated were selected from "the juvenile, aged, diseased and helpless (*bāla-vṛddha-vyādhita-anāthānām*)" Similar grounds of release are also mentioned in RE. V. Good conduct in jail might also merit release according to Kauṭilya [*Ib.*].
33. Asoka's concern for the *Ājīvikas* as expressed in PE. VII and also in the grant to them of the cave-dwellings.	33. Kauṭilya [III 20] shows his Brahmanical prejudice against them by branding them along with the Buddhists (*Sākyajīvakādīn*) as being unworthy of entertainment at any ceremony connected with the gods or ancestors (*devapitṛikāryeshu*).
34. *Devī Kumālānam* in PE. VII.	34. The word *Devī* for queen is also used by Kauṭilya [I. 10], as well as the word *Kumāra* for a prince [I. 20].
35. Asoka's control over the harem through his officers called Dharma-*Mahāmātras* and *Strī-adhyaksha-Mahāmātras* as described in RE. V, XII and PE. VII.	35. Kauṭilya [I. 20] acquaints us with the administrative arrangements for the royal harems of the day. The *Antaḥpura* with its inmates, the *avarodhas* (cf. *oro-*

Asoka's Editcts.	*Kauṭilya's Arthaśāstra.*
	dhana of RE. VI), was placed under a military guard, the *Antarvaṁśikasainya*, and civil officers, the *Abhyāgārikas*, comprising both males and females, who regulated all communications between the harem and the outside world. It may be noted that Kauṭilya does not permit the *muṇḍa* and *jatila* ascetics (probably the Buddhists and Jains) access to the harem. He calls the chief officer of the harem *Antarvaṁsika* [V. 3] corresponding to *strī-adhyakshmahāmātra*.[1]

This Note I have adapted from my Article on the subject contributed to the Lahore Session of the All-India Oriental Conference for 1930.

INDEX OF NAMES

A

B

C

R

S

T

INDEX OF SANSKRIT WORDS

A

Abhayavana, 110.
Abhiyāna, 63.
Abhyāgārika, 64.
Ābhyantara, 117.
Āchāra, 49, 51.
Adevamātrika, 74.
Adhirāja, 1.
Adhyakshas, 52, 54, 88.
Adhyaksha-sthāna, 64.
Agada, 167.
Āgantu, 108, 119.
Agni śaṁyoga, 69.
Agnishṭha, 138.
Agniyoga, 113.
Agnyāgāra, 56, 58.
Agramahishī, 82.
Agrāmātya, 81.
Agronomoi, 89.
Āhata, 214.
Āhitaka, 127.
Ahorūpahara, 101.
Ajasrapaṇya, 114.
Ājñā, 72.
Ākarādhyaksha, 105.
Akshapaṭala, 99.
Akshaśālā, 108.
Alaṅkārabhūmi, 64.
Āmaṁ, 112.
Anekamukham, 114.
Anīkastha, 86, 88, 128, 177, 200.
Anirvāhya, 116.
Anisṛishṭatāriṇaḥ, 113.
Aṅkuśa, 137.
Anta, 37.
Antapāla, 84, 86, 92.
Antarāla, 155, 183.
Antarvaṁśīka, 64, 86.
Anugraha, 129, 181.
Anujñā, 158.
Anuloma, 154, 162.
Anvāyana, 116.
Apaviddha, 154.
Āpūpa, 211.
Āpūpika, 121.
Ārālika, 65.
Ārāma, 197, 200.
Āraṭṭas, 22.
Ardha, 213.
Arishṭa, 119.
Ārya, 87.
Āryaputra, 52.
Āsana, 65.
Āsava, 119.
Ashṭāprud, 212.
Āśrāvaṇa, 85.
Āstaraka, 65.
Āstaraṇa, 120.
Asuravijaya, 59.
Aśvadamaka, 86, 88, 128, 200.
Aśvamedha, 1.
Aṭasī, 104.
Āṭavī, 168.
Āṭavika, 84, 156, 169.
Ātithya, 117.
Ātivāhika, 115.
Aṭṭālaka, 69, 140, 176.
Audanika, 133.
Aupachārika, 178.
Auparika, 85.
Aupasthāyika, 83.
Aupaśāyika, 178.
Aupāyanika, 105, 116.
Aushadhavarga, 109.
Avalikhana, 101.
Avaskara, 137.
Aveśana, 135.
Avikshepa, 88.
Āyudhajīvī-saṁgha, 23.
Āyudhīya, 198.

B

Bāhirika, 70.
Bāhirikadeya, 94.
Bahumukham, 115.
Bali, 94, 105, 132.
Bandhaka, 87.
Bandhanāgāra, 96, 136.
Bhāga, 94, 106, 130.
Bhuśiravijñāna, 105.

S

T